LIBRARY OF HEBREW BIBLE/
OLD TESTAMENT STUDIES

715

Formerly Journal for the Study of the Old Testament Supplement Series

Editors
Laura Quick, Oxford University, UK
Jacqueline Vayntrub, Yale University, USA

Founding Editors
David J. A. Clines, Philip R. Davies and David M. Gunn

Editorial Board
Sonja Ammann, Alan Cooper, Steed Davidson, Susan Gillingham,
Rachelle Gilmour, John Goldingay, Rhiannon Graybill, Anne Katrine Gudme,
Norman K. Gottwald, James E. Harding, John Jarick, Tracy Lemos,
Carol Meyers, Eva Mroczek, Daniel L. Smith-Christopher,
Francesca Stavrakopoulou, James W. Watts

NARRATIVE ETHICS IN THE HEBREW BIBLE

Moral Dilemmas in the Story of King David

Eryl W. Davies

t&tclark
LONDON • NEW YORK • OXFORD • NEW DELHI • SYDNEY

T&T CLARK
Bloomsbury Publishing Plc
50 Bedford Square, London, WC1B 3DP, UK
1385 Broadway, New York, NY 10018, USA
29 Earlsfort Terrace, Dublin 2, Ireland

BLOOMSBURY, T&T CLARK and the T&T Clark logo
are trademarks of Bloomsbury Publishing Plc

First published in Great Britain 2022
This paperback edition 2023
This paperback edition published in 2023

Copyright © Eryl W. Davies, 2022

Eryl W. Davies has asserted his right under the Copyright, Designs and Patents Act, 1988,
to be identified as Author of this work.

All rights reserved. No part of this publication may be reproduced or transmitted in any form or by
any means, electronic or mechanical, including photocopying, recording, or any information storage
or retrieval system, without prior permission in writing from the publishers.

Bloomsbury Publishing Plc does not have any control over, or responsibility for, any third-party
websites referred to or in this book. All internet addresses given in this book were correct at the
time of going to press. The author and publisher regret any inconvenience caused if addresses have
changed or sites have ceased to exist, but can accept no responsibility for any such changes.

A catalogue record for this book is available from the British Library.

Library of Congress Control Number: 2021930666.

ISBN:	HB:	978-0-5676-9963-3
	PB:	978-0-5676-9966-4
	ePDF:	978-0-5676-9964-0

Series: Library of Hebrew Bible/Old Testament Studies, volume 715
ISSN 2513-8758

To find out more about our authors and books visit www.bloomsbury.com
and sign up for our newsletters.

I'r plant
Manon, Llinos,
Gethin, Osian,
ac i'r ŵyr
Lewys Dafydd

Contents

Preface	ix
Abbreviations	xi
INTRODUCTION	1
Chapter 1	
NARRATIVE ETHICS	4
'Story' or 'History'?	5
The Purpose of the David Narratives	10
Ambiguity in Biblical Narrative	11
Evaluation of Biblical Narrative	15
Nabal, Abigail and David (1 Samuel 25)	17
Evaluation of Characters in 1 and 2 Samuel	22
Martha Nussbaum's Approach to Ethics	23
Chapter 2	
LIES AND LOYALTY (1 SAMUEL 19:11-17; 20:1-34)	32
Deception: Michal and Saul (1 Samuel 19:11-17)	33
Deception: David and Jonathan (1 Samuel 20:1-34)	35
The Ethics of Deception	37
Deception in the Hebrew Bible	38
Deception in Moral Philosophy	42
Measure for Measure	45
Loyalty	48
Loyalty: Michal and Saul (1 Samuel 19:11-17)	48
Loyalty: Jonathan and David (1 Samuel 20:1-34)	53
Moral Dilemmas	55
Conclusion	57
Chapter 3	
ADULTERY AND MURDER (2 SAMUEL 11)	59
Adultery and Murder	61
The Characterization of David	66
The Narrator's Evaluation of David's Character	66
Scholarly Evaluations of David's Character	73

The Characterization of Bathsheba	76
Why Was the Story Preserved?	88
Conclusion	90

Chapter 4
NATHAN AND DAVID (2 SAMUEL 12:1-25) 92
    Nathan's Parable and its Sequel 93
    Nathan's Parable and the Story of David and Bathsheba 96
    The Death of Bathsheba's Child (12:15b-25) 103
    A Nussbaumian Reading of the Story 104
    Conclusion 107

Chapter 5
THE RAPE OF TAMAR (2 SAMUEL 13) 108
    The Rape of Tamar 111
    The Legal Aspects 119
    The Characters in the Story 125
        Tamar 126
        Jonadab 130
        David 132
        Absalom 135
        Amnon 139
    Conclusion 140

Chapter 6
ETHICAL CRITICISM AND THE CHARACTER OF YAHWEH
(2 SAMUEL 12:7-25; 24:1-17) 143
    Ethical Criticism and the Hebrew Bible 144
    The Character of Yahweh in 1 and 2 Samuel 149
    The Character of Yahweh in 2 Samuel 12:7-25 154
    The Character of Yahweh in 2 Samuel 24:1-17 159
    Conclusion 163

Chapter 7
CONCLUSION 166

Bibliography 172
Index of References 186
Index of Authors 191

Preface

I wish to express my thanks to Andrew Mein and Claudia V. Camp for their interest in the volume and for accepting it for publication in the Library of Hebrew Bible/Old Testament Studies series. I am also grateful to the staff at Bloomsbury Publishing, and in particular Lily McMahon, Editorial Assistant, for responding to my queries and for her help, advice and guidance along the way.

Although this volume has been a long time in the making, much of it was written during a period of global pandemic, when it has not always been easy to access the relevant literature on the subject. I therefore wish to express my special thanks to the staff at both Bangor University library and the National Library of Wales, Aberystwyth, who have been unfailingly helpful in ensuring that the necessary books and articles were at my disposal.

Finally, I wish to express my thanks to Eirian, my wife, for her constant encouragement and support during the writing of this volume. The book is dedicated, with love, to our children and to our grandson, who was born on the day this volume was sent to press.

Eryl W. Davies
January 2021

ABBREVIATIONS

AB	Anchor Bible
AnBib	Analecta biblica
BDB	Brown, F., S.R. Driver, and C.A. Briggs, *A Hebrew and English Lexicon of the Old Testament*, Oxford: Clarendon Press, 1907
BETL	Bibliotheca Ephemeridum Theologicarum Lovaniensium
Bib	*Biblica*
BibInt	*Biblical Interpretation*
BIS	Biblical Interpretation Series
BJRL	*Bulletin of the John Rylands Library*
BLS	Bible and Literature Series
BWANT	Beiträge zur Wissenschaft vom Alten und Neuen Testament
BZAW	Beiheft zur Zeitschrift für die alttestamentliche Wissenschaft
CBC	Cambridge Bible Commentary
CBQ	*Catholic Biblical Quarterly*
CBR	Currents in Biblical Research
CJPhil	*Canadian Journal of Philosophy*
ExpT	*Expository Times*
FOTL	Forms of the Old Testament Literature
HBM	Hebrew Bible Monographs
HUCA	*Hebrew Union College Annual*
IBC	Interpretation: A Bible Commentary for Teaching and Preaching
ICC	International Critical Commentary
Int	*Interpretation*
JBL	Journal of Biblical Literature
JBR	Journal of Bible and Religion
JHI	Journal of the History of Ideas
JPhil	Journal of Philosophy
JR	Journal of Religion
JSOT	Journal for the Study of the Old Testament
JSOTSup	Journal for the Study of the Old Testament, Supplement Series
JSS	Journal of Semitic Studies
JTS	Journal of Theological Studies
KJV	King James Version
LHBOTS	Library of Hebrew Bible/Old Testament Studies
LXX	Septuagint (the Greek Old Testament)
MLR	*Modern Language Review*
MT	Masoretic Text

NCB	New Century Bible
NEB	New English Bible
NIV	New International Version
NovT	*Novum Testamentum*
NRSV	New Revised Standard Version
NS	New Series
OBT	Overtures to Biblical Theology
OTL	Old Testament Library
PhilRev	*Philosophical Review*
REB	Revised English Bible
RSV	Revised Standard Version
SBT	Studies in Biblical Theology
SJOT	*Scandinavian Journal of the Old Testament*
SSN	Studia Semitica Neerlandica
StBL	Studies in Biblical Literature
TBC	Torch Bible Commentaries
TynB	*Tyndale Bulletin*
VT	*Vetus Testamentum*
VTSup	*Vetus Testamentum*, Supplement Series
WBC	Word Biblical Commentary
ZAW	*Zeitschrift für die alttestamentliche Wissenschaft*

Introduction

Until comparatively recently the ethics of biblical narrative has remained a largely neglected area of research.[1] It is not that the *ethics* of the Hebrew Bible has been neglected; indeed, since the early 1970s there has been a remarkable resurgence of interest in the ethics of both the Hebrew Bible and New Testament.[2] Nor is it the case that the *narrative* of the Hebrew Bible has been overlooked; on the contrary, the emergence in biblical studies of narrative criticism (Powell 1993; Resseguie 2005) and narratology (Bal 1985; Moore 2016) has brought a renewed interest in issues

---

1. Bruce C. Birch observed that 'in spite of the centrality of the narrative storytelling traditions in the OT, they have seldom been considered for their moral address' (1988: 76; 1991: 52). Birch goes on to note that the New Testament has suffered far less from this neglect, since the Gospel accounts of the life, death and resurrection of Jesus are at the very heart of its witness.

2. Writing in 1970, Brevard Childs was able to claim that 'in spite of the great interest in ethics...there is no outstanding modern work written in English that even attempts to deal adequately with the biblical material as it relates to ethics' (1970: 124). When Christopher Wright broached the subject of the ethics of the Hebrew Bible in a volume published in 1983, he felt no need to apologize for adding another volume to the literature 'since the subject of Old Testament ethics has scarcely any literature to add to' (1983: 9). Similarly, when Cyril Rodd expressed an interest in examining the ethics of the Hebrew Bible in 1956, he was told that it was a 'non-subject' that had no future (2001: ix). However, by the last quarter of the twentieth century, and the beginning of the twenty-first, the situation had changed dramatically. In 2004, Christopher Wright published a further study on the ethics of the Hebrew Bible, a study which extended over 500 pages, and which contained a bibliography listing almost 400 books and articles specifically devoted to the field (2004: 481–99). In 2009, the third (and final) volume of John Goldingay's critically acclaimed *Old Testament Theology* was devoted to the subject of ethics, and this study contained over 900 pages and well over 800 items in its bibliography (2009: 840–72). A similar resurgence of interest seems to have occurred with regard to the ethics of the New Testament. In 1997, Richard B. Hays's magisterial volume, *The Moral Vision of the New Testament*, appeared, listing some 500 works in its bibliography, and Hays himself conceded that this represented only a fraction of the literature on the subject (1997: 471–84).

such as plot, structure, characterization, compositional technique and point of view.³ However, it is only in recent years that attention has focussed on the narratives of the Hebrew Bible in order to examine their ethical import, biblical scholars generally preferring to examine other genres, such as the legal material (Kaiser 1983; Lalleman 2004), the prophetic oracles (E.W. Davies 1981; Mein 2001), or the wisdom literature (Otto 1994).⁴ Such neglect is all the more surprising when one considers that narrative occupies such a substantial part of the Hebrew Bible. As John Barton has observed, given that 463 pages of the NRSV take the form of narrative, 'if there is a moral vision in the Old Testament, then surely we might expect to find it there' (2003: 2). Thus, the appearance in recent years of extended discussions of the ethics of biblical narrative by Waldemar Janzen (1994), Gordon Wenham (2000), Mary Mills (2001), Robin Parry (2004), Athena Gorospe (2007), and S. Min Chun (2014) is warmly to be welcomed, and there is every indication that narrative is increasingly being regarded as an important locus of moral deliberation in Hebrew Bible studies. After all, the biblical writers were primarily storytellers, and they knew – perhaps without even knowing that they knew – that stories were capable of educating morally and often did so more powerfully and effectively than the imposition of legal stipulations. In cultures the world over, stories, whether historical or fictional, whether composed in prose or poetry,⁵ have always been an important resource of moral teaching, and it should occasion no surprise that the biblical authors should have viewed narrative as an ideal vehicle for ethical reflection.

The present volume, then, is intended as a contribution to the on-going interest in the ethics of biblical narrative. It must be emphasized at the outset that the intention is not to mine the Hebrew Bible in order

---

3. For an overview of the literary-critical scholarship relating to the narrative traditions of the Hebrew Bible and New Testament, see the important volume edited by Danna Nolan Fewell (2016).

4. It is worth noting that the ethics of the Psalms has been rather neglected, though in recent years a few studies have appeared which deal with the ethical significance of individual psalms (cf. Clements 1999) or with the Psalter as a whole (Wenham 2005, 2012; E.W. Davies 2021a).

5. The fact that the narratives of the Hebrew Bible nearly always take the form of prose is striking, since narratives in the ancient world usually took the form of poetry (cf. Linafelt 2016). Robert Alter comments that 'it is peculiar, and culturally significant, that among ancient peoples only Israel should have chosen to cast its sacred national traditions in prose' (1981: 25). Indeed, Alter was able to claim that the biblical writers 'were among the pioneers of prose fiction in the Western tradition' (1981: 157).

to reconstruct the moral norms embraced in ancient Israel.[6] Rather, its aim is to provide a deeper understanding of the values and moral vision embedded in the biblical narrative texts. In order to provide a focus for our discussion it will be convenient to examine some of the stories relating to David in 1 and 2 Samuel, since these seem to be particularly appropriate for ethical reflection. While scholars have tended to focus on the historical, political, theological, and literary aspects of these chapters, they also raise serious problems of moral evaluation for the reader, which have not always been explored in sufficient detail.

The following chapters will not be concerned with issues that have tended to dominate the historical-critical approach, such as the date, authorship and provenance of the text. These are often irresolvable problems, and such conclusions as have been reached are frequently based on highly speculative hypotheses.[7] This is not in any way to disparage the historical-critical approach, for it has undoubtedly produced many valuable insights, and the more complete and reliable our knowledge of the world from which the Hebrew Bible emerged, the sharper our insights will be into the ethical significance of the text. Nevertheless, one of the weaknesses of the historical-critical approach was that it often resulted in the fragmentation of texts without a concern for the meaning of the narrative as a whole; hence, the discussion in the following chapters will be unashamedly literary in its approach, and will largely focus on the final, canonical shape of the text. Our intention in what follows is not to provide a running commentary on all the stories in which David plays a role; many of the individual narratives about him could be (and in many cases, have already been) the subject of full-length articles or even volumes in their own right. The aim, rather, is to enhance the reader's understanding of the moral issues underlying the stories considered and to tease out their ethical implications. In doing so, it is hoped that the discussion will bring to the fore issues applicable to many other narratives in the Hebrew Bible.

---

6. For those interested in the ethics of ancient Israel, the Hebrew Bible remains our primary source of information, but how far it can be regarded as a reliable source of information in this regard has been a matter of considerable debate. The difficulty of attempting to reconstruct the moral norms that existed in ancient Israel has been emphasized by John Barton (2003: 116–19), partly because different ethical beliefs were held by different groups within Israel at different times.

7. David Gunn has drawn attention to the weakness of the historical-critical approach when applied to the narratives of the Hebrew Bible: 'It is no exaggeration to say that the truly assured results of historical critical scholarship concerning authorship, date and provenance would fill but a pamphlet' (1987: 66).

Chapter 1

NARRATIVE ETHICS

The aim of the present chapter is to explore some of the issues that arise in discussions of the ethics of biblical narratives. Two issues, in particular, will occupy our attention in the chapters that follow, namely, the ambiguity surrounding the actions and intentions of the various characters in the narratives under consideration, and the equally complex issue of evaluating their conduct and motivations. In the stories concerning David in 1 and 2 Samuel, the narrator introduces different and even conflicting narrative possibilities into the text, and so much is left unsaid concerning the thoughts and feelings of the protagonists that we are invited – and, indeed, required – to read between the lines and to make decisions that the text resolutely refuses to make on our behalf. Since the narratives are often purposefully ambiguous, the task of evaluation is by no means as straightforward as we might imagine, and in the following chapters it will be necessary to consider how characters are evaluated both within the narrative itself and by subsequent commentators. Moreover, in the course of the volume, it will be argued that applying philosophical insights to the stories concerning David may serve to challenge traditional readings, offer alternative interpretations, and suggest different perspectives on some familiar narratives. In this regard, Martha Nussbaum will prove to be a helpful, discerning, and insightful conversation partner. By adopting the type of approach advocated by Nussbaum in relation to Greek tragedy and contemporary fiction, our aim is to open up the text to a multiplicity of readings and thus avoid any temptation to draw a single, straightforward moral 'lesson' from the text or to provide neat, simplistic solutions to the ethical problems faced by the characters. First, however, it may be salutary to consider whether the narratives concerning David are historically reliable or merely a literary creation, and why these narratives were recorded and preserved in the tradition.

'Story' or 'History'?

Although the focus of this volume will be on literary presentation rather than historical reconstruction, it seems appropriate to consider at the outset whether the events concerning David recorded in 1 and 2 Samuel actually happened, albeit perhaps in embellished or embroidered form, or whether the stories about him were simply the product of the imagination of the narrator, and designed merely to entertain the reader? Does the 'warts-and-all' portrait of David reflect the historian's scrupulosity or the artist's eye for intricate characterization? Is the presence of doublets in the narrative a case of history repeating itself or an indication of the narrator's contrived, artistic pattern-making? The narrative may be 'history-like', to use Hans Frei's term (1974), but is it *history*? The issue of historicity is not entirely irrelevant to the present study, for if the stories concerning David are deemed to be purely historical, purporting to render an account of incidents that actually happened during his lifetime, it might be deemed presumptuous, and even misguided, to attempt to analyse them in terms usually applied to prose fiction in order to elucidate their ethical ramifications.[1]

During the last fifty years or so, there has been something of a crisis in the historiography of ancient Israel, with scholars often taking diametrically opposing views. In some respects, the discussion has become increasingly polarized, as has been evident in the fractious debate between the so-called maximalists and minimalists.[2] On the one hand, some scholars have sought to question the historical reliability of most of the biblical corpus, and have argued that the biblical text cannot be used to recreate the history of ancient Israel; on the other hand, a number of scholars have argued equally forcefully in support of the basic historicity of the biblical narratives.

Perhaps nowhere has the dispute been so apparent as in the discussion of the historical value of the so-called Succession Narrative, or Court History, encountered in 2 Samuel 9–20 and 1 Kings 1–2.[3] Julius Wellhausen (1885: 262) praised the 'essentially historical character' of the story, and he was

---

1. Carly Crouch raises a pertinent issue when she asks: 'Is it a legitimate interpretative move to investigate the moral logic of a text whose interests are elsewhere?' (2016: 345).

2. For a sober and judicious account of the controversy, see Collins 2005: 27–51.

3. The term 'Succession Narrative' goes back to Leonhard Rost's classic study (originally published in 1926), but the term is not altogether satisfactory, since there is not a 'succession' in the strict sense here; for that reason, the more neutral term 'Court History' or 'Story of David' seems more appropriate. Cf. Jensen 1992: 40–1.

followed by Gerhard von Rad, who considered the story of the succession to the throne of David to contain 'genuine historical writing – the oldest historical writing in the Old Testament'.[4] Robert H. Pfeiffer claimed that it was a work 'unsurpassed in historicity' (1948: 357), while Georg Fohrer regarded the David narratives as 'based on a detailed knowledge of the events' (1970: 226). Gene M. Tucker believed that they represented 'Israelite history writing at its very best', adding that the last part of the reign of David was 'one of the best documented periods in the history of Israel' (1971: 36). John Bright claimed that the sources behind 1 and 2 Samuel were 'of the highest historical value' and he suggested that much of the material was contemporaneous, or nearly so, with the events described (1972: 179). Many scholars regarded the Court History as having been written in the early years of Solomon's reign and suggested that it may even have been produced by an eyewitness of the events described. Thus, in his commentary on 1 and 2 Samuel, H.W. Hertzberg claimed that the author of these chapters must have been someone 'who was very close to the happenings described' (1964: 378), and Norman Whybray agreed with the 'well-nigh universally held and extremely probable view that the book was written by a man who had been personally acquainted with David and his court' (1968: 54). Julius A. Bewer even went so far as to claim that the writer was present in all the situations depicted, arguing that the graphic details were sufficient token of the historical reliability of the narrative.[5] More recently, Walter Brueggemann, in his examination of 1 Sam. 21:1-6, 2 Sam. 12:16-23, 23:13-17, insisted that the memories of David in these passages 'were not fabrications nor imaginations, but memories of how David really lived and understood himself' (1969: 494). At the other extreme, scholars have claimed that there is no evidence whatsoever that the author of the Court History was a contemporary or near-contemporary, still less an eyewitness, of the events recorded; on the contrary, the

4. Von Rad 1966: 192. Von Rad contrasted the story of David with accounts (which he branded as 'sagas') such as those concerning Gideon in the book of Judges. The former contained no miraculous elements and little by way of divine intervention; consequently, the Court History could be regarded as reflecting a 'new type of history writing', more secular in outlook, in which events just followed their natural, ineluctable course. In a similar vein, Christopher R. North argued that in the 'Court History' of David 'we pass for a while from the mystic twilight of saga into the clear daylight of history proper' (1946: 34).

5. Bewer 1962: 30. David Gunn criticized Bewer's unfounded optimism, noting that for readers of the *Iliad* or of a modern historical novel, 'the lack of substance in this argument will be immediately apparent' (1978: 31). James S. Ackerman similarly observed that the appearance of realism in a narrative can just as easily be the hallmark of a gifted writer as of an eyewitness to the events (1990: 59).

stories concerning David probably emerged no earlier than the postexilic period, and consequently their historical value must be regarded as highly questionable.[6] Moreover, the absence of substantial corroborative external sources or archaeological evidence merely added to the doubts concerning the historical value of the narratives about David, and this led some scholars to regard them as little more than a work of fiction.[7]

The problem with such polarized views as those expressed above is that they presuppose that biblical narrative must fall into one of two neatly demarcated and opposed categories: they must be regarded as either history or fiction. In fact, however, the distinction between the two genres is often blurred.[8] Fact and fiction are invariably present to some degree in works of literature, from the epics of Homer to the plays of Shakespeare, and in this regard the literature of the Hebrew Bible is no exception. History is far more intricately related to fiction than is often supposed, and both share a range of common strategies: historians resemble writers of fiction in employing, as sometimes they must, a series of imaginative incidents in order to reconstruct the past and give the events described a certain narrative shape and pattern; on the other hand, references to historical characters and events abound in fiction (such as in the novels of Hilary Mantel), and storytellers may incorporate in their narrative many facts while owing no allegiance to the commitments binding on the historian.

---

6. Van Seters, for example, argued that the Court History was a post-Deuteronomistic addition to the story of David dating from the postexilic period (1983: 290–1). For a discussion of the various proposals concerning the date of the Court History, see Barton 2004.

7. See, for example, Garbini 1988; Thompson 1992; Lemche 1998.

8. This is no less true of contemporary fiction. Thomas Keneally's *Schindler's Ark* (later turned into the film *Schindler's List*) was based on a true and extraordinary story of a German businessman who used his position as an employer of forced labour in Nazi-occupied Poland to save the lives of countless Jews. Interestingly, the volume was published as non-fiction in the USA but won the Booker prize for fiction in the UK (cf. Lodge 1992: 202–3). Another example is Truman Capote's *In Cold Blood: A True Account of a Multiple Murder and its Consequences*, published in 1966, which dealt with multiple murders and the families who were the victims. Capote testified that the work was based on official documents or interviews pertaining to the real-life cases discussed. But some considered him guilty of literary embellishments, since he proceeded to describe the thoughts and feelings of the protagonists, and consequently a work that was originally published in the USA as non-fiction came to be subsumed under the category of 'fiction' in the 1980s by its British publishers (cf. Cobley 2001: 181–2). Such cases merely show the fragile distinction between the historian's empirical report and the novelist's imaginary account.

The blurring of fact and fiction, of 'story' and 'history', is well illustrated in Meir Sternberg's interpretation of one of the best-known episodes in 2 Samuel, namely, the parable of the ewe lamb recorded in 12:1-6. Nathan here seems to be recounting an event to David whereby a poor man was seeking redress from the king for an injustice perpetrated against him by his wealthy neighbour, and David – believing that the event did actually happen – fulminates against the rich man's rapacity; but when Nathan utters the words 'You are the man!' (v. 7), the narrative, in one fell swoop, is transferred from the 'history' of an injustice to a fictional tale of injustice. The parable of the ewe lamb may serve as a pertinent reminder that in any biblical narrative 'fiction' and 'history' may be equally present, or equally absent, or present and absent in varying degrees.[9]

The view taken in this volume is that the stories about David are not a work of complete fiction disguised as factual events, but nor does the account correspond to historical and topographical fact in every detail. It is not improbable that the author put his 'historical' characters into situations that they never actually experienced and imagined encounters between characters that never took place. After all, it is clear that the narrator included material that was, in Meir Sternberg's words, 'not just undocumented but undocumentable' (1985: 32), such as the thoughts, feelings and motives of the protagonists, or the verbatim dialogue during occasions when only those present could have known what was said (such as Nathan's private rebuke of David in 2 Sam. 12:7-12, or the dialogue between Tamar and Amnon in 2 Sam. 13:10-16). The narrator probably had certain events to guide him which were firmly embedded in tradition – the rise of David to the throne, his success in making Jerusalem the capital, and the fact that he was succeeded by his son, Solomon. At the same time, however, the narrator exercised a great deal of artistic freedom in articulating the traditions at his disposal, so that the end product was an amalgam of history and fiction. Robert Alter regards the stories about David as providing a particularly good example of the interweaving of historical detail and fiction, and he concludes that 'fiction was the principal means which the biblical authors had at their disposal for realizing

---

9. Sternberg 1985: 30. The issue of whether David believed that he was listening to a real or a fictional case is discussed below (pp. 98–100). Some argue that it is unlikely that he would have been so angry with a fictive character as he would have been with a man of flesh and blood ('the man who has done this deserves to die'; 2 Sam. 12:5); others, however, contend that the anonymity of the characters in the story would have been a cue for David to regard the story as fiction.

history'.[10] Since the narratives concerning David are not strictly speaking historical but largely imaginative re-enactments of history, they may justifiably be characterized as 'historicized fiction' or as 'fictionalized history'.[11]

It is not without significance, then, that some recent scholars who have written on the Court History have been anxious to overturn the cherished distinction between history and fiction in the narrative. David Gunn, for example, delicately treads a middle ground by arguing that while the narrative 'shows clear signs of traditional composition and contains subject-matter and motifs that belong pre-eminently to the world of the story-teller' (1978: 33), it is not unreasonable to suppose that there were 'genuine historical antecedents' to the story, but that it acquired non-historical characteristics during the process of transmission (p. 49). The author, he claims, 'believed himself to be recounting in essence what actually happened, whether or not it *was* precisely what happened' (p. 61). Norman Whybray's view was broadly similar. He claimed that the Court History was akin to an 'historical novel' (1968: 47); the theme was historical, but the treatment was that of a novelist (pp. 10–11).[12] Whether it was to be considered primarily as a work of history or as a work of fiction was 'a matter of degree' (p. 7). More recently, Rachelle Gilmour

---

10. Alter 1981: 32. Alter develops his idea by reference to Shakespeare: 'The author of the David stories stands in basically the same relation to Israelite history as Shakespeare stands to English history in his history plays. Shakespeare was obviously not free to have Henry V lose the battle of Agincourt, or to allow someone else to lead the English forces there, but, working from the hints of historical tradition, he could invent a kind of *Bildungsroman* for the young Prince Hal; surround him with invented characters that would serve as foils, mirrors, obstacles, aids in his development; create a language and a psychology for the king which are the writer's own achievement, making out of the stuff of history a powerful projection of human possibility. That is essentially what the author of the David cycle does for David, Saul, Abner, Joab, Jonathan, Absalom, Michal, Abigail, and a host of other characters' (1981: 35–6).

11. Alter 1981: 25. Alter does not explain the distinction between the two, but presumably the precise categorization will depend on whether it is the factual or fictional element that predominates. Burke O. Long argues that the authors of 1 and 2 Kings presented a picture of Israel's past with 'imaginative creativity' (1985: 405), and he criticizes 'the modern biblical historian who habitually overlooks the role of fictionalizing imagination in [Israel's] historiography' (p. 416).

12. Interestingly, Otto Eissfeldt had come to a similar conclusion, regarding 2 Sam. 13–20 and 1 Kgs 1–2 as 'a composition presented and embellished with great narrative skill, a composition which has in it something of a *good* historical novel' (1966: 141; his italics).

has observed that the subject matter of the narratives contained in 1 and 2 Samuel suggests history, while the mode of telling, with its rich characterization and complex themes, 'more closely resembles a modern idea of story' (2016: 192).

The Purpose of the David Narratives

Norman Whybray's view that the stories relating to David are akin to an historical novel 'rather than a work of history properly speaking' (1968: 47) raises the issue of the purpose of the narrator in recounting the events of David's life. It seems probable that many of the stories concerning David had an apologetic purpose, namely, to justify or legitimate David's ascent to the throne. But it is likely that the narratives were also told in order to entertain the reader. Indeed, David Gunn has argued that this was the primary purpose of the storyteller, although he insists that the stories were not designed as entertainment of the type designed merely to amuse the reader or to while away the occasional hour; rather, they were intended as 'serious entertainment' that demanded the active engagement of those being entertained, challenging their intellect, their emotions, and their understanding of themselves (1978: 61). This is broadly the view advanced in the present volume, although it will be argued in the chapters that follow that many of the stories, while undoubtedly entertaining, were also intended to provide moral edification and to refine moral insight. Indeed, it is possible that some of the stories concerning David were told not primarily for whatever historical memories they contained but because of the moral instruction that the narrator wished to impart.[13] The account of Nathan's parable (discussed in Chapter 4) suggests that it was part of the literary culture of the time to tell stories as a way of provoking a moral response and encouraging readers in the art of moral perception. The story of David's illicit affair with Bathsheba, for example, was probably intended to provide a source of sober reflection on human behaviour. It conveyed to its readers the basic truth that choices matter, and that acting impulsively without weighing up the consequences of one's action can lead to all kinds of complications and to repercussions that were neither intended nor anticipated. Moreover, the story served as a warning that sin has a dynamic of its own, and that attempts at concealment cannot succeed, for the all-seeing eye of the omnipotent deity will ensure that moral failures will not go unpunished.

13. April Westbrook has argued that the stories concerning the female characters in 1 and 2 Samuel were intended to provide readers with multiple opportunities for ethical evaluation of David and the hierarchical system that he represented (2015: 21).

But the stories also yield moral insight for contemporary readers of the life of David, for the past does not belong just to those who lived in it, but to those in the present who are willing to infuse it with meaning. For this reason, the stories about David resonate far beyond the particular time and place in which they were composed. The narratives capture with vivid and subtle nuance the complexities of the human experience, and since the characters who populate them share the same needs, emotions and frailties as ourselves, learning about their predicaments often helps us to understand and contemplate our own. The world of the text is not too far removed from the world of lived experience, and we can recognize something of our own lives in the lives of the characters we encounter in the biblical narrative. As such, the stories invite a certain self-scrutiny, and in the character of David we may see mirrored some of our own weaknesses and vulnerabilities; indeed, we may find, in the process, that these narratives tell us 'more than we want to know about David and more than we can bear to understand about ourselves' (Brueggemann 1990: 272).

Ambiguity in Biblical Narrative

Part of the fascination of biblical narratives lies in their ambiguity. Motives, instead of being transparent, are shrouded in mystery; plots, instead of being clear and coherent, are riddled with gaps and omissions; characters, instead of being paragons of virtue or embodiments of evil, are complex, multi-faceted entities, their actions often volatile and their behaviour frequently unpredictable. Of course, it is precisely these troublesome omissions, ellipses and non-sequiturs that evoke our curiosity and interest, and it is the very complexity of characterization that gives the story an air of verisimilitude and leaves the reader wanting more. Although the biblical narrators appear omniscient, they display their omniscience with a frustrating selectivity, withholding information about events, character traits, and motives.[14] The biblical stories, through the most rigorous economy of means, lead us to ponder such issues as the complexity of motive and the ambiguities of character. As readers we are called upon – indeed, compelled – to speculate about what makes the characters 'tick', to fill in the gaps, and give voice to the silences of the text, often blissfully unaware that this is what we are doing.

---

14. James Ackerman emphasizes the reticence of the biblical narrators to provide information concerning the inner thoughts and motivations of the characters: 'As opposed to Homer, who tells us everything, the art of biblical narrative challenges us with what we are not told but must attempt to discern' (1990: 41).

In the Abraham cycle, for example, the motive of the protagonist is often left in a penumbra of doubt, and while the reader must draw his or her own inferences from the text, much inevitably remains a matter of conjecture. Did he pass off his wife, Sarah, as his sister (Gen. 12:10-20; 20:1-18) in order to save his own skin, or did he have more altruistic reasons for his action, knowing that if he were to die in Egypt he would have no son and could not, therefore, be a blessing to the nations (Gen. 12:2-3)? Was he motivated by a selfish desire for self-preservation or by a genuine desire to see the divine promise fulfilled? A further quandary appears in the story of his intercession on behalf of Sodom and Gomorrah (Gen. 18:22-33), for here, too, his motive is not entirely clear. Did he intercede out of a genuine concern for the fate of the innocent or because he knew that his nephew, Lot, was among the inhabitants (cf. Mills 2001: 32)? Just as different interpretations are possible concerning his motive, so conflicting views of his character emerge from the narrative. Indeed, it is by no means certain whether he is intended as a good or bad role model for the reader. In some texts he appears as a noble and pious man of unwavering faith, acting in silent trust that God would fulfil his promise; in other texts, however, he appears as a callous, cold-hearted parent and a callow, unworthy husband, prepared to sacrifice his son and lie about his wife in order to ensure his own safety.[15] Thus, readers of the Abraham narratives are bound to ask some searching questions about the patriarch's behaviour. Why is the man who obediently leaves Ur, trusting completely in God's promises (Gen. 12:4-5), so sceptical when informed by God that Sarah was pregnant, despite her advanced years (Gen. 17:17)? Why is it that the man who was prepared to plead with God in the case of Sodom and Gomorrah (Gen. 18:22-33) appears seemingly willing to sacrifice his own son without a similar plea for justice and mercy (Gen. 22:1-19)?[16] How is it that the man who acts in the most

---

15. Mary Mills (2001: 25–47) argues that the different interpretations of Abraham's character depend on whether we view the Abraham cycle in its entirety or whether we focus exclusively on individual stories. While the broader context suggests a pious man of faith and one of sound moral integrity, some of the individual narratives suggest that his behaviour impacts badly on his household. Hence her conclusion that Abraham is viewed as 'a saint in his piety and as a savage in his parenting' (p. 47).

16. Cf. Magonet 1997: 21. Mary Mills notes the ambiguity in the story of the binding of Isaac: 'to sacrifice a child must either be the height of moral vision and ethical behaviour or the most corrupt and unethical action possible' (2001: 32). She concludes that neither Abraham nor God emerge from the episode with their reputations untarnished (p. 38).

disreputable way with regard to his handmaid, Hagar (Gen. 21:8-14), has the gall to argue with God that the judge of all the earth should do what is right (Gen. 18:25)?

It would be interesting to know how the original readers would have regarded such stories. In the narrative concerning Jacob and Esau, for example, which of the two brothers would they have regarded as the more blameworthy (Gen. 25:29-34)? Was it Esau, whose precipitate actions ('he ate, drank, rose and went away'; v. 34) show the utter contempt in which he held his birthright? Or was it Jacob, the shrewd calculator who resorted to trickery to get his own way? Would they have condemned him for cheating his brother or admired him as a man who patently seemed far better suited as the bearer of the birthright (cf. Berlin 1994: 39)? And in the later story in which Jacob is deceived into marrying Leah instead of Rachel (Gen. 29:21-30), would they have sympathized with the tricked trickster or delighted in seeing him receive his just deserts? It would also be interesting to know where the narrator stood ethically as such events were recounted, for it is by no means clear who gains and who loses the moral approbation of the text. The narrators present us with many different voices but deny us the authorial guidance as to which (if any) we should be listening to. They seem deliberately to invest their stories with an aura of ambiguity, leaving us in doubt about their precise applicability, while at the same time teasing our minds into active thought and deliberation. As John Goldingay observes, such ambiguity can be 'creatively provocative' (1995: 39), for the stories leave us with questions to resolve, moral options to be counterbalanced, conflicting possibilities to be considered, and various perspectives to be untangled. From the ethical point of view, the stories are often notoriously non-committal, but it is this ethical ambiguity that makes the biblical narratives such fascinating objects of study, for a narrative with a clear moral is not likely to be morally interesting.[17] The so-called moral of the story is often open to interpretation, and it is precisely because the interpretations are so varied that the reading experience is so rewarding and enriching. The stories are not limited to a single, clear message or 'moral lesson'; rather, as Mary Mills has observed, they occupy a 'no-man's land of indeterminacy' (2001: 247–8).

It is this ambiguity inherent in the text that makes the 'model morality' enamoured by some scholars unsatisfactory, for it oversimplifies the story, suggesting that a straightforward 'moral lesson' can be drawn.

---

17. The portrait of David in Chronicles is largely devoid of moral ambiguity, and as a consequence it is morally less interesting.

Indeed, it is quite possible that the story may carry more than one 'message' and that different readers of the same text may arrive at different moral conclusions. Biblical morality must allow for a diversity of interpretations and we must not settle for a single, unified reading that produces a bland, one-dimensional ethic. The task of the exegete is to demonstrate that a story can generate a whole repertoire of meanings and a rich montage of different perspectives, and to show that a single narrative may be subject to a wide range of interpretations, since phrases, events and characters lend themselves to different readings. As Meir Sternberg reminds us, the Bible 'habitually generates ambivalence' (1985: 38), and the events and characters depicted are seldom presented in black and white terms; on the contrary, as often as not, they are shrouded in shades of grey. Since the characters are such complex, multi-dimensional entities, portrayed in their imperfections as well as their virtues, it is not simply a matter of imitation or avoidance; just like people we meet in everyday life, they do not fit neatly into the binary good/evil stereotype.[18] They mirror our own strengths and weaknesses and thus reflect the moral tensions that belong to the very nature of human existence. This is why the stories have such a powerful and enduring hold on the imagination.

The story of David's affair with Bathsheba, discussed in Chapter 3, provides an excellent example of a narrative that is fraught with ambiguity. Here, the narrator appears deliberately to withhold the information that is required by the reader in order to render judgments about the characters, their motives and actions. Did Bathsheba deliberately attempt to attract the king's attention by bathing in full view of the royal palace? Did she respond willingly to David's invitation or was she acting under duress? Should she be viewed as the archetypal scheming temptress or as the innocent victim of male lust? Furthermore, was Uriah, her husband, aware of the adultery, and, if so, did David suspect that he knew? The gaps between what is told and what must be inferred seems to have been deliberately and carefully contrived by the narrator to leave the readers with an element of doubt, inviting them to arrive at different – and perhaps conflicting – interpretations of the motives and intentions of the principal characters.

---

18. Gordon Wenham argues that it is misguided to view the characters depicted in the Hebrew Bible in black and white terms, for such narratives deal 'with a world where there are few perfect saints and few unredeemable sinners; most of its heroes and heroines have both virtues and vices, they mix obedience and unbelief' (2000: 15).

The effect of the narrative's ambiguity is to draw its readers into the fictive world of the story, setting in motion their own decision-making processes, and forcing them to come to their own moral judgment concerning the culpability or innocence of the characters portrayed. Such ambiguity allows for a readerly interaction with the characters that a more explicitly detailed account would not have made possible, for it enables us to enter the story in a spirit of imaginative speculation, teasing out its compressed or implicit meanings. In an important article on the function of literary ambiguity in the David–Bathsheba story, Gale Yee makes the following observation:

> The ambiguity of the narrative calls forth a reader response in such a way that the moral purpose of the story is emphasized. The story, precisely in its ambiguity, engages its readers to make moral judgments implicitly at every point of the narrative. The author's technique of leaving ambiguous motives which the readers especially desire to be crystal clear forces the readers to become more actively involved with the characters and the morality of their actions. Therefore, the "inner world" of the characters is not irrelevant to the story's moral goal… It is relevant because its detailing is purposefully left ambiguous so that the readers assume their own moral posture towards the story. (1988: 251)

As Yee points out, the narrator's own evaluation of the events recorded in the David–Bathsheba affair is deliberately left until the end of the story, by which time readers will inevitably have come to their own conclusions. When they are informed that 'the thing that David did was evil in the sight of the LORD' (2 Sam. 11:27b), the divine displeasure will hardly come as a surprise, for they will surely have already come to a similar conclusion themselves, and the narrator's judgment merely confirms what the reader has already decided. Yet even the narratorial evaluation itself is ambiguous, for it is not clear whether 'the thing' refers to David's adultery with Bathsheba or his murder-by-proxy of her husband. Here again, therefore, the reader is invited to consider different possibilities.

The ambiguous nature of the narratorial judgment leads us to consider another aspect of narrative ethics that will be considered in the course of the present volume, namely, the issue of evaluation.

Evaluation of Biblical Narrative

The process of evaluating the moral stance of a biblical narrative is often a complex and difficult enterprise. Occasionally, the task is made easier by the omniscient narrator, who attempts to guide our perception of a particular character or event by including a comment that is explicitly evaluative. Thus, for example, we are told that Noah was a righteous man, blameless in his generation, who walked with God (Gen. 6:9), and Job is similarly said to be 'blameless and upright', and is described as a man 'who feared God and turned away from evil' (Job 1:1, 8). Of course, the narrator's explicit and authoritative evaluation is by no means always positive, for the storyteller reserves the right to be censorious when the occasion is deemed appropriate. For example, we are informed that the people of Sodom were 'wicked' (Gen. 13:13), and that Nabal was 'surly and mean' (1 Sam. 25:3); Rehoboam did what was 'evil' (2 Chron. 12:14), and Jehoshaphat is said to have acted 'wickedly' (2 Chron. 20:35). But such direct and unambiguous evaluations are comparatively rare in biblical narrative, and evaluative judgments usually take a more indirect form by allowing one character in the story to comment on the moral disposition of another.[19] Boaz, for example, deems Ruth to be a 'worthy woman' (Ruth 3:11), and his estimate of her character is confirmed by her actions in the story; similarly, when Jacob concedes that Tamar's actions had been justified (Gen. 38:26), we realize that his estimation of her character is entirely appropriate. It sometimes transpires that the character making the evaluation is Yahweh himself and, in such cases, we may suppose that the viewpoint expressed coincides with that of the storyteller. Thus, when the narrator claims, for example, that Manasseh 'did what was evil in the sight of the LORD' (2 Kgs 21:16), or that Hezekiah 'did what was right in the sight of the LORD' (2 Kgs 18:3), it is not unreasonable to assume that the omniscient storyteller, who presumes to know God's mind, concurs with the divine assessment.[20]

In all the above examples, the narrator, whether directly or indirectly, provides some kind of guiding light to assist the reader in determining which character to admire and which to deplore. In most narratives, however, readers are deprived of the authoritative narratorial 'voice over'

---

19. Adele Berlin refers to this strategy as 'embedded evaluation', the narrator having the characters themselves do the evaluation either by their own words or actions (1994: 105). S. Min Chun (2014: 173) distinguishes between 'embedded ethics' (i.e. the ethical perspective of the narrator) and 'embodied ethics' (i.e. the ethical perspective of the characters).

20. Berlin similarly concludes that the evaluation proffered by God in biblical narratives is presumably the same as that of the narrator: 'I say this because I cannot think of any passage in which the narrator disagrees with God's evaluation or judgment… [O]ne often gets the impression that the narrator is reflecting the way God would evaluate events if he had been the one telling the story' (1994: 148 n. 28). For a different view, however, see Parry 2004: 238–9.

to guide their response; instead, the narrator appears as a neutral recorder of events, and readers are invited to make a moral evaluation that the text resolutely refuses to make on their behalf. Indeed, the narrator's attitude to a character or event appears at times so scrupulously neutral that even the most shocking occurrences are reported with an off-hand indifference. In passages such as Genesis 19 or Judges 19, where the actions depicted are particularly heinous, the intrusive authorial voice is nowhere to be heard, and it is left to the reader to supply the moral outrage that the events described clearly invite. By withholding judgment, the narrator, in effect, invites us to do our own reflection on the story.

Since the narrator is so good at making sense of the events described, we are generally well-disposed to accept the point of view offered, and it takes a conscious effort of detachment for the reader not to identify with the author's point of view or with the ideology that underlies it. The flow of the story encourages us to accept the values it propagates, and so powerful are the rhetorical devices deployed by the narrator that readers are not always conscious that they are being manipulated.[21] As an example of the narrator's ability to manipulate the reader's response, it will be convenient to examine, briefly, the story of Nabal, Abigail and David recounted in 1 Samuel 25.

Nabal, Abigail and David (1 Samuel 25)

By this point in the narrative of 1 Samuel, David is being pursued by Saul and is leading a fugitive's life in the Judaean wilderness. He hears that Nabal, a wealthy landowner, was shearing his sheep in Carmel, and David sends word to inform him that his men had protected Nabal's shepherds and his flocks, and he now wanted to be rewarded for their work. The message that David relays to Nabal seems deliberately designed to intimidate him, for it implies that his men had *hitherto* refrained from doing any harm to Nabal's flocks or to his shepherds (v. 7), and if he wanted this situation to continue he should give 'whatever you have at hand to your servants and to your son David' (v. 8). It is difficult to come to any other conclusion than that David – in true mafioso-style – was here engaged in some form of extortion, and that he was, effectively, running a protection

---

21. Rhetorical Criticism shows how the use of language and literary technique is used by the biblical narrators to manipulate their readers into drawing certain conclusions, so that even when no explicit narratorial judgment is offered, it may be possible to infer the authorial point of view by probing the way in which the story is told. Chun provides an insightful discussion of the discourse-linguistic features in the story of Josiah in 2 Kgs 22:1–23:30 that serve to convey the author's stance (2014: 172–225).

racket.²² Nabal, not unreasonably, refuses to pay him any money, since David had not been engaged by him to provide such protection; indeed, he had not even heard of David, and he supposed that he must be a runaway slave turned robber or extortioner (v. 10). Nabal insists that it is his own men, who have done an honest and decent day's work, that should be rewarded, not some nameless nobody who had the impudence to demand money in return for his unsolicited services: 'Shall I take my bread and my water and the meat that I have butchered for my shearers, and give it to men who come from I do not know where?' (v. 11). When Nabal's contemptuous reply is conveyed to David, he becomes angry and determines to avenge the insult by killing not only Nabal himself, but all his male relatives (vv. 13, 21-22). He sets out with an armed force of four hundred men, and a bloodbath is only avoided by the timely intervention of Abigail, Nabal's wife, who comes to meet David, presenting him with extravagant gifts, and interceding on her husband's behalf. She urges him to refrain from embarking on a rash and ill-considered punitive expedition, for by indulging in such unbridled vengeance David would be guilty of shedding innocent blood, and his action would probably impede his ascent to the throne (vv. 28-31). David relents, aborts his attack on Nabal and, following Abigail's advice, leaves it to God to exact vengeance. When Nabal hears from Abigail about the fate that he had so narrowly averted, the shock proves too great for him, and he suffers a stroke which leaves him paralyzed.²³ Yahweh strikes him dead, whereupon David marries Abigail and appropriates her husband's status and wealth.²⁴

22. For the view that David was engaged in some form of extortion, see Ackroyd 1971: 195; Lemche 1979: 12; Gunn 1980: 96–8; McKenzie 2000: 97; Brueggemann 1990: 176. Bruce Birch, however, objects to this interpretation, claiming that such a view 'seems more influenced by old gangster movies than by the biblical narrative' (1998: 1166). However, as April Westbrook has observed, the violent raids executed by David later (1 Sam. 27:8-11) serve to confirm the plausibility of his threats here (2015: 66 n. 5). Thus, Mark Biddle is probably correct when he comments that 'it is difficult to escape the conclusion that, in fact, the only threat to Nabal's flocks had been David himself' (2002: 637).

23. For an overview of various attempts to offer a medical diagnosis of the nature of Nabal's illness ('his heart died within him; he became like a stone'; v. 37), see Boyle 2001: 403–5.

24. Since Nabal was a Calebite, a member of an important tribe in the south, closely associated with Judah, alliance by marriage to such a group would be vital for David's eventual position, for he was later to be made king at Hebron, the main town of the Calebite area (2 Sam. 2:1-4; cf. Judg. 1:20). See Levenson 1978: 24–8; Levenson and Halpern 1980: 507–11.

Now, the above broad outline of the story would surely predispose the reader to sympathize with Nabal, and to regard David's unseemly shenanigans in a decidedly negative light.[25] That David was prepared to wipe out Nabal and his male servants simply because Nabal refused to reward him for a service that he had never asked for suggests the action of a precipitate and violent man who was prepared to wreak vengeance simply in order to salve his wounded ego. We, like Nabal, would surely regard David's behaviour with disgust, and his use of a crude vulgarism as he refers to the male members of Nabal's family ('those who piss against the wall'; v. 22) does little to enhance our estimation of his character.[26] The fact that Nabal is put to death by Yahweh merely heightens our sympathy with a man whose actions merely reflect what any self-respecting and legitimate landowner would have done in the circumstances.[27]

This particular narrative is of interest for our purpose because it demonstrates how the narrator was able to use all the tactics at his disposal to ensure that the reader would *not* side with Nabal, nor think poorly of David.[28] In order to persuade the reader to accept his point of

---

25. This narrative is widely regarded as foreshadowing the darker side of David's character, which later emerges clearly in the story of David and Bathsheba, discussed in Chapter 3. For the parallels between the two narratives, see Boyle 2001: 414; Berlin 1994: 30; Nicol 1998 (but note the reservations of Esler 2020: 179–80). Steven McKenzie argues that the David–Bathsheba story is essentially the same as the Nabal–Abigail narrative 'only without the cover-up' (2000: 156). Jon Levenson sees in 1 Sam. 25 'a proleptic glimpse, within David's ascent, of his fall from grace' (1978: 24).

26. English translations rather prudishly avoid translating the Hebrew literally, preferring instead to deploy the more anodyne term 'male' (though cf. KJV's 'any that pisseth against the wall'). Some suggest that the term is pejorative, implying that the male members of Nabal's family were no better than dogs that urinate against a wall; for criticisms of those who argue in favour of a pejorative connotation of the term, however, see D.E. Smith 2010. It may be significant that Nabal is identified as a 'Calebite' (v. 3) which, in addition to denoting his ancestry, was perhaps intended as a deliberate play on the Hebrew word for 'dog' (*keleb*); cf. Leithart 2001: 526.

27. This narrative inevitably raises questions regarding the moral nature of Yahweh as a character in the story, for even if Nabal is deemed to have acted unwisely, he surely did not deserve to be struck dead by God. As David Gunn has observed, 'retribution here is not decided on moral grounds' (1980: 102). The moral aspect of God's character is discussed in Chapter 6.

28. Walter Brueggemann claims that the narrator 'stacks the cards against Nabal in David's favor' (1990: 177), and Steven McKenzie observes that the narrator 'goes to great lengths to explain how David was innocent of any wrongdoing' (2000: 33).

view, the narrator declares his sympathy openly, emphasizing at the outset that Nabal was a surly, churlish, mean-spirited man, in stark contrast to his wife, Abigail, who was 'clever and beautiful' (v. 3).[29] Should the reader have any misgivings about the narrator's negative evaluation of Nabal's character, we are told that even his own servants regarded him as 'so ill-natured that no one can speak to him' (v. 17). And if any doubts should persist in the reader's mind, then they are surely dispelled when Abigail, Nabal's own wife, regards him as a fool by name and a fool by nature (v. 25), who was not to be taken seriously.[30] Abigail's disparagement of her husband is matched by her adulation and admiration of David: he was a warrior, 'fighting the battles of the LORD', and was one in whom 'evil shall not be found' (v. 28). She even flatteringly refers to David's future under Yahweh's blessing, and she has the prescience to foresee that David was destined to become 'prince over Israel' (v. 30).[31] Indeed, throughout the story, Abigail's conduct is contrasted sharply with that of her husband; she behaves in an exemplary manner, and appears

29. As Jon Levenson has observed, the pair are 'irremediably mismatched' (1978: 16), and the description of Abigail is as 'unambiguously laudatory as that of her husband is derogatory' (1978: 18). On the contrast between the two characters, see Kessler 2000: 411–12. Adele Berlin considers the portrayal of the characters as 'exaggerated stereotypes' (1994: 30), and claims that the entire story can be reduced to the tried and tested formula '"fair maiden" Abigail is freed from the "wicked ogre" and marries "prince charming"' (p. 31).

30. For a detailed discussion of the name and its implications, see Barr 1969: 21–8. Of course, it is unlikely that Nabal was his real name (for who would give their child a name meaning 'fool'?). McKenzie (2000: 97) suggests that his real name may have been Ithra (cf. 2 Sam. 17:25) or Jether (cf. 1 Chron. 2:17). The storyteller, however, clearly regarded the name Nabal as providing an insight into the man's true nature, and by assigning him this name the narrator effectively contributed to his 'character assassination' in the story (cf. Levenson 1978: 13).

31. April Westbrook argues that Abigail here assumes the functions of a prophet, although she is not overtly described as such in the text. Abigail rightly predicts that David will acquire the throne, and that he will avoid unnecessary bloodshed of Nabal's household. Moreover, she foresees that the Davidic dynasty will be an 'enduring' house (v. 28), a prediction that was later to be repeated by Nathan, who *is* clearly identified as a prophet within the text (2015: 69–71). H.W. Hertzberg (1964: 203–4) similarly regards Abigail as representing 'the prophetic voice', and George Nicol considers that Abigail's form of speech 'is almost prophetic in quality and content' (1998: 132). As many commentators have observed, Abigail's clear perception of David's destiny stands in sharp contrast to her husband, who does not even know who David is. As Robert Gordon observes, 'Abigail is as perspicacious as Nabal is obstinately blind' (1980: 46).

as a paragon of eloquence, charm and sophistication, imbued with intelligence and shrewd common sense, whereas her husband is foolish, brusque and mean, and was the kind of man who would participate in a debauched and self-indulgent feast at which he would become so inebriated that he was unapproachable until the following day (v. 36). Moreover, in order to refute any suggestion that David had engaged in a morally questionable scam, even Nabal's shepherds agree that the protective presence of David's men had, indeed, been an asset ('they were a wall to us both by night and by day, all the while we were with them keeping the sheep'; v. 16).[32] There was no question that David and his men had acted egregiously; on the contrary, they had provided Nabal with a perfectly genuine and legitimate service. And while Nabal dies, unmourned, at the end of the story, it is made clear that David was not implicated in his death, since that was due to the direct intervention of Yahweh: 'the LORD has returned the evil-doing of Nabal upon his own head' (v. 39).

By the end of the story, not only does Nabal's wife and servants think poorly of him, but so do we as readers; in fact, we may well feel that he had been niggardly in refusing to recompense David for ensuring that his flocks and shepherds were safe. That the narrator has succeeded admirably in orienting the reader to embrace his point of view is clear from the gloss which some scholars have put on the story. Thus, for example, John Kessler is content to read the text as the narrator would want us to read it, and he views David's request as entirely reasonable, while Nadab's refusal is both offensive and irrational. He argues that the latter's undoing was entirely the result of his own folly, while David showed great restraint and wisdom in relenting from the vengeance that he had planned to exact upon the household of Nabal. Viewed through the narrator's ideological lens, Nabal 'is seen to be ungrateful, greedy, stubborn, disrespectful of social norms, and generally a graceless boor with an inflated view of his own importance', while 'David's activity is *irreproachable*', for 'he proves to be respectful of social norms, open to reason, capable of self-restraint, and blameless' (2000: 414). George G. Nicol similarly comes to David's defence, arguing that 'David acts honourably and with a high degree of chivalry in this affair' (1998: 136 n. 21). Walter Brueggemann even concludes that the narrator has succeeded in demonstrating that the death of Nabal was, indeed, 'a merited outcome' (1990: 175). That scholars

---

32. David Gunn asks whether Nabal's servants were here 'really recalling a genuine favour or merely dressing up a racket in the interests of practical survival? We simply cannot be sure' (1980: 98).

have been so willing to follow the interpretative direction suggested by the narrator is a testament to the storyteller's craft in persuading the reader to embrace his own 'take' on the incident.

Evaluation of Characters in 1 and 2 Samuel

Our aim in the chapters that follow will be to assist readers in their evaluative response to some of the other stories relating to David as recorded in 1 and 2 Samuel by highlighting the moral problems and ambiguities within the text.[33] At times, the narrator provides no explicit evaluation of the actions and behaviour of the characters, and it will be argued that such reticence on the storyteller's part was deliberate; it is as if the narrator is saying, in effect, you decide! The account of the lies and deceptions perpetrated by Michal and Jonathan in 1 Sam. 19:11-17 and 20:1-34, discussed in the next chapter, falls into this category, for the reader is left to consider the values that should guide human conduct, and to ponder over some agonisingly difficult moral questions without any explicit authorial guidance. In the account of David's affair with Bathsheba and his murder-by-proxy of her husband (2 Sam. 11), discussed in Chapter 3, attention will be paid not only to the way that the narrator has evaluated David's behaviour, but also how subsequent commentators have evaluated the character of both David and Bathsheba. Chapter 4 will be concerned with David's reaction to Yahweh's judgment rendered through the prophet Nathan, and it will be argued that the grief that he displays upon realizing that his punishment entailed the death of the child born of the illicit union (2 Sam. 12) may lead to a different evaluation of David's character on the part of the reader. The account of the rape of Tamar, discussed in Chapter 5, is devoid of explicit authorial judgment but the nature of Amnon's character is revealed through his speech, actions and gestures, and the voicing of any moral criticism is left to one of the characters, for it is Tamar who identifies his actions as 'an outrage' and who warns him not to be like 'one of the scoundrels in Israel' (2 Sam. 13:12-13). Often, as here, the conceptual viewpoint of the narrator and reader will coincide, but sometimes the reader may want to challenge or reject, rather than endorse, the author's evaluation. Chapter 6 will argue that the involvement of God in human affairs is worthy of critical examination, and that Yahweh, no less than any other character, should not be exempt from moral scrutiny.

33. For a detailed and insightful analysis of the ambiguity and complexity in the narrator's method of conveying moral, political and theological evaluation in 1 and 2 Samuel, see Gilmour 2011: 155–223.

Martha Nussbaum's Approach to Ethics

In recent years, John Barton has argued that Martha Nussbaum's studies of ancient Greek tragedy and modern novelists, such as Henry James and Marcel Proust, might provide a helpful approach for the study of ethics in biblical narrative (1995; 2000: 54–7). Nussbaum, a philosopher in the Aristotelian tradition, attempts to bring literary works into the arena of modern philosophy, arguing that fictional narrative is an eminently suitable object for ethical investigation. Nussbaum does not, of course, claim that works of fiction should replace moral philosophy, or that Plato and Kant should suddenly give way to James and Proust in the University curriculum; she does insist, however, that ethical insight should not be the sole preserve of moral philosophers, for she believes that the imagined characters and events of literary fiction can give expression to profound moral truths.[34] Indeed, she goes so far as to argue that the richly textured world of the novel is, in some respects, preferable to the lofty heights of philosophical abstraction. At the very least, moral philosophy has lost much through the absence of dialogue with literary thought, and she contends that 'if philosophy is a search for wisdom about ourselves, philosophy needs to turn to literature' (1990: 290).

At this point it may be helpful to unpack some of Nussbaum's arguments concerning the relative merits of moral philosophy and fiction. Nussbaum readily concedes that moral philosophers can produce impeccably logical and reasoned arguments; the problem, however, is that they are concerned, for the most part, with general rules, and general rules cannot always accommodate the complex requirements of a specific situation. The advantage of fiction, on the other hand, is that it is closely allied to the world of particulars and to concrete experiences; its concern is with the vicissitudes and idiosyncrasies of individual cases and, as such, it demands of the reader a nuanced and finely tuned responsiveness to such cases. In this regard, Nussbaum is clearly indebted to Aristotle, who argued that a system of rules set up in advance can encompass only situations that have been seen before; the real world, on the other hand, confronts us with ever new configurations, ever new situations, in which

---

34. That the novelist, through imagined characters and situations, can give expression to moral insights is clear, for example, in the work of Iris Murdoch. Her novels feed on her views as a moral philosopher in that they exemplify in imagined individuals her abstract ideas of good and evil.

we must determine for ourselves the proper course to take.³⁵ It is for this reason, according to Nussbaum, that the rule-book mentality espoused by some moral philosophers is seriously deficient, and she deploys a colourful analogy to make her point: 'A doctor whose only resource, confronted with a new configuration of symptoms, was to turn to the textbook would be a poor doctor; a pilot who steered his ship by rule in a storm of unanticipated direction or intensity would be incompetent' (1990: 71). In other words, we must confront the moral dilemmas with which we are faced with responsiveness, imagination and flexibility. Nussbaum is at pains to emphasize that this does not mean that ethical decisions should simply be *ad hoc*, rejecting all guidance from the past; after all, the good navigator 'does not go by the rule book' but nor does 'she...pretend that she has never been on a boat before' (1990: 75). That is, general rules may in some cases be useful or necessary, but they should not, by themselves, be regarded as sufficient guides for the moral life.³⁶ It is for this reason that Nussbaum prefers to turn to works of fiction for moral enlightenment, for the ethical values enshrined in such works resolutely refuse to be reduced to generalities or rules of thumb; rather, they invite us to view the world in all its bewildering complexity, presenting us with texts that display the sheer difficulty of moral choices, while inviting us to come to a decision, having pondered for ourselves the various options available.

But works of fiction, according to Nussbaum, require commentary, for sensitive and informed commentary can unpack the complexity of fictional accounts in a helpful way. Readers need commentary also because they might miss some clues hidden in the text, or pass over subtle hints within the composition, or overlook certain interpretative possibilities while assiduously pursuing others. Sensitive commentary also enables readers to revise previous readings, but above all, it can aid them in the art of perception. For Nussbaum – as for Aristotle – moral

---

35. Nussbaum contrasts Aristotle's views in this regard with those that prevailed in Sparta: Spartan morality emphasized a system of inflexible rules to which all citizens must be thoroughly subservient; they were not to attend, in their decision-making, to the particularity of individual situations (1990: 98).

36. Aristotle expressed grave reservations about universal principles as arbiters of ethical correctness. Nussbaum refers to the emphasis of both Aristotle and Henry James on the 'ethical crudeness of moralities based exclusively on general rules', and their insistence that ethics must demand 'a much finer responsiveness to the concrete' (1990: 37). Nussbaum does not deny the universalizability of ethical judgments; it is just that when contexts change universal principles are not likely to be of much usefulness.

knowledge was not simply an intellectual grasp of certain propositions or of particular facts; it was about intuitive perception, a faculty which, according to Nussbaum, moral philosophers have all too often tended to neglect.[37] This is why fiction can make a significant contribution to moral deliberation, for stories and novels involve an intuitive approach and an improvisatory response that allows readers to ponder a complex situation flexibly, prepared, if necessary, to alter their *prima facie* conception of the good in the light of a new, shared experience.[38] Moral philosophy, on the other hand, seeks to extricate us from such complexities and bewilderment by setting up a watertight system of rules and methods of calculation that claims to be able to settle all troublesome cases, in effect, before the fact (1990: 141).

Another important aspect of Nussbaum's contribution is her insistence that reading involves an emotional as well as an intellectual capacity.[39] Emotion has a vital role to play within the ethical life and has a good claim to be regarded as a significant aspect of the moral process. Stories about love, longing, fear, loss, conflict, hope, despair, guilt, and the complex inter-relations between them, enable us to learn something about ourselves and our own emotional repertoire. In order for this to happen, however, we must allow the characters to interact with us not only through the intellect but through our emotion: we must fear their danger, grieve at their loss, delight in their success, and feel their anxiety when faced with the uncertain outcomes of life. As will become apparent in our discussion of the aftermath of the David–Bathsheba affair (Chapter 4), a sensitive reading of the story will only come about if the reader is prepared to grasp the emotional impact of the narrative: David's frantic anxiety about the fate of his child, his feeling of guilt and need for atonement, his sense of sinfulness and his

---

37. Nussbaum claims that 'philosophers who have defended the primacy of intuitive perception are few' (1990: 141).

38. The notion of improvisation – a favourite Jamesian as well as Aristotelian concept – is important in Nussbaum's thinking: 'Good deliberation is like theatrical or musical improvisation, where what counts is flexibility, responsiveness, and openness to the external' (1990: 74). For a detailed discussion of her concept of improvisation, see Nussbaum 1990: 148–67.

39. Nussbaum is particularly critical of Plato in this regard, who argued that ethical learning must proceed by separating the intellect from our emotion. She observes that the tendency to downplay the role of emotion in philosophical discourse emerges again in the seventeenth century, and 'can be traced back at least as far as Locke, who writes that the rhetorical and emotive elements of style are rather like a woman: amusing and even delightful when kept in their place, dangerous and corrupting if permitted to take control' (1986: 16).

fear of judgment (2 Sam. 12:12-23). As we become emotionally involved, we inevitably recognize our affinity with the characters and become, in effect, participants in their lives and in their moral dilemmas. The stories elicit in us an acknowledgment of our own imperfections, and as we read, we realize that they are saying something about ourselves, our own lives, and our own choices. As a result, the narrative dwells in us at an unconscious level; indeed, it may even (without our fully realizing it) engender in us a change, and since our interaction with the characters resides well beyond the time spent on the page, the change may well turn out to be a 'matter of prolonged therapy' (1990: 295).

The importance of the interaction between the text and the reader is vividly illustrated in Nussbaum's illuminating discussion of Dickens's novel, *David Copperfield*. In the novel, the reader is told that David's father had left him a collection of novels that he avidly read and reread, 'reading as if for life'.[40] Nussbaum takes this to mean that David was in no sense a detached, objective reader but was, rather, a 'passionate participant' in the stories that he encountered (1990: 354), bringing to them his own hopes and fears as he contemplated the bewildering complexities of life. According to Nussbaum, the young David Copperfield may be regarded as an example of how all readers should appropriate works of fiction: they, too, must immerse themselves in the story and enter the lives of the characters they encounter, imagining possible connections between their own situations and those of the protagonist so that, in the act of reading, readers become, in Proust's words, readers of their own selves (2003: 276).

In this regard, it is interesting to observe that some biblical scholars have referred to another David – the David who hears and responds to Nathan's parable in 2 Sam. 12:1-6 – as providing readers with a similar example of how we should respond to the narratives recorded in the Hebrew Bible.[41] As Jan Fokkelman has remarked, David here takes up position as that of the 'good listener' who 'existentially participates in the truth' of the parable (1981: 81), and the anger and indignation he

---

40. Dickens 1966: 106. One of the chapters in Nussbaum's *Love's Knowledge* bears the title 'Reading for Life' (pp. 230–44). Her detailed discussion of *David Copperfield* is found on pp. 335–64.

41. For the notion of David as the 'model reader', see Pyper 1996. Many literary critics have pondered the significance of the fact that Dickens named his seemingly virtuous protagonist, David, and Copperfield's odious rival, Uriah, in effect reversing the 'good' and 'bad' characters in the 2 Sam. 11 account. As Eitan Bar-Yosef has observed, the novel 'subverts the very essence of the biblical story' (2006: 961). The affinity between the two narratives has been discussed in detail by Jane Vogel (1977: 1–19); see, also, Lasine 2012: 233–9.

experiences upon hearing of the outrageous behaviour of the rich man who stole the poor man's ewe lamb betrays his intense involvement in the story. Indeed, such was the impression that the story made upon him that he was able to identify with the poor man even to the extent of becoming angry on his behalf, and his hyperbolic reaction upon hearing the case ('the man who has done this deserves to die'; 12:5) suggests that he had cast aside any pretension to appear as the objective, dispassionate judge, adjudicating a case that had been brought before him for resolution.[42] As John Barton has perceptively observed, Nathan's parable is itself a parable of the way the entire David story (and, it might be added, biblical narratives in general) is meant to work for us (1998: 32–6). As we identify with the various individuals and their predicaments, we are invited to recognize the affinity – or lack of affinity – between ourselves and the characters of the story.[43] Viewed in this light, biblical narrative is – as Barton recognized – decidedly anti-relativistic: David belongs to our world as much as to his own.[44] Although many elements in the narrative are alien to us in various ways, and are distant from us in time and place, the stories uncover universal tendencies through the presentation of particular people and particular situations, and learning about their predicaments often helps us to understand our own. Just as David was invited to find analogies between Nathan's parable and his own life, and to draw the appropriate conclusion, so we are encouraged to think reflectively about what we read and to engage in an exercise of self-scrutiny.[45] In the process we, like David, may come to recognize some unwelcome and unpalatable truths about ourselves, and in this way the act of reading becomes a moral activity in its own right.

42. As A.A. Anderson has observed, David hardly appears here as the level-headed, objective judge, for 'however precious a pet lamb may be to a poor man, its thief could hardly be put to death' (1989: 161). Horst Seebass similarly points to the incongruity of such a sentence applied to a simple case of theft (1974: 203–4).

43. Stuart Lasine expresses the hope that the appropriate response he would draw from this narrative is that 'David is a mirror of someone I've tried *not* to become. If Nathan were to tap me on the shoulder, I would hope he'd say, "You're *not* the man!"' (2012: 232).

44. Barton 1998: 28–31. Barton makes the following important observation: 'I do not think the study of biblical texts will survive very long unless this general point of view is accepted; they will otherwise become, first, blank canvasses on which we paint our own pictures, and then uninteresting ancient fragments not worth bothering with at all' (1998: 29).

45. As Walter Brueggemann observes, by letting the text work on us, readers existentially participate in its truth, for the narrative permits our 'self-indictment, a sensing of our own fault before anyone need speak it to us' (1990: 286). Bruce Birch

Applying some of Nussbaum's insights to the narratives of the Hebrew Bible raises a number of interesting questions. Can reading such narratives be just as fruitful for the ethicist as reading the works of moral philosophers? To what extent can certain truths about human life be fittingly stated only in narrative form? Are there moral truths that the plainness of traditional moral philosophy lacks the power to express? Can biblical narratives, so often plundered for their aesthetic value or theological insights, be viewed also as vehicles for ethical reflection? Barton has rightly recognized that the narratives in the Hebrew Bible cannot be called 'philosophical' as such, but he suggests that they might 'deal, in their own way, with some of the issues that concern, or have concerned philosophers'.[46]

This, in turn, raises the possibility that the ethics of the Hebrew Bible can be brought into fruitful engagement with extra-biblical modes of thought. Of course, the tendency has frequently been to move in the opposite direction, emphasizing that biblical thought contrasts sharply with modern philosophical approaches, the morality enshrined in the Hebrew Bible being regarded as based on divine revelation and therefore incompatible with that based on human reason.[47] It may be, however, that biblical morality and moral philosophy share some common insights, and it is at least conceivable that some modern theories of philosophy have already been anticipated in the biblical text.[48] For example, utilitarianism – the notion that the morally right action is to be determined by its likely consequences – is regarded as one of the most important

---

has emphasized the transformative power of biblical narratives, while appreciating that they can only exercise that power if they are reflected upon in light of our own experience: 'If we cannot see ourselves in the stories we encounter, they have little power to shape and transform us' (1988: 78).

46. Barton 1995: 67. Barton suggests that the narratives of the Hebrew Bible can be analysed along the lines that Nussbaum suggests with regard to classical Greek tragedy, although he modestly admits that he has not 'progressed very far towards making her classical key turn in the biblical lock' (1995: 67).

47. Walter C. Kaiser, for example, draws a sharp contrast between the ethics of the Hebrew Bible and philosophical ethics, describing the former as personal, theistic, universal, and future orientated (1983: 4–13).

48. It may be that some modern theories of justice, too, have been anticipated in the Hebrew Bible. For example, the modern notion of retributive justice is anticipated in the *lex talionis*, the concept of a life for a life often being used to justify the imposition of the death penalty in some states in the USA. Similarly, the notion of compensatory justice, whereby the injured party (or his or her family) has a claim against the wrongdoer, is anticipated in such passages as Exod. 22:1-6.

insights of modern times. The morally right action is the one that produces the greatest amount of positive consequences for everyone concerned. Now, Abraham's intercession on behalf of the inhabitants of Sodom can be regarded as a precursor of the consequentialist ethic (Gen. 18:22-33). Abraham carefully weighs the interests of all concerned and urges God to adopt a course of action most likely to maximize the interests of those affected. The issue at stake is whether the just punishment of the wicked majority is more important than the unjust punishment of the righteous minority. For Abraham, as for contemporary utilitarians, the rightness of an action is determined by a sober assessment of its anticipated consequences. Stories such as that encountered in Gen. 18:22-33 may suggest that there exists in the Hebrew Bible what Barton calls 'philosophical narratives', that is, narratives that deal in their own way with philosophical themes. Barton rightly concedes that the Hebrew Bible lacks anything that could be called 'moral philosophy', if by that we mean the type of abstract theoretical discussions we encounter in Plato, but it certainly contains narratives that invite the reader to ponder moral issues that might otherwise remain abstract and unfocussed.[49]

In conclusion, it must be emphasized that applying the insights of Martha Nussbaum to the narratives of the Hebrew Bible is not intended as an attempt to annex biblical texts to foreign modes of ethical discourse for the sake of it; rather, it is to suggest that it is possible to have a fruitful and constructive dialogue between biblical ethics and modern philosophy for the mutual enrichment of both. Indeed, it may be that biblical teaching has often remained peripheral to the community at large precisely because it has not interacted with modern philosophical concepts. Yoram Hazony has argued forcefully that the failure to appreciate the Bible as a work of philosophy rather than simply as a work of revelation has had far-reaching implications in almost every intellectual, educational and cultural setting in which the Bible features:

> It affects the standing of the Hebrew Scriptures in the public schools, where they are neglected or banned outright because they are seen as works of revelation, not reason. And it affects their status in the religious schools, too…where teachers and administrators confer in bafflement over how to transmit a love of the Bible to the next generation despite the fact that

---

49. Barton claims that the tendency to regard classical Greece as the first culture in the world to reflect systematically on ethical issues may need to be revised, since it is arguable that the cultures of the eastern Mediterranean and Mesopotamia did think about ethics in a more systematic way that is commonly assumed (2014: 1–4).

these texts are works of revelation, not reason. It also dictates the way the Hebrew Bible is treated in the universities, where professors of philosophy, political theory, and intellectual history consistently pass over the ideas of the Hebrew Scriptures as a subject worth researching and teaching to their students, since they see their work as the study of works of reason, not revelation. And what is true for the schools and universities is true for the rest of our culture as well. Outside of religious circles, the Bible is often seen as bearing a taint of irrationality, folly, and irrelevance, the direct result of its reputation as a consummate work of unreason. This taint ensures that for most educated people, the Bible remains pretty much a closed book, the views of its authors on most subjects unaccessed and inaccessible.[50]

In the chapters that follow, it will be argued that many of Nussbaum's insights may prove helpful in negotiating the moral complexity of some of the narratives concerning David. In Chapter 2 it will be shown how moral philosophy helps not only to contemplate the sheer difficulty of moral choice – in this case between truthfulness and loyalty – but also to resolve the dilemma of establishing priorities between conflicting obligations. In Chapters 3 and 5 the account of David's adultery with Bathsheba and the murder of her husband, Uriah (2 Sam. 11:1-27), and the story of the rape of Tamar by her half-brother, Amnon (2 Sam. 13:1-39), will be analysed adopting the method deployed by Martha Nussbaum in relation to Greek tragedy. This will involve reading both stories, first sequentially, and then providing a sensitive and reflective commentary that will, hopefully, unpack the ethical complexities of the narratives in a helpful way. Nussbaum's emphasis on the role of emotion in the reading experience will be applied to the narrative concerning David and Nathan in 2 Sam. 12:1-25, discussed in Chapter 4. Far from being an objective spectator of the events recounted in the parable uttered by the prophet, David becomes emotionally involved in the story and identifies with the poor man, experiencing his sense of injustice. Moreover, David's reaction upon learning of the death of the son born of the illicit union between him and Bathsheba will lead to an appreciation of the emotional impact of the story, and this may prompt us to reconsider our evaluation of David's character as we contemplate the change in his behaviour and disposition. Nussbaum's emphasis on the importance of ethical criticism in relation

---

50. Hazony 2012: 3. Hazony proceeds to criticize recent works by modern moral philosophers (such as Anthony Kenny, Gilbert Harman and Bernard Williams) which consider various influences on the Western philosophical tradition but do not make even a passing reference to the Hebrew Bible, despite the constant exposure of Western thought to the Hebrew Scriptures over more than twenty centuries (2012: 17–18).

to works of literature emerges most clearly in her favourable review of Wayne Booth's volume, *The Company We Keep* (1990: 230-44), and she quotes with approval Henry James's repeated insistence on the reader's duty to become 'finely aware and richly responsible' (1990: 37). The responsibility of biblical scholars to apply ethical criticism to the stories of the Hebrew Bible will be discussed in Chapter 5 by focussing on two narratives in which the character of God plays a prominent role in the story of David (2 Sam. 12:7-25; 24:1-17).

Chapter 2

LIES AND LOYALTY
(1 SAMUEL 19:11-17; 20:1-34)

Biblical narratives often provide a fascinating exploration of moral dilemmas where ethical obligations appear to conflict with one another. The two narratives contained in 1 Sam. 19:11-17 and 20:1-34 provide an interesting case in point. In both narratives the protagonists are forced to establish priorities between conflicting alternatives, for they face a situation where they must choose between loyalty and betrayal, and between truth and falsehood. The two narratives, in turn, lead the reader to consider the values that should guide human conduct, and to ponder over some agonisingly difficult moral questions. Can certain circumstances mitigate or extenuate a lie and remove moral blame? How should one react when certain ethical values – in this case, loyalty and truth-telling – collide? Should respect for the truth trump family loyalty and family solidarity? These are just some of the issues raised by the two narratives in question. In what follows, the text of both passages will be examined, along with the contribution of moral philosophers, ancient and modern, which will hopefully help to elucidate the ethical quandaries faced by the characters in the story.[1]

---

1. Shira Weiss (2018), in a thought-provoking and illuminating study, has adopted a similar approach to that deployed in the present chapter by examining how contemporary philosophical analysis can shed light on some of the narratives encountered in the Hebrew Bible. Interestingly, a substantial part of her volume (pp. 120–94) is concerned with the 'ethics of deception', although there is little by way of discussion of the narratives in 1 and 2 Samuel. She maintains that 'a philosophical analysis of numerous episodes, in light of the arguments advanced in the debate over deception, affords alternative interpretations, elucidates the complex moral problems raised by the stories, and contributes to an enhanced understanding of the biblical text which allows for a more informed evaluation by the reader' (2018: 129).

Deception: Michal and Saul (1 Samuel 19:11-17)

The narrative contained in 1 Sam. 19:11-17 recounts Saul's attempt to kill David, and Michal's intervention that facilitated his escape. The ethical interest of the passage focuses on Michal's deception of Saul's messengers (v. 14) and her subsequent justification of her action to her father, who was incensed at the thought that his own daughter had enabled his enemy to escape. The narrative records that Saul's messengers had been sent to keep watch over David's house during the night so that Saul (or his messengers) could kill him in the morning.[2] Aware of the danger to David's life, Michal warns him to escape and lets him down through the window. She then takes an idol and lays it on the bed, covering it with clothes and putting a net of goats' hair[3] on its head, to make it appear that David was sleeping in bed.[4] When the messengers come to capture him, she tells them that he was ill. Saul, seeing that his messengers had failed

---

2. MT reads, literally, 'to guard him and kill him in the morning', but it is not clear whether it was the messengers or Saul himself who intended to kill David. RSV follows LXX, and reads 'that he (i.e. Saul) might kill', a reading favoured by some commentators (e.g. McKane 1963: 120); however, the reading of NRSV is preferable, which takes the messengers as the subject of the verb *lahamîtō*.

3. The Hebrew term *kĕbîr* occurs only here in the Hebrew Bible, and its precise meaning is uncertain. Kyle McCarter (1980: 326) compares Song of Songs 4:1 ('your hair, like a flock of goats') and thinks that the term here may refer to a wig, possibly made of goats' hair. NRSV's 'net of goats' hair' is conjectural, but probably approximates to the meaning of the term. See, further, Rowe 2011: 187 n. 244; Bodi 2005: 100–1.

4. Some have argued that the idol, or teraphim, would not have been placed in the bed to make it appear that David was lying there since such objects would have been too small to serve as a realistic substitution for a person. W.F. Albright, for example, observed that no idols of comparable size to a man have been found in excavations of the holy land (1946: 114). It is therefore argued that it is more likely that the idol would have been placed beside the bed, as was customary when people were ill, since it was believed that such figurines had special healing powers (so, e.g., Ackroyd 1971: 157–8). Scholars who favour this interpretation assume that the term 'teraphim' is derived from the root *rp'*, 'to heal', and that their purpose was to serve as a protective talisman; see S. Smith 1931. According to this explanation of the term, the messengers would have seen the idol beside the bed and would have immediately recognized its significance, and taken it as confirming the truth of Michal's statement that David was ill (cf. Rowe 2011: 167). The problem with this interpretation, however, is that it does not explain why Michal should have placed goats' hair on the head of the figurine, for this surely suggests that it was intended to be mistaken for a person. It is interesting to note that the rabbis understood the teraphim in this context to assume

in their mission, instructs them to bring David to him – even with the bed if necessary! – 'that I may kill him' (v. 15). When the messengers return and enter the bed chamber, they realize that they had been duped, and Saul castigates his daughter for her duplicity: 'Why have you deceived me like this, and let my enemy go, so that he has escaped?' (v. 17a).[5] Michal responds by denying any complicity, and claiming that she had acted under duress, since her husband had threatened to kill her if she did not help him to escape (v. 17b).

Even within this short narrative there are two attempts deliberately to mislead. The first lie uttered by Michal ('he is sick'; v. 14) is compounded by deception, for the act of placing the idol in the bed was clearly a ruse designed to confirm the veracity of her statement. It cannot be proved that her response to her father's question in v. 17b was also a lie, for there is no report of David's words to her, and so the possibility must remain open that he had, indeed, threatened to kill her.[6] It seems more probable, however, that Michal fabricated the death threat from David to exonerate her actions; after all, she had clearly lied to the messengers, and so one may suppose that she would have had no compunction about lying again to cover her tracks.[7] Michal's response to Saul's accusation that she had deceived him was to deceive him even more!

---

human form, and supposed that the idol had been placed in, rather than besides, the bed (cf. Bodi 2005: 102). For a discussion of the significance of the teraphim in the present passage, see van der Toorn 1990: 205–8.

5. Viewed in the light of the present narrative, the question posed by Saul in 1 Sam. 24:19 seems ironical: 'For who has ever found an enemy, and sent the enemy safely away?' Well, the answer is clear: his own daughter, for one!

6. So, e.g., David Clines, who observes that we know that Michal's answer to the messengers, 'he is sick' (v. 14), is a lie, because we have just learned from the narrator that David is not in bed but has escaped through the window; we *assume* that Michal's answer to Saul is also a lie, 'but we do not *know* that', since 'there has been no report of David's speech against which we could check it' (1991: 39; cf. White 2007: 456). Diana V. Edelman claims that Michal's response concerning the alleged threat to her life in v. 17b may well have been a true statement of the actual course of events (1991: 147–9). However, such a scenario seems inherently improbable since, as Matthew Newkirk has observed, 'it is illogical that after David received warning of apparent danger from Michal, he would need to threaten her to assist him in escaping the very danger of which she had warned him' (2015: 66).

7. Cf. Robert Alter (1999: 121), who observes that the purported death threat by David 'is of course pure invention by Michal in order to make it seem that she was forced to help David flee'. In a similar vein, John Mauchline suggests that 'Michal lied to Saul in what she considered a good cause' (1971: 143).

It is somewhat surprising that the ethical import of the narrative has been virtually ignored by commentators, although it is clearly a story involving such crucial moral issues as truth and falsehood, loyalty and deception. The story is generally viewed as a straightforward account of how a resourceful wife, at great cost to herself, orchestrated her husband's escape.[8] If the ethical ramifications underlying the passage are mentioned at all, the discussion tends to be brief and peremptory, and Michal's attempts to dissemble are usually viewed positively, given that David had little choice but to escape from Saul's unambiguously murderous intentions.[9] Yet, the narrative raises profound questions about the ethics of deception and the conflict of loyalties that merit further consideration. Before such issues are examined in detail, however, it may be salutary to examine a longer narrative contained in the following chapter (1 Sam. 20) where, once again, the ethics of truth-telling and loyalty come to the fore, although in this case the protagonists are David and Jonathan.[10]

Deception: David and Jonathan (1 Samuel 20:1-34)

Previous incidents in David's encounter with Saul had convinced him that his life was in repeated danger,[11] and in the present narrative David, in 'a protest of injured innocence' (Auld 2011: 231), asks Jonathan what he had done to inflame his father's anger (v. 1). Jonathan, who had previously convinced Saul that David had done nothing to sin against him (1 Sam. 19:4), confidently reassured David that he was not in danger of losing his life. However, Saul's hostile intentions were all too plain to David, who

---

8. The narrative has inevitably provided fertile soil for feminist biblical critics, for it is Michal's prescience that enables David to escape; it is she who takes the initiative, and it is her composure and sense of urgency that saves David's life. David, by contrast, seems blissfully unaware of the gravity of the situation until alerted by his wife; he is mute and compliant throughout, and 'his only role is acquiescence' (Rowe 2011: 122).

9. As Clines has observed, 'hardly a writer can be found who does not approve of Michal's deception', and even when she is viewed as betraying her own father, 'there is rarely a whiff of criticism for her behaviour' (1991: 41–2).

10. A number of parallels between the two stories have been noted by various scholars, and these have been conveniently tabulated by S. Ackerman 2005: 185–6.

11. Saul had already made three attempts on David's life. On the first occasion, David managed to evade Saul's spear (1 Sam. 18:11); on the second occasion, Saul attempted to kill him by the hand of the Philistines (1 Sam. 18:25); and on the third occasion Michal actively assisted him to escape the clutches of Saul's assassins (1 Sam. 19:11-17).

realized that his death was 'only a step' away (v. 3), and he suggests that it was his own friendship with Jonathan that was the reason for Saul's concealment of his true intentions.

David thus devises a plan by which to determine Saul's true feelings towards him.[12] At the new moon festival, the following day, David was expected to be seated with Saul at the feast, but instead of joining the king, David would hide in the countryside. If Saul were to ask Jonathan why David had not attended, Jonathan was to lie on his behalf, informing him that David had requested permission to go to Bethlehem to attend the annual family sacrifice.[13] Saul's reaction would reveal his disposition towards David: if Saul were to bear no malice or animosity for this minor discourtesy, then David would accept that all was well between them, but if Saul became angry, then David's fears will have been confirmed. In the event, Saul does not appear to be particularly perturbed by David's absence on the first night of the feast since he assumes that some unforeseen or unavoidable circumstance may have prevented him from attending. Indeed, Saul himself surmises that David's failure to attend was probably because of some ritual uncleanness that would have rendered him temporarily unfit for cultic participation.[14] Saul even repeats his supposition ('he is not clean, surely he is not clean'; v. 26), as if to underline its plausibility. David's continued absence from the feast on the second day, however, raises Saul's suspicion, and Jonathan repeats the lie that he had been told by David to say, even amplifying it as if to make it all the more plausible: 'He [David] said, "Let me go; for our family is holding a sacrifice in the city, and my brother has commanded me to be there. So now, if I have found favour in your sight, let me get away, and see my brothers." For this reason he has not come to the king's table' (v. 29). On hearing this, Saul becomes angry and, realizing that

---

12. Alter notes that David could hardly have been in any serious doubt as to Saul's disposition towards him, given Saul's previous attempts to kill him; he thus approves of Robert Polzin's suggestion that David's real intention was 'to provoke Saul to an angry outburst that would remove Jonathan's misconceptions, not his own' (1999: 124).

13. The new moon and full moon were common occasions for family celebrations, at which special sacrifices were offered. The ritual calendar of Num. 28:11-15 prescribes the monthly offerings for the new moon, and its observance is occasionally alluded to in the Hebrew Bible in connection with the Sabbath (cf. Hos. 2:13; Isa. 1:13). See, further, Hallo 1977; de Vaux 1961: 469–70.

14. The main types of ritual uncleanness, and the appropriate means of purification, are set out in detail in Lev. 11–15; cultic uncleanness may arise from several factors, such as touching a dead body, or emitting various bodily discharges.

this was a conspiracy against him, announces that David deserves to die (v. 31). The story ends with Jonathan recognizing what David – and we as readers – had suspected all along, namely, that David's initial fears concerning Saul's intentions had been well-founded.[15]

The Ethics of Deception

The way in which these two narratives deal with the morality of truth-telling and loyalty requires detailed consideration, especially since commentators generally seem to lack any awareness that a moral problem exists, and consequently feel little need to examine the behaviour of the characters or to explore its ethical ramifications. The moral issue at stake can be stated very succinctly: while everyday morality dictates that telling the truth and being loyal to one's family are commendable qualities, in these two narratives neither Michal nor Jonathan are criticized even though both are represented as telling a lie and betraying their own father.[16] One might have expected their actions to have offended the moral sensibilities of the narrator, but just when we might expect a word of censure, the narrator 'keeps his lips sealed' (Alter 1992: 67).

The issue of family loyalty will be discussed in more detail below; first, however, it will be convenient to focus on the lies perpetrated by Michal and Jonathan in the two narratives under discussion. These two texts are by no means the only instances of duplicity in 1 and 2 Samuel,[17] and numerous examples occur elsewhere in the Hebrew Bible; yet, the biblical authors seldom explicitly condemn such questionable behaviour.[18]

---

15. Cf. Walter Brueggemann, who comments that 'it is high narrative art to interest us so passionately in something we had already known' (1990: 152).

16. As Jan Fokkelman observes, Michal's deception does not receive the disapprobation that one might have anticipated, for despite her attempt to conceal the truth, 'the bad outcome that one would expect for Michal fails to materialize' (1986: 265). Most scholars assume that Michal's action is evaluated positively by the narrator and that she is presented 'in a favourable light' (McKane 1963: 121; cf. M.J. Williams 2001: 61–2). The midrashim, in general, praise Michal's action in helping to save David's life in 1 Sam. 19:11-17 but condemn her when she reprimands him for his unseemly dancing before the ark in 2 Sam. 6:16-23 (cf. Bodi 2005: 89).

17. Matthew Newkirk claims that there are no fewer than 28 episodes involving deception in 1 and 2 Samuel, and he maintains that these two books contain the highest density of narrative episodes involving deception in the Hebrew Bible (2015: 2). Harry Hagan notes that there are 18 instances of deception in the Succession Narrative alone (1979: 302).

18. Newkirk notes that there are eight episodes in 1 and 2 Samuel where the tactic used to deceive is a lie, yet the lie is viewed positively in each case (2015: 178–80).

Their reticence to pass judgment, however, is probably due to their realization that moral issues can seldom be seen in black and white terms, and that truth-telling (and its opposite) never takes place in a vacuum; rather, it always occurs in a concrete situation and – depending on the circumstances – deliberate acts of deception may be considered as morally permissible or even praiseworthy. It was not a question of whether lying *per se* should be regarded as acceptable or unacceptable, as something to be either condemned or condoned; rather, the issue was whether it was justified *in the particular circumstances described.*

In this regard, the biblical narratives raise questions that have been debated at length by moral philosophers, past and present. Is there a moral obligation always to tell the truth? Can certain circumstances – such as when an innocent life is threatened – mitigate or extenuate a lie and remove moral blame? Is a lie more excusable if told (as in the case of Michal and Jonathan) for altruistic reasons, such as to avoid harm to others rather than oneself? Is a lie told in a moment of desperation (Michal) any less reprehensible than a calculated, strategic lie (Jonathan)? Is it right for a lesser evil to be perpetrated (lying) to avoid a possible greater evil (murder)? Is it worse to induce another to tell a lie (as David does) than to do so oneself? And what should one do when values – in this case, truth-telling and loyalty – clash? Is deception more culpable if it involves a breach of trust? By posing such questions the biblical authors invite us to identify with the moral dilemmas of the characters, and in the process our own moral faculties are sharpened and refined.

Deception in the Hebrew Bible

Before considering how moral philosophers might regard the behaviour of Michal and Jonathan in the narratives under consideration, it may be helpful to briefly outline the teaching of the Hebrew Bible concerning the dual aspects of lying and deception. One might instinctively suppose that such mendacity as that exhibited by Michal and Jonathan falls short of the morally upright behaviour adumbrated in the Hebrew Bible, but the biblical teaching concerning truth-telling and deception is by no means as straightforward as one might expect. Indeed, James Barr has argued that 'absolute truthfulness in matters of every kind…is not evident as an ideal in much of the Old Testament'.[19]

---

19. Barr 2006: 18. Barr claims that the emphasis on truth and on the avoidance of lies is much more prominent in the New Testament than in the Hebrew Bible. He suggests that the story of Ananias and Sapphira in Acts 5, for example, 'treats lying

The starting-point for scholarly discussion of the ethics of truth-telling in the Hebrew Bible has usually been the ninth commandment of the Decalogue: 'You shall not bear false witness against your neighbour' (Exod. 20:16). However, this is not a prohibition against lying in general but refers specifically to false testimony in a court of law that might lead to a wrongful conviction and an unjust verdict.[20] Other legal texts in the Pentateuch similarly prohibit deception in specific circumstances, such as surreptitiously moving the boundary stone to acquire more land (Deut. 19:14; 27:17) or using false weights and measures (Lev. 19:35-36; Deut. 25:13-15). There is no blanket prohibition of lying as such in the Hebrew Bible, though there is clearly a moral presumption in favour of truth-telling.[21] Such a presumption is encountered in the Psalms (5:6, 9; 58:3; 109:2), and in the wisdom literature (Prov. 6:16-19; 12:22; Job 31:5-6) as well as in the prophets (Isa. 5:18) but – surprising though it may seem – the relevant texts seldom categorically condemn lying and deception *per se*, only to the extent that they result in injustice and cause a disruptive or negative impact on the welfare of the community.[22] The Hebrew Bible recognizes the desirability of truthful behaviour, but truth is hardly the cornerstone without which the entire edifice of biblical morality would fall. The primary moral virtue in the Hebrew Bible is justice rather than truth.

That there is a certain moral ambiguity about dishonesty and deception in the Hebrew Bible is further confirmed by the fact that numerous instances of deception and dissimilation occur in the Pentateuchal

---

and deceit with a severity unparalleled in earlier Scripture' (2006: 17). In Rev. 22:15 liars are equated with dogs, fornicators, and murderers, and 1 Tim. 1:9-10 includes liars and perjurers among the 'godless and sinful' whom the author castigates.

20. Cf. Phillips 1970: 142; Patrick 1986: 56–7. As Barr wryly comments, the fact is that '"thou shalt not make any sort of untrue statement at any time" is not to be found in the Ten Commandments, although one might like to put it there' (2006: 16). For a helpful discussion of the ninth commandment of the Decalogue, see Brueggemann 2004.

21. Hannah Arendt argues that except for Zoroastrianism none of the major religions included lying (as distinct from 'bearing false witness') in their catalogue of grave sins, and that lying only came to be considered as a serious offence with the arrival of Puritan morality (1968: 232).

22. Maurice E. Andrew concludes that falsehood in the Hebrew Bible is not only an utterance of something that is not true but refers, also, to that which causes harm in various ways, and which brings 'discord and injury instead of the wholeness and enrichment which is necessary for full life' (1963: 431). See, also, Newkirk 2015: 44–52.

narratives that do not appear to provoke Yahweh's wrath or the moral censure of the narrators.[23] Abraham lies concerning the status of his wife, Sarah (Gen. 12; 20; 26); Jacob deceives Esau concerning his birthright, only to be deceived himself by being given Leah as a wife instead of Rachel (Gen. 25; 31); Tamar deceives Judah, only for the patriarch to concede that she was in the right (Gen. 38); Joseph deceives his brothers when they come to visit him in Egypt (Gen. 42; 44); and the Hebrew midwives deceive Pharaoh and are rewarded by being given families themselves (Exod. 1:15-21).[24]

Given that deception is tolerated, or even applauded, in these narratives, depending on the motive of the perpetrator,[25] it will come as no surprise that God himself occasionally indulges in deception to bring about the demise of an individual or a nation deserving judgment (cf. Roberts 1988). In Exod. 3:18, Yahweh tells Moses to request from Pharaoh permission to take a three-day journey into the desert to offer sacrifices, though it was clear that the Hebrews had no intention of returning to Egypt once they had left,[26] and the story of Micaiah ben Imlah (1 Kgs 22:5-23) indicates that God could sometimes work through lying messengers and lying

---

23. For a detailed discussion of these narratives, see Weiss 2018: 120–94. W.A. Irwin discusses various narratives depicting human and divine deception in the Hebrew Bible, and observes that the striking element is not only their frequency but their 'unconcerned acceptance, if not indeed tacit approval' of deception 'as the norm of human life' (1929: 367).

24. Michael J. Williams claims that 'most of the pericopes of Genesis involve deception to one degree or another, even those that involve Israel's venerated matriarchs and patriarchs' (2001: 4). Ora Horn Prouser goes so far as to claim that 'in biblical narrative there are very few major characters who do not participate in some sort of deceptive practices, either as the liar or as the dupe' (1994: 15). While this seems something of an exaggeration, it does underline the prevalence of deception in the narrative texts of the Hebrew Bible.

25. Matthew Newkirk, in particular, has emphasized the link between the deceiver's motive and the corresponding evaluation of the act by the biblical narrator: when the aim of the deceit is to cause unjust harm or death to another, or when the deceiver is lying in his or her own interest, the deception is viewed negatively; however, if the intention is to *prevent* harm, or if the lie is intended to benefit someone else, then it is viewed positively (2015: 187–91).

26. Some scholars, such as Nahum Sarna, argue that the reason for requesting the three-day journey was simply to make clear that the 'intended sacrifice, which would be anathema to the Egyptians, would take place well beyond the recognized range of Egyptian cultic holiness' (1991: 19). The problem with this interpretation, however, is that there is no indication in the narrative that such a celebration occurred or was intended to occur. See, further, Esau 2006.

spirits to achieve his purpose. The prophet Jeremiah accuses God of being 'like a deceitful brook' (Jer. 15:18), and alleges that he was guilty of duplicity: 'Ah, Lord GOD, how utterly you have deceived this people and Jerusalem, saying, "It shall be well with you", even while the sword is at the throat!' (Jer. 4:10).[27]

A further striking example of God's duplicity occurs in a passage that bears a strong resemblance to the narrative concerning Jonathan and David discussed above. 1 Samuel 16:1-5 describes how Yahweh, having rejected Saul as king, instructs Samuel to go to Bethlehem, since he had chosen one of Jesse's sons to be king instead. Samuel fears that his journey to Bethlehem might arouse Saul's suspicions, and he protests that his life may be in danger should the king discover the true nature of his visit. Yahweh instructs Samuel to deceive any inquirers by telling them that he had come merely to offer a sacrifice, not to anoint a rival king. The elders of Bethlehem are afraid when Samuel appears, and he is given access to the city only because he repeats verbatim the deceptive words that Yahweh had provided for him.[28]

It is evident from the brief outline above that there is some ambiguity in the Hebrew Bible regarding the morality of deception and dissimilation. While there is a clear presumption in favour of telling the truth, one cannot ignore the narratives that contain an acknowledgment that, in certain circumstances, duplicity could be viewed as morally legitimate, and even, on occasion, desirable. The deceptive practices perpetrated by some of Israel's venerated ancestors – Abraham, Isaac and Jacob – are viewed by the biblical narrators with a certain equanimity, and there seems at times to be a grudging approval of those who deploy deception to achieve their goal. Moreover, although the Hebrew Bible characterizes Yahweh as a God of truth who does not lie (cf. Num. 23:19), he

---

27. The Targumists, ever anxious to portray God in a favourable light, could not allow Jeremiah to suggest that Yahweh actually deceived the people of Israel; they thus modified the text of Jer. 4:10 by introducing 'prophets of falsehood' as the agents of deception. See Dray 2010: 251–2.

28. As Walter Brueggemann observes, Samuel, in effect, was to deceive Saul in obedience to a divine command: 'This may not be a blatant lie authorized by Yahweh, for Samuel does take an animal for the occasion, but this is clearly an authorized deception. Yahweh will lie, if necessary, in order to move the kingship toward David' (1990: 121). Marti J. Steussy similarly observes that the 'sacrifice' was little more than a divinely endorsed ruse (2000: 147). Stephen Chapman seeks to play down the element of divine deception by suggesting that God merely instructed Samuel 'to engage in some light subterfuge' (2016: 146). For the element of divine deception in this narrative, see Newkirk 2015: 58–60.

can also be viewed as the wilful source of false prophecy and as a deity who occasionally appears implicated in deception, either directly or by approving those who engage in the practice. Such ambiguity serves as a salutary reminder that ethical issues need not always be framed in terms of a dichotomy between 'right' and 'wrong', and that the morality of truth-telling cannot always be determined by hard and fast rules that will apply to all situations.

Deception in Moral Philosophy

At this point it may be salutary to consider how moral philosophers, ancient and modern, might judge the behaviour of Michal and Jonathan in the narratives under consideration. It will be convenient to begin with Augustine, who argued that God forbade all lies, though he was prepared to concede that some lies were more reprehensible than others, and he sought to distinguish between the most grievous lies and those that could more easily be pardoned. In his essay, 'Lying', Augustine divided lies into eight types, and classified them according to the intent or justification with which the lie was told. He concluded that in seven categories, the lie was told unwillingly in order to achieve a specific goal, and these, he considered, were not to be regarded as 'lies' in the strict sense; it was only the eighth category, where an untruth was told simply 'for the pleasure of lying and deceiving', that constituted the 'real lie'.[29] Thus, Augustine was prepared to defend Abram's action when, fearing for his life, he told Abimelech that Sarah was his sister (Gen. 20:2); in this case, claimed Augustine, Abram merely 'concealed something of the truth' (Deferrari 1952: 151–2; cf. Adler 1997: 436). Since the lies uttered by Michal and Jonathan in the two narratives under discussion were told not for their own sake but to achieve a specific goal, namely, to ensure the safety of a husband and friend, it is likely that Augustine would have encountered little difficulty in justifying their duplicity.

A more absolutist position was advocated by Thomas Aquinas, who wrote: 'All lies are by definition wrong...since words should by definition signify what we think, and it is perverse and wrong for them to signify what is not in our mind'.[30] A similar view was espoused much later, and

---

29. Deferrari 1952: 109. Augustine laid a particular emphasis on the intention of the speaker: 'For, a person is to be judged as lying or not lying according to the intention in his own mind, not according to the truth or falsity of the matter itself' (Deferrari 1952: 55). It seems that in Augustine's scheme, all lies are sinful but (to paraphrase Orwell) some lies are more sinful than others.

30. *Summa Theologiae* IIa IIae, Q. 69, 1 and 2; quoted in B. Williams 2002: 102.

in a quite different religious and cultural context, by Immanuel Kant, at least in his later writings, for he held that lying was always wrong, and was a derogation of duty of all rational human beings.[31] Indeed, lying was not to be regarded as simply one form of wrongdoing among others, but as the basic source of all moral corruption, for it contributed to the insidious and progressive adulteration of human communication and trust. In his notorious essay, 'On the Supposed Right to Lie from Altruistic Motives', Kant claimed that 'truthfulness…is the formal duty of an individual to everyone, however great may be the disadvantage accruing to himself or to another… For a lie always harms another; if not some other particular man, still it harms mankind generally, for it vitiates the source of law itself' (1950: 346–7). In the same essay, Kant considers a case that bears a remarkable similarity to the one we have encountered in 1 Sam. 19:11-17. He envisages a situation whereby a would-be murderer inquires about the whereabouts of his intended victim, who happens to be a friend whom one was hiding in one's house. Kant argued that even in such exceptional circumstances, lying to the prospective killer could not be morally permitted, irrespective of the disastrous consequences that might ensue from one's readiness to assist the aggressor.[32] According to Kant, therefore, there could be no exoneration for the behaviour of Michal and Jonathan in the two narratives considered; lying was inherently wrong and permitted of no exception or qualification.

To some extent, it is possible to appreciate the logic of Kant's position, if only on the basis of the 'slippery slope' argument. After all, if it is permitted for us to lie once, why should we not lie again and again? Indeed, the Michal episode vividly illustrates how lying begets lying, and how one lie often necessitates another to avoid detection.[33] However, although Kant's position has the virtue of clarity and simplicity, it has usually been regarded by most moral philosophers as too rigid and inflexible, and they have tended to reject his dogmatic and uncompromising stance, arguing that the problem with such an absolute prohibition was that it

---

31. Thomas L. Carson claims that Kant is 'probably the most well-known defender of an absolute prohibition against lying in the history of Western philosophy' (2010: 4).

32. Cf. Kant's oft-quoted statement: 'The duty of truthfulness makes no distinction between persons to whom we may owe this duty and those toward whom we may repudiate it, but is an unconditional duty which is valid in all circumstances' (1950: 349).

33. Michal's behaviour validates the truth of the old adage that it is easy to tell a lie, but hard to tell only one!

made no allowance for the moral complexity that real circumstances often present.[34] Hence, Kantian morality has occasionally been depicted as 'fundamentally pharisaical in spirit' since the philosopher seems to care 'only about an unthinking conformity to rules and the narcissistic cultivation of own's own sense of moral purity'.[35] Rejecting such a rigorist and uncompromising approach, most modern moral philosophers argue that truthfulness cannot be elevated into an absolute principle that allows no room for exceptions, such as lying to prevent harm to an innocent person. They readily acknowledge that lies are not universally reprehensible, and that a distinction can be drawn between benign lies (of which they approve) and malevolent lies (which they condemn).[36] According to this view, therefore, non-malfeasance or the avoidance of harm is a principle that can be appealed to in order to justify a lie and override the opposing principle of veracity. Since the lies told by Michal and Jonathan were intended, directly or indirectly, to avert an evil act, namely, the threat to David's life, their behaviour could be morally justified.

The classic utilitarian position holds that the rightness or wrongness of an act is determined solely by the consequences of the act. Thus, in contrast to the absolutist position of Kant, utilitarians would claim that lying and deception can sometimes be regarded as permissible. For example, if lying to deceive someone was necessary to save the life of an innocent person, then lying would clearly have better consequences than

---

34. Gerald R. Miller and James B. Stiff observe (though without reference to Kant) that 'only the most stubborn ethical absolutist would undertake to defend the proposition that it is *never* justifiable to communicate deceptively' (1993: 1–2).

35. Sussman 2011: 226. Sussman, however, concedes that such a characterization of Kant's position is not entirely fair, and he attempts to come to Kant's defence, arguing that although his conclusions are 'wildly implausible', they do have 'substantial motivation within Kant's practical philosophy' (p. 230). Others have sought to defend Kant by pointing to his advanced age when he wrote his essay, and that the rather bizarre position that he advocated was due to the failing intellectual powers of his later years, since in his earlier writings his approach to the issue of deception was by no means so rigid, extreme and legalistic. See Mahon 2011; Benton 1982: 135–44. For Kant's earlier musings on the subject, see his *Lectures on Ethics* 224–29. These lectures were reconstructed and published on the basis of student notes based on lectures that Kant delivered during 1784–5, some twelve years before the publication of 'A Supposed Right to Lie'; see Bok 1989: 37–9.

36. Cf. the comments of Alan Strudler: 'It is always morally unacceptable to deceive a person in a way that breaches his trust, unless that deception is necessary to defend against a grave wrong' (2011: 152).

not lying, and in such circumstances could be justified.[37] It is likely that utilitarians would have little problem in justifying the lie told by Michal and the deception perpetrated by her, even though, strictly speaking, her duplicity was not told to save David's life (since he had already escaped!). Whether they would approve of the lie uttered by Jonathan, however, is a moot point since, in assessing the rightness or wrongness of an action, utilitarians consider whether there was a better alternative course of action that the agent could have performed instead; if there was, then the act was wrong, if there was not, the act was right. In the case of David and Jonathan, there were other forms of action that could have resolved the issue of Saul's attitude towards David, and in this case the lie would be regarded as dubious from the ethical point of view.

Ironically, the biblical writers would probably have agreed with the arch atheist Friedrich Nietzsche, who asked, 'Why must we have truth at any cost anyway?' Nietzsche opposed the blanket condemnation of 'lying as wrong' and saw deception as an inevitable part of the matrix of human relations, neither good nor evil as such, and inviting sympathy and understanding rather than condemnation and blame. As Nietzsche remarked, in some circumstances lying was 'a necessity of life' and was 'part of the terrifying and problematic character of existence' (1967: 451).

Measure for Measure

As readers of biblical narrative, we enjoy the advantages of overview and retrospect, and in considering the ethical implications of the deceptions perpetrated by Michal and Jonathan we may well be reminded of the duplicity exhibited by Saul himself in the chapter immediately preceding the two narratives under consideration. Here, Saul offered Merab, his elder daughter, to David as a wife on condition that he engaged in battle with the Philistines. Saul's internal monologue makes it clear that this was simply a ploy to have David killed without having to kill him himself: 'For Saul thought, "I will not raise a hand against him; let the Philistines deal with him"' (1 Sam. 18:17). Further confirmation that Saul had no intention of giving Merab to David in marriage is found in v. 19, which states that when Merab 'should have been given to David, she was given

---

37. One common objection to the utilitarian approach is that it is occasionally too permissive about the morality of lying and deception. If it is a clear-cut case, such as that of saving an innocent life, then few would regard it as objectionable; the problem arises as to whether lying and deceiving can be justified if they produce *just slightly better* consequences than not lying and deceiving others. Cf. Carson 2010: 94–5.

to Adriel the Meholathite as a wife'. Saul then proceeded to offer his other daughter, Michal, to David as a wife, and demanded as a bride-price 'a hundred foreskins of the Philistines' (v. 25). The depth of Saul's duplicity is even more apparent in this instance, for he hypocritically commands his servants to tell David that 'the king is delighted with you, and all his servants love you; now then, become the king's son-in-law' (v. 22). Once again, Saul's real intention is expressed in his internal monologue: 'Saul thought, "Let me give her to him that she may be a snare for him and that the hand of the Philistines may be against him"' (v. 21), a clear indication that Saul was hoping 'that his foreign enemies would do his dirty work for him' (McKenzie 2000: 81). As if to emphasize Saul's intention even further, the narrator makes it plain that 'Saul planned to make David fall by the hand of the Philistines' (v. 25).

When this narrative is juxtaposed with chs. 19 and 20, an interesting moral conundrum emerges, for one may well wonder, from an ethical point of view, whether some 'measure for measure' principle is at work in these chapters.[38] Saul deceives David twice (with Merab and Michal in 1 Sam. 18:17-25), and Michal deceives Saul twice in 1 Sam. 19:11-17. Recollection of Saul's own duplicity invites us to reconsider the deceptions perpetrated by Michal and Jonathan, for it raises a profound ethical issue: is it justified to repay lies with lies, deception with deception? Is deceiving the deceiver simply a case of giving him what he deserves?[39] In brief, has Saul, in deceiving David, not forfeited his right to be dealt with honestly? Was it right to repay him in kind and to emulate the type of wrongdoing of which he himself was guilty? Saul had disguised his murderous intention under the cloak of a lie; thus, by being lied to by his own children, was he not receiving the treatment that his own behaviour merited? Considering the deceptions perpetrated by Michal and Jonathan in this broader context poses an ethical dilemma: were they merely

---

38. Yael Shemesh (2003) provides a discussion of the ways in which biblical stories express the notion of measure for measure and argues that this concept is particularly conspicuous in the narratives concerning David. David Marcus similarly perceives a pattern of 'retributive deception' in the stories of intrigue involving David in 1 and 2 Samuel (1986: 164). Matthew Newkirk, on the other hand, contends that the 'measure for measure' principle is not sufficiently prevalent in these books to support such an argument, since in most cases the deceiver never reappears in the narrative as the deceived (2015: 192–3).

39. Augustine, of course, would not approve, for he argued that reciprocating a lie with a lie was no different from reciprocating robbery with robbery or adultery with adultery (cf. Bok 1989: 124–5, 252).

treating Saul as he deserved to be treated, or were both stooping to the lowest common denominator by reciprocating lies with lies, deceit with deceit?

Moral philosophers emphasize that in cases of duplicity consideration should be given to the person who is misled or betrayed by the lie, for deception involves the person lied to as well as the person who lied (cf. Bok 1989: 20–8). In discussions of such narratives as those encountered in 1 Sam. 19:11-17; 20:1-34, it is often the motive and intent of the liar that is considered in determining the lie's acceptability; what is usually forgotten is that good motives and intentions from the liar's perspective may not be so judged by the recipient of the lie. Thus, it seems appropriate to consider the two narratives in question from Saul's point of view.[40] Indeed, both narratives provide a graphic illustration of the way that a lie can destroy relationships and incite violence and vengeance. Seen from Saul's perspective, the shared expectation of mutual trust is destroyed, and his anger at the friendly relationship between David and Jonathan is understandable. To have his own son and future heir join David, his avowed enemy, in a conspiracy against him must have resulted in a feeling of profound humiliation. As a father, he could have expected loyalty from his son, and it was natural for him to feel slighted at such a blatant breach of trust. The poet and feminist theorist Adrienne Rich has perceptively observed that 'to discover that one has been lied to in a personal relationship...leads one to feel a little crazy' (1979: 186), and many commentators have noted that the vehemence and violence exhibited by Saul upon realizing that he had been lied to gives the impression of a king who had almost gone mad, having lost all sense of reason and decorum.[41] In depicting Saul's violent reaction in 1 Sam. 20:30-33, and the crude and barely coherent words that he utters, the narrator conveys the acute

---

40. David Clines raises the possibility that the story concerning Michal would be viewed very differently if one attempted a re-evaluation of the characters of David and Saul, regarding the latter as a victim of fate and viewing David 'as a selfish prig rather than as a man after God's own heart' (1991: 42–3). J.A. Barnes very effectively demonstrates how one's own perspective determines one's moral evaluation of an individual by positing the universal attitude adopted towards spies: 'Those who spy *on us* are popularly regarded as morally despicable; they deserve harsh penalties when discovered. Those who spy *for us* are silent heroes whose achievements we regret we cannot honour openly' (1994: 24; my italics).

41. Steven L. McKenzie claims that Saul is portrayed as 'paranoid and unbalanced' (2000: 86); the depiction of his irrational behaviour was no doubt intended to discredit Israel's future king.

sense of personal injury that Saul must have experienced upon realizing that his own son was in league with the enemy. Aware that the normal expectation of truthful exchange between members of his own family had been compromised, he – not surprisingly – feels angry, resentful and disappointed, and the self-deluded king is left to ponder that the easiest person of all to deceive is oneself.

Loyalty

Having examined the lies uttered by Michal and Jonathan in 1 Sam. 19:11-17 and 20:1-34, it will now be necessary to discuss the issue of family loyalty that comes to the fore in both passages. The lies uttered by the two characters is not the only – and perhaps not even the most important – moral issue to be considered, for what is equally at stake in both are issues of filial obedience and family loyalty. Both Michal and Jonathan are children of Saul, but both are said to 'love' David (1 Sam. 18:1, 20). The question that arises, therefore, is: where should their loyalties lie? How should Michal have been expected to behave as Saul's daughter and David's wife? And how should Jonathan have been expected to behave as Saul's son and David's friend? Of course, the issues of loyalty and mendacity are, to some extent, inseparably intertwined in both narratives, for being loyal to one person meant deceiving another. Before exploring the ethical ramifications further, it will be convenient to discuss the issue of loyalty in the two narratives under consideration.

Loyalty: Michal and Saul (1 Samuel 19:11-17)

Michal is depicted in 1 and 2 Samuel as the pawn in a ferocious power-struggle between two unscrupulous and manipulative men, and in 1 Sam. 19:11-17 she is forced to decide, as the daughter of Saul and the wife of David, wherein her true loyalty lies.[42] In the event, she opts to be loyal to her husband. Jonathan Rowe, however, has argued that her decision in this regard was by no means as obvious and straightforward as commentators tend to suggest. While Western readers assume that Michal's loyalty would naturally have been to her husband, Rowe amasses much anthropological data to support his contention that in traditional societies, such as that of ancient Israel, the primary social obligation of a married

---

42. Jan Fokkelman (1986: 263) notes that whereas in previous chapters Michal is termed the 'daughter of Saul', in 1 Sam. 19 she is designated as David's wife, which immediately suggests to whom she would ultimately be loyal.

woman would have been to her parents: 'Many commentators, assuming modern Western notions of family dynamics, fail to perceive that Michal's fidelity to her husband would be very unlikely in any clash of obligations' (2011: 164-5). In Israel, the duty to honour one's father and mother was paramount, and thus a married woman's natural inclination would have been to support her father against her spouse.[43] Rowe argues that this is supported by the present narrative, for the fact that the messengers seemed to take Michal's word on trust suggests that they had assumed that Saul's daughter would have sided with her father against David. That this was also Saul's own assumption is implied in v. 17a, for he evidently expected his daughter to prioritize loyalty to him over loyalty to her husband;[44] moreover, Michal's response in v. 17b seems to suggest that she should not have acted as she did, and she finds herself compelled to tell another lie to justify her actions. It was thus perfectly natural, logical and reasonable for Saul to ask Michal why she had contravened father–daughter solidarity: 'Why have you deceived me like this, and let my enemy go, so that he has escaped?' (v. 17a).

Rowe quite properly recognizes that an understanding of the relevant 'cultural context' (i.e. our knowledge of the established attitudes regarding a daughter's obligation to both father and husband in ancient Israel) is just one side of the coin, for one must also consider the issue of 'individual choice' (since people do not always choose to act in culturally accepted ways). Michal may have acted as a free agent without adhering to the expected cultural norms, and Rowe argues that this is precisely what she did by bucking the trend and choosing to be loyal to her husband (pp. 79-85).

Rowe thus argues that original readers of the story would have assumed that when a woman such as Michal was faced with the dilemma of helping her husband to escape or siding with her father, she would most naturally have opted for the latter. Her decision to support her husband was, therefore, 'one that implied readers would have found counter-intuitive, even shocking' (p. 120), and her action would have been viewed by them as 'startlingly unexpected' (p. 204). Whereas modern readers tend to be scandalized more by Michal's mendacity than by her choice of allegiance,

---

43. Rowe (2011: 149) points to Num. 30 in support of his argument, since this chapter suggests that even after marriage a father (or husband) could commute the woman's vows; he believes that this demonstrates the continued influence of the father in the life of the married woman.

44. Fokkelman similarly notes that Saul 'entertained the illusion that the bond of blood would be the decisive factor for her, and not the bond of marriage' (1986: 269).

original readers of the story would have viewed the matter the other way around: her lie was merely an incidental consequence of her prior choice to be loyal to David (p. 190).

Now Rowe is clearly right in warning against the imposition of modern Western categories of thinking on the very different society in which the narrative concerning Michal was written and read (p. 84); however, his attempts to gauge how implied readers would have understood the text do not seem convincing. In the first place, it is by no means clear that in ancient Israel a married woman's first loyalty would have been to her father rather than her husband. That one was expected to show complete loyalty to one's father and mother in the case of children or unmarried adults is undoubtedly true (Exod. 20:12), but surely one's allegiance would change after marriage, and a woman's natural loyalty would thenceforth have been to her husband. That this was so is suggested by the story concerning Rachel in Genesis 31, an episode that is often compared with that narrated in 1 Sam. 19:11-17, for here the married daughter sides with her husband rather than her father.[45] Furthermore, Rowe's contention that a married woman would have remained loyal to her father 'since any other course of action would leave her, already isolated in her husband's household, without support from her natural kin' (p. 165) seems questionable; indeed, if that had been Michal's expectation, she was soon to be disabused, for she subsequently enjoyed little support from her father's house. As Jan Fokkelman (1986: 272) has remarked, 'she is thrown back to the status of an object when Saul… gives her in marriage to another', no doubt the king's way of wreaking revenge on the daughter who had outwitted him.

---

45. Keith Bodner (2008: 206–8) notes a network of correspondences between Gen. 31 (where Jacob flees from Laban, and Rachel steals her father's teraphim) and 1 Sam. 19:11-17 (where David flees from Saul, and Michal aids his escape by means of the teraphim): both episodes feature a deceptive father-in-law (Laban and Saul), younger daughters (Rachel and Michal), fugitive husbands (Jacob and David), and hidden idols (Rachel hides the teraphim under her camel's saddle to fool her father, and Michal hides it in David's bed to trick her father's messengers). Bodner even goes so far as to argue that the Deuteronomist configures the portrait of Michal on the Rachel model, noting that both stories feature 'aggressive initiative by a younger daughter against her father in favor of her husband' (p. 207). Robert Alter (1999: 120) similarly notes that both stories 'feature a daughter loyal to her husband and rebelling against a hostile father'. For the similarities between Gen. 31 and 1 Sam. 19:11-17, see, further, Auld 2011: 225; Fokkelman 1986: 274–6.

Rowe points out that Saul regarded David as his enemy ('Why have you…let my enemy go?'), and that there was a shared assumption and a cultural expectation that enemies should be killed (pp. 126–7). On this basis, Rowe argues that Michal's reply to Saul was far shrewder than commentators have usually supposed, for her claim that David had threatened to kill her was intended to present him as a violent husband and as *her* enemy (pp. 144–5). She thus calculatedly positions herself on Saul's side to make her father believe that, despite any doubts he might have harboured concerning her loyalty in the matter of the teraphim, she ultimately remained the dutiful and faithful daughter. Michal manipulated the received understanding of acceptable social practice to change her father's conception of her action, from that of betrayer to that of an innocent, wounded party. Far from being disloyal to her father, she had been the victim of intimidation and had little choice but to let his (and her!) enemy escape.

Now, Rowe's argument that in the cultural context of its time it was believed that enemies deserved to die may well be correct, but if the putative 'enemy' was one's own husband, then surely different considerations would have come into play. Rowe, however, resolutely rejects such a possibility and insists that, despite Saul's murderous intentions towards David, readers would have expected Michal to demonstrate absolute loyalty to her father and would not have expected her to warn her husband of Saul's actions (p. 166). Even if Rowe is correct in arguing that a daughter would have been loyal to her father for years after marriage, it surely beggars belief that she would have remained so had she known that her father intended to kill her husband.

Finally, Rowe's interpretation is based on a dubious exegesis of the text. He maintains that, since family solidarity for a newly married woman meant loyalty to her father's house, it would have seemed entirely plausible, for the implied reader, 'that Saul believes Michal's assertion of unwilling complicity' and her contention that 'her husband could act against her' (p. 168). The problem with this interpretation is that Saul's response to Michal's words are not recorded, and so it must be a matter of conjecture as to whether Saul believed her or not. Indeed, if anything, the balance of probability must be that he did not, for why would Saul, who clearly regarded himself to have been deceived in the matter of the teraphim, have considered her words about David's threat to her life as any more credible? Rowe is forced to concede that Saul's 'apparent acceptance'(!) of Michal's second lie is understandable, for 'both he and she may be viewed as not desiring to validate the truth of the matter for the sake of their continuing relationship' (p. 188). But is it plausible to conclude that Saul was colluding in the lie because he had a stake in not knowing the truth? It seems that Rowe's contention here is based on an argument from silence. That Michal is depicted as the dutiful wife who renounces her allegiance to her father because of her devotion to her husband is clear; what is not clear is that such an act was regarded as a breach of established convention and a deliberate transgression of accepted societal norms. The fact that David's attempts to get the better of Saul were facilitated by members of Saul's own family would probably have occasioned as little surprise for the original audience as for contemporary readers of the story.

Before concluding our discussion of loyalty in 1 Sam. 19:11-17 it is, perhaps, worth considering the extent of David's loyalty to Michal. There can be little question of Michal's loyalty to her husband, for her only concern was for his safety, while she remained behind to face the wrath of her father. But whether her loyalty to David was reciprocated is doubtful, for David made no attempt to take her with him or return to her later when the danger had subsided. Indeed, after facilitating David's escape, we do not hear of Michal again until much later, but it is clear that she was destined to become 'practically a husbandless woman, an ever-waiting and neglected wife' (Bodi 2005: 44). While Michal is said to have loved David,[46] there is no indication of his feelings towards her; as Jan Fokkelman has remarked, this was very much a 'one-sided love relationship' (1986: 273). Indeed, the narrative suggests that David took her as his wife merely to further his own political ambitions.[47] This is the story of a woman who, in her love and devotion to her husband, was willing to renounce her allegiance to her father, only to find that her love, loyalty and devotion were not to be reciprocated.[48]

46. Cf. 1 Sam. 18:20, 28. Alter notes that this 'is the only instance in all biblical narrative in which we are explicitly told that a woman loves a man' (1981: 118). As Fokkelman (1986: 269) rightly observes, Saul made a 'hopelessly wrong evaluation by paying inadequate attention to the love factor'.

47. As April Westbrook has observed, 1 Sam. 18:26 makes it abundantly clear that what pleased David was not so much having Michal as a wife, but being the king's son-in-law, suggesting that David had merely used her to further his own political ambition (2015: 54). A similar point is made by Cheryl Exum: 'It would be much more to Saul's advantage if David loved Michal – but that is precisely what the text leaves unsaid, suggesting that David's motives are as purely political as Saul's' (2016: 6). Cf. Alter 1981: 120.

48. Susan Ackerman notes the contrast between David's reaction to Michal and his reaction to Jonathan. David is never said to respond emotionally to Michal's love for him, whereas he is evidently as emotionally committed to Jonathan as Jonathan is to him (2005: 184–5).

Loyalty: Jonathan and David (1 Samuel 20:1-34)

The issue of trust and loyalty is also at the heart of the story concerning Jonathan and David in 1 Samuel 20. We are alerted at the outset that family ties will be an important factor in the narrative that follows, for in his address to Jonathan, David refers to Saul not by name, or as the king, but as 'your father': 'What have I done? What is my guilt? And what is my sin against your father that he is trying to take my life?' (v. 1). Jonathan clearly harboured the illusion of being his father's confidante, and believed that he would have been fully informed of everything that Saul was planning; he would therefore have been able to warn David if he had sensed that his life was in imminent danger. David, however, felt that such confidence was misplaced, for he knew that Saul was aware of the friendship between them and would probably have deliberately withheld information from his son. Jonathan had no doubt as to where his loyalties lay ('whatever you say, I will do for you'; v. 4); nevertheless, David sees fit to remind Jonathan that he was bound to him in a 'sacred covenant' (v. 8a; cf. 18:3),[49] almost as though he feared that Jonathan might be intimidated by his father to abandon his covenant promise. David, in turn, emphasizes his own loyalty to Jonathan, and acknowledges that the punishment for disloyalty was death, whether it was disloyalty to the king or to the heir apparent (v. 8b). Jonathan responds by reassuring him that his friendship with David supersedes family ties, and if he were to discover that his father intended David any harm, he would certainly alert him to the fact. Verse 13b explains why Jonathan's loyalty to David was such as to override even family loyalty: he recognized that David was Yahweh's choice to succeed his father, an admission that would eventually be acknowledged by Saul himself (1 Sam. 24:20). Jonathan seeks an assurance from David that he would remain loyal to him and his household when he would eventually become king (vv. 14-15), and he binds David to this undertaking by an oath (v. 17).[50] The covenant

---

49. MT reads, literally, 'covenant of Yahweh'; that is, Yahweh was a witness to the covenant and was expected to oversee its implementation (cf. vv. 23, 42).

50. That Jonathan should seek some reassurance that the covenant love towards himself and his family would survive unimpaired when the tables were turned and David became king is understandable, for the Jehu story in 2 Kgs 9–10 shows that usurpers to the throne were prone to wipe out the survivors of the previous royal house as an act of political expediency, lest they became an alternative focus of loyalty at a later time. That David did not act in such an unscrupulous way is evident from his anger at the death of Ishbosheth in 2 Sam. 4, and his benevolence towards Jonathan's son, Mephibosheth, in 2 Sam. 9.

between them is reiterated, and Jonathan swears loyalty to David, since 'he loved him as he loved his own life' (v. 17).

The events that transpire at the new moon festival clearly demonstrate Saul's attitude towards David. When Saul realizes that his rival has not appeared even by the second day of the feast, he is outraged and cannot even bring himself to utter David's name when he asks Jonathan: 'Why has the son of Jesse not come to the feast, either yesterday or today?' (v. 27).[51] Jonathan responds by telling him that he had given permission for David to attend a family sacrifice, since David's brother[52] had requested him to be there (vv. 28-29).[53] The pretext does little to dispel Saul's mistrust, and in an intemperate outburst he warns Jonathan that by placing his loyalty to the 'son of Jesse' above loyalty to his own father, his prospects of ascending to the throne, as the hereditary successor, had been jeopardized (vv. 30-31). The effect of Saul's violent reaction, however, is merely to bring David and Jonathan closer together, and the chapter ends with the reciprocity between them expressed in the most succinct terms: 'they kissed each other, and wept with each other' (v. 41).[54]

As Walter Brueggemann has observed, this chapter invites us to reflect 'on the cost of loyalty and the terrible ambiguities within which loyalty must be practiced' (1990: 153). The covenant of love that Jonathan had established with David, and the obligations which that created, was to bring him into conflict with the ancient obligation based on kinship. It was a covenant that constrained him to act against his own – and his father's – interests, for by ensuring that David's life was not in danger he was paving the way for David's accession to the throne, a privilege that in the normal course of events might have been expected to come to him (v. 31). But the story also illustrates how the shared expectation of mutual trust is destroyed for both Jonathan and Saul because of the conspiratorial relationship between the two friends. For his part, Jonathan was to discover that his belief that he enjoyed the confidence of his father had

---

51. Matthew Newkirk notes that while Saul refers to David as the 'son of Jesse', the narrator (vv. 27, 33, 35) and Jonathan (v. 28) call him by his name, thus aligning Jonathan's point of view with that of the narrator (2015: 72).

52. LXX and 4QSam^b read the plural 'brothers' here, which may be original (cf. the use of the plural, 'brothers', later in the verse).

53. As William McKane notes, this was the most plausible explanation that could have been concocted 'since kin obligations were among the most primary and urgent' in ancient Israel (1963: 128–9).

54. Fokkelman (1986: 350) notes that this is 'the only kiss in the whole of Samuel which is a mutual kiss' and, as such, the expression forms 'the emotional climax of the entire episode'.

been misplaced, and if there was any doubt at all that the rapprochement between father and son had irretrievably broken down, such doubts are removed when Jonathan experiences what David had already experienced twice – the spear of an outraged king being thrown at him (v. 33).[55] From Saul's perspective, there was a similar breach of trust, for he regarded Jonathan's friendship with David as an act of blatant disloyalty that prevented him from serving his father with undivided allegiance. Saul viewed events simply in terms of politics and self-interest, and such altruism as that exhibited by his son was intolerable, for he was forced to see his hopes of establishing a dynasty disappear once and for all. The fact that Jonathan had given permission for David to attend a family gathering merely added insult to injury, for if kinship obligation had been paramount for David, why should it not have been so for Jonathan also? Why should Jonathan allow his friendship with David to override the loyalty that he owed to his father? In depicting Saul's violent reaction in vv. 30-33, the narrator conveys the acute sense of personal injury and loss of trust that he would have experienced by such a breach of faith with his own son.

The two narratives, 1 Sam. 19:11-17 and 1 Samuel 20, depict characters having to wrestle with a dual loyalty: that owed to a father and that owed to a husband and friend. In the event, the allegiance that David commands is shown to be stronger than the filial loyalty of Saul's own children. Given Saul's undisguised hostility towards David, there is a certain irony in the fact that his own family were responsible for David's survival.

Moral Dilemmas

The two narratives discussed above raise an issue that has been much discussed by moral philosophers, namely, the dilemma of establishing priorities between conflicting obligations.[56] According to Kant, moral action was necessitated by a single prevailing duty, and it was part of

---

55. David Jobling (1978: 24 n. 9) suggests that there is a certain merging of identities and roles in the portrayal of Jonathan and David, and at this point in the narrative the identification is total, since 'an act directed at one is an act directed at the other' (p. 14). Fokkelman also notes the similarity between Jonathan and David 'which is almost an identification' when the two friends are exposed to exactly the same threat (1986: 325). Steven McKenzie suggests that the narrator's intention was to cast Jonathan as David's alter ego, so that 'when Jonathan volunteers to abdicate the throne for David, he is really just acting on behalf of another version of himself' (2000: 84).

56. See, for example, the discussions in L.V. Anderson 1985; Lemmon 1962; McConnell 1978; Conee 1982; and Marcus 1980.

the very notion of a moral rule or principle that it could never conflict with another moral rule. It was in the nature of morality as understood in Kantian terms that 'a conflict of duties and obligations is inconceivable' (1964: 23). Martha Nussbaum, however, has argued convincingly that moral obligations *do* sometimes collide, and she believes that one need only turn to Greek tragedy to find plenty of examples of 'moral conflicts' or 'conflicts of duties' (1986: 63–79). Sophocles' play, *Antigone*, for example, expresses the tragedy of irreconcilable conflict, for there is no obviously correct choice between Antigone's contradictory duties to the god Hades and to her uncle, Creon; indeed, the tragedy of the play consists in the very necessity of choice and in the bleak recognition that however Antigone chooses, she will have to sacrifice a significant value. Morality, according to this view, is not like solving a puzzle where all that one must do is to find the right answer, for, as often as not, there *is* no 'right' answer to many moral deliberations; it is rather a matter of carefully weighing the alternatives, since valid reasons can be given in favour of whichever decision is taken, though circumstances dictate that one decision must override the other.

The narratives in 1 Sam. 19:11-17 and 1 Samuel 20 provide excellent examples of the kind of moral quandary to which Nussbaum refers, for they invite the reader to consider the problematic resolution of a moral dilemma, namely, whether respect for truth should trump family loyalty and family solidarity. Both narratives portray a scenario where values conflict and where one value must be sacrificed for the sake of the other. There is no suggestion, of course, that the value that must be sacrificed does not matter; it is merely that in the particular circumstances described it may be outweighed by more important considerations. Neither passage presents us with a simple morality tale, with good and evil neatly juxtaposed for our edification; rather, the choice presented in both is between competing virtues, and the question posed is which should have priority. The message of both is not 'you shall never under any circumstances lie or be disloyal, no matter how much harm truth or loyalty might produce'; rather, they invite us to consider the possibility that lying or being disloyal may sometimes be required in the service of a higher good. The lack of explicit evaluation and the suppression of authorial judgment are there for a purpose, for the narrator, by presenting such a moral quandary, is saying, in effect: you decide! The narratives withhold moral judgment, and that is precisely their point. We, as readers, like our fictional surrogates, are presented with a conflict of values, and as we become emotionally involved with the characters and engage with the narrative world that they inhabit, we are challenged to reflect upon our own values and priorities.[57] As Jonathan Rowe has rightly perceived, the ethical conundrums presented in the narratives of the Hebrew Bible 'are by no means merely hypothetical curiosities but...constitute many people's daily dilemmas' (2011: 2), and in pondering over those dilemmas our ethical sensitivities are refined, and our moral discourse is enriched.

Conclusion

The two narratives discussed in this chapter have focussed on the recurrent themes of deception and loyalty, and an attempt has been made to consider the biblical stories in light both of the general teaching of the Hebrew Bible concerning lies and deception, and the debates among moral philosophers concerning the morality of truth-telling. In both narratives we are forced to reflect on the nature and value of truth and to come to some judgment concerning the acceptability (or otherwise) of deception. Both narratives, in fact, provide a challenge to our basic assumptions about what constitutes moral conduct and, in the process, they raise a veritable plethora of agonisingly difficult questions. Should one always act on the basis of strict and rigid moral principles? Can deception occasionally be tolerated as a prudent aberration in a world where there is a *prima facie* duty to tell the truth? Does morality occasionally require what it normally forbids? Do all moral claims have equal force at any one time? And what should one do when moral conflicts and competing values have to be resolved, and when obeying one principle involves transgressing another?

Narratives such as those discussed in this chapter are important precisely because there is no formulaic response to such questions; they recognize that life's decisions are often not straightforward, and nor are they resolved by hard and fast rules that will apply to every situation. Instead of generalizing about deception in the abstract, the narratives

---

57. As Sissela Bok has observed, whether to lie, equivocate or exaggerate are choices made in everyday life, and such choices are often difficult because duplicity can have different purposes and results: 'Should physicians lie to dying patients so as to delay the fear and anxiety which the truth might bring them? Should professors exaggerate the excellence of their students on recommendations in order to give them a better chance in a tight job market? Should parents conceal from children the fact that they were adopted?... And should journalists lie to those from whom they seek information in order to expose corruption? We sense differences among such choices; but whether to lie, equivocate, be silent, or tell the truth in any given situation is often a hard decision' (1989: xv–xvi).

focus our attention on specific examples, inviting us to reflect upon the motives and intentions behind the lies, as well as the context in which they occur and the effect they have on the interpersonal relations between the characters. Our judgment regarding the legitimacy of deception need not, of course, be the same in the two narratives, for in each case we must consider whether the end justified the means. In the case of Michal the deception was deployed to hide information that David's enemy would find useful; it was an understandable decision – what moral philosophers might term a 'protective lie' – intended to defend an innocent person against a threat to his life. In this case, the deception was deployed as a defensive device and may therefore be deemed acceptable. In the Jonathan episode, on the other hand, there were surely ways of discerning Saul's attitude towards David without resorting to deception, in which case the act must be regarded as morally dubious.

The narratives also lead us to consider the issue of loyalty, and they provide an illuminating insight into the complex nature of loyalty within human relationships, and what happens when moral obligations collide. In 1 Sam. 19:11-17, Michal is confronted with a conflict between fealty to her father, love for her husband, and the commitment to truth. In 1 Samuel 20, the issue is whether the reciprocal duties of loyalty between father and son should prevail over that between two friends. Both narratives lead us to ponder the effect of a breach of trust between the deceiver and the deceived, and what occurs when the normal expectation of trusting exchange between family relations has been compromised. But the narratives also invite the reader to consider the necessity of establishing priorities when faced with a moral dilemma, and the need to weigh up conflicting alternatives when two obligations collide.

Chapter 3

ADULTERY AND MURDER
(2 SAMUEL 11)

The story of David's adulterous affair with Bathsheba and its aftermath is one of the best-known narratives in the Hebrew Bible and, as befits a story of intrigue, sex and violence, it is one that has captured the imagination of readers throughout the centuries. This episode in David's life has often been viewed with a mixture of dismay and astonishment: dismay that David, Yahweh's chosen king, could have stooped so low as to commit adultery and murder, and astonishment that the Hebrew Bible could have narrated the episode with such uncompromising frankness and openness.[1] The two chapters concerning David's encounter with Bathsheba and its aftermath (2 Sam. 11–12) are generally regarded as a pivotal turning-point in David's life, for they mark an abrupt transition in the king's fortunes. Prior to ch. 11, David is presented as a pious, successful and victorious king, but his ill-fated liaison with Bathsheba and his callous murder of her husband unleash a long chain of disasters that will befall David and his family.[2] A life under divine blessing henceforth becomes a life under

---

1. Cf. Hertzberg 1964: 309. Jan Fokkelman notes that David's plan to kill Uriah is 'the darkest blot on the portrait of Israel's most famous king' (1981: 60), a view echoed in 1 Kgs 15:5, which states that 'David did what was right in the sight of the LORD, and did not turn aside from anything that he commanded him all the days of his life, except in the matter of Uriah the Hittite'. As is well known, the Chronicler, who otherwise follows the text of Samuel chapter by chapter, omits this episode in David's life altogether, no doubt because of the serious blemish it casts on his reputation.

2. As Robert Gordon notes, because of his behaviour in the matter of Bathsheba and Uriah, 'the David of 2 Samuel 12–20 is a man under judgment, reaping publicly, through his family, the fruit of his cloistered sin' (1986: 252). R.A. Carlson argues that the misfortunes that befall David in 2 Sam. 13–1 Kgs 2 were interpreted 'as retribution "in full measure" for David's crime in 2 Sam. 11f.' (1964: 190). Following the

divine curse. Due to his egregious behaviour in the matter of Bathsheba and Uriah, the David of subsequent chapters (2 Sam. 12–20) is a man subject to God's judgment.

Part of the interest of the story is that it is widely regarded as a fine example of Hebrew storytelling,[3] and the very compactness of the narrative contributes to the sense of high drama as the events unfold.[4] As Robert Alter has observed, the writer 'has pulled out all the stops of his remarkable narrative art in order to achieve a brilliant realization of this crucially pivotal episode'.[5] But it is also clearly a story that lends itself to a detailed ethical analysis, for in the course of two chapters we are confronted with adultery, deception, betrayal, murder, and even the death of an innocent child precipitated by Yahweh.[6] The ethical interest of the story lies, at least in part, in its intentionally structured ambiguity, for as readers we are constantly invited to fill in the gaps in the text and to speculate as to why the characters act as they do.[7] Did Bathsheba deliberately attempt to attract the king's attention? Was her husband, Uriah,

---

Bathsheba affair, Tamar is raped, Amnon is murdered, Absalom usurps the throne, the country suffers a three-year famine, and the census taken by David results in a plague that afflicts the entire nation.

3. Robert Scholes and Robert Kellogg cite the story of David and Bathsheba as an example of 'primitive narration' (1966: 166-7), a view which does less than justice to the intricate artistry and sophisticated literary style of the story.

4. Within a single chapter Bathsheba has an adulterous affair, becomes pregnant, loses her husband, marries David, and bears a child by him.

5. Alter 1999: 249. Alter claims that the cycle of stories about David represents 'one of the most stunning imaginative achievements of ancient literature' (1981: 35).

6. Alter is critical of scholarly attempts to break up chs. 11–12 into two self-contained, isolated units, arguing that the powerful literary integrity of the text speaks for itself: 'The deployment of thematic key words, the shifting play of dialogue, the intricate relation between instructions and their execution, the cultivated ambiguities of motive, are orchestrated with a richness that scarcely has an equal in ancient narrative' (1999: 249).

7. Antony F. Campbell argues that no other story in the Hebrew Bible is 'so steeped in ambiguity', for here 'questions abound; answers are largely absent' (2005: 113). In a similar vein, Alter claims that 2 Sam. 11 is 'one of the richest and most intricate examples in the Bible of how ambiguities are set up by what is said and left unsaid in dialogue, of how characters reveal themselves through what they repeat, report, or distort of the speech of others' (1981: 76). For the view that ch. 11 'exemplifies the literary art of intentional ambiguity', see Bodner 2005: 78. Gale Yee provides a detailed discussion of ambiguous elements in this chapter, and notes three major ways in which such ambiguities are elicited by the narrator: by creating tension between the actions and motivations of the characters, by using the same

aware of the adultery? Were his actions a deliberate ploy to foil the king's designs? The answer to such questions remains largely in the realm of speculation, and the moral power of the story comes as much from our ignorance as from our knowledge of what has transpired. In what follows, an attempt will be made to apply to the story the method deployed by Martha Nussbaum in relation to Greek tragedy.[8] According to Nussbaum, ethical insight comes from reading the story, first sequentially, and then by providing a sensitive and reflective commentary that will, hopefully, unpack the ethical complexities of the narrative in a helpful way.

Adultery and Murder

The opening of ch. 11 provides the background and historical setting for what follows. The affair between David and Bathsheba is said to have happened in 'the spring of the year, the time when kings go out to battle' (v. 1).[9] One afternoon, David sees from the roof of his palace a beautiful woman bathing,[10] and the sight immediately inflames his desire for her. David inquires as to the identity of the woman and is informed that she

words for different characters to produce character contrasts, and by the subtle and not so subtle differences between narrative and dialogue (1988). See, also, Sternberg 1985: 190–222. On the technique of 'gap-filling' in narrative generally, see Iser 1971.

8. John Barton (1995: 75; 1998: 19–36) suggests that the account of David's adultery with Bathsheba and the ensuing disasters that befall his family is one ideally suited to be analysed and commented upon in the style of Martha Nussbaum's *Love's Knowledge* (1990) and *The Fragility of Goodness* (1986).

9. The reference is to the period between the heavy winter rains and the spring harvest, when the lull in agricultural duties was viewed as an appropriate time to engage in large-scale military operations; cf. 1 Kgs 20:22, 26; 2 Chron. 36:10. See, further, Mauchline 1971: 247; A.A. Anderson 1989: 152–3. The received consonantal text reads 'messengers' (*mal'ākîm*) instead of 'kings' (*mĕlākîm*), but the fact that 'kings' is the reading preserved in the LXX, Targum and Vulgate (and in 1 Chron. 20:1) strongly supports the view that 'kings' represents the original reading. It is possible that the reading of the MT is a scribal attempt to salvage something of David's reputation, since the implication that David stayed home while his troops went out to battle could have been regarded as reflecting badly on him; cf. Gordon 1986: 252–3; Esler 2011: 313, and the comments below, pp. 66–7. For a detailed discussion of the textual ambiguity in 11:1, see Bodner 2005: 77–88, who argues that the ambivalent element in the opening verse serves to prepare the reader for a host of ambiguities that will follow in the rest of the chapter.

10. Graeme Auld observes that one of the features of 1 and 2 Samuel is the attention given to the appearance of some of the main characters: the attractiveness of David, Tamar, Absalom and Abigail are commented upon by the narrator (2011:

was 'Bathsheba, daughter of Eliam, the wife of Uriah the Hittite' (v. 3).[11] Given that Bathsheba was married to one of David's own warriors, one might have expected the information to restrain him from pursuing the matter any further, but David merely sends messengers to bring her to the palace, where he has sexual intercourse with her. Bathsheba then returns home and, in due course, she dispatches messengers to inform the king that she was pregnant.[12] The note, in parenthesis, to the effect that Bathsheba was 'purifying herself after her period' (v. 4b), breaks the otherwise chronological line of development; the detail, seemingly pointless, becomes significant for the subsequent narrative, for it clearly incriminates David in making her pregnant, and indicates that Uriah could not have been the father of the child that was eventually born.[13]

454–5). For a discussion of the various representations of beauty in the books of Samuel and Kings, see Avioz 2009; Sternberg 1985: 354–64; and for a general discussion of the ideologies of male beauty in the Hebrew Bible, see Macwilliam 2009.

11. As Walter Brueggemann has observed, Bathsheba 'is identified by the men to whom she belongs' and has no existence of her own (1990: 273). Some have surmised that the Eliam referred to here is the same as Eliam, son of Ahithophel the Gilonite mentioned in 2 Sam. 15:12; 23:34 (so Mauchline 1971: 249; Hertzberg 1964: 309–10; Bodner 2005: 96; Bailey 1990: 87), in which case Bathsheba would have been the wife of one of David's officers and the daughter of another, implying that she came from a politically influential family. Alter observes that it is unusual to identify a woman by both her husband and father, and he suggests that in this case the reason was that both were members of David's elite corps of warriors (1999: 250). However, it is by no means certain that the Eliam mentioned here was the son of Ahithophel, and the identification has rightly been questioned by some commentators (cf. A.A. Anderson 1989: 153; Gordon 1986: 253; McCarter 1984: 285).

12. As Cheryl Exum observes, not every act of sexual intercourse issues in pregnancy, but 'as fate would have it, this one does' (1992: 127). Bathsheba's 'I am pregnant' are the only words she utters in the entire story that follows. Alter comments on the 'stringent efficiency' of the biblical narrative at this point, leaping from the sexual act to the discovery of the pregnancy (1999: 251).

13. Many scholars have argued that the point of the circumstantial clause may also have been intended to suggest that Bathsheba's intercourse with David took place at a propitious time for conception (cf. the Talmudic tractate *Nid.* 31b), ovulation usually taking place between ten and fourteen days after the onset of menstruation; cf. H.P. Smith 1899: 318; Krause 1983; McCarter 1984: 286; Bach 1993: 71; McKenzie 2000: 157–8; Bailey 1990: 88; Hertzberg 1964: 310; A.A. Anderson 1989: 153. This may be an anachronistic reading of the text, however, since it is questionable whether it was known at the time that fertility occurred in the middle of a cycle (cf. Kirk-Duggan 2003: 58). For the view that v. 4 does not refer to menstrual cleansing, see Chankin-Gould et al. 2008.

David then commands Joab, the commander of his army, to send Uriah home from the battlefield, ostensibly in order to obtain first-hand information concerning the progress of the Ammonite campaign; his real motive, however, was to find a way in which paternity of the child could be attributed to Bathsheba's husband. To that end, David instructs Uriah to go home and 'wash your feet' (v. 8),[14] and in order to induce in Uriah a sense of obligation to comply with his wishes, David offers him a gift.[15] However, Uriah, as a dutiful soldier on active service, would have been bound by a vow of sexual abstinence;[16] he thus refuses the invitation to go home and he sleeps, instead, at the entrance of the king's house and in the company of the king's servants (v. 9).[17] When David is informed that

14. The word 'feet' here is usually understood as a euphemism for the genitalia (cf. Ruth 3:4, 7), although some have understood 'wash your feet' in a more literal sense, meaning no more than 'refresh yourself after your journey' (H.P. Smith 1899: 318; cf. Gen. 18:4; 43:24) or 'make yourself comfortable' (cf. Hertzberg 1964: 310). However, Uriah's response to David in v. 11 suggests that he understood the sexual import of David's instruction, and that David's words in v. 8 amounted to permission from the king for him to return home to sleep with his wife.

15. William McKane notes that this was a 'sinister present', the kind of gift 'which is given to tie the hands of the man who receives it and to make it difficult for him not to do the giver's bidding' (1963: 232).

16. Meir Sternberg claims that the supposed prohibition of sexual relations laid on Israelite soldiers in war is 'a figment of the scholarly imagination', since nowhere is this mentioned among the laws of purity devolving on soldiers in Deut. 23:10-15. Indeed, he claims that the present narrative establishes its non-existence, since David would hardly instruct Uriah to return home and expect him to violate a taboo; moreover, if such a taboo existed, it is unclear why Uriah did not cite the duty of celibacy instead of claiming that his refusal was due to his solidarity with his fellow-soldiers (1985: 526–7 n. 15). However, there is evidence to suggest that soldiers on active duty were expected to maintain a regimen of sexual abstinence, and this was a rule which David himself claimed to have followed scrupulously (1 Sam. 21:5-6; cf. McCarter 1984: 286). Daniel Bodi suggests that David, by inviting Uriah to sleep with his wife, may have been inciting him to break a sexual taboo and thereby commit a serious breach of ritual law, while at the same time attributing paternity of the child to him; if so, David 'would assume here truly Machiavellian traits' (2010: 62). William McKane (1963: 229; cf. Gordon 1986: 254) suggests that the expression 'wash your feet' alludes to the ritual ablution associated with release from the vow of sexual abstinence taken by those engaged in war; however, there seems little evidence to support this interpretation, and it has not generally been accepted by commentators.

17. It is stated twice that Uriah did not go down to his house (vv. 9, 13), and the insistence on this point is important for the narrative, since it eliminates any possibility of saddling Uriah with the paternity of Bathsheba's child. Ironically, had Uriah obeyed the king's invitation, he would have saved his life (cf. Bodi 2010: 66).

Uriah did not return home, he asks him for an explanation (v. 10). Uriah, the honourable soldier, responds that he could not, in all conscience, go home, eat, drink and lie with his wife while his fellow-soldiers were fighting in battle (v. 11). Having failed in his first attempt to get Uriah to return home and sleep with his wife, David plies him with drinks in the hope of undermining his scruples, but once again the ruse proves unsuccessful (v. 13).

David makes one last, crude attempt to extricate himself from his awkward predicament by devising a merciless and cold-blooded plan to engineer Uriah's death. He writes a letter to Joab, instructing him to place Uriah in the area where the battle would be at its fiercest, and to leave him there, unsupported, 'so that he may be struck down and die' (v. 15). Ironically, Uriah himself was to carry the letter that was to seal his fate.[18] Joab obeyed his instructions, but only up to a point:[19] he knew that if he had carried out David's command to the letter, it would have been obvious to all present that Uriah had been deliberately left to die, and this would undoubtedly have created a sense of intolerable insecurity in the ranks and would have affected the morale of the troops.[20] Ruthless as ever in his approach to *Realpolitik*, he knew that he must make it appear that Uriah's death was simply one of the casualties of war, which meant that other faithful soldiers would have to die as part of the cover-up. Joab reckoned that it was better for many besides Uriah to be killed than for the conspiracy to be revealed, and so he decided to implement the spirit, as opposed to the letter, of David's instruction. He therefore sent a detachment of his troops, with Uriah among them, to carry out an assault on the city, and in the violent clash that followed, Joab lost some of his men, including Uriah (v. 17). Joab knew that he would have to notify the king of Uriah's death, but that he would also have to inform him of the disparity between the plan and its implementation. He was only too aware that the tactics that he had adopted were militarily unwise, but he also

---

18. David Gunn (1978: 46) notes that the motif of a person being made to carry their own death warrant is one that frequently occurs in folklore, although this is the only instance of the motif in the Hebrew Bible. See, further, Gunkel 1987: 145; McCarter 1984: 287; Bodi 2010: 66–8.

19. As Meir Sternberg has observed, there is a subtle disparity between 'the order of execution and the execution of the order' (1985: 214).

20. John Mauchline notes that Joab was not a man to shrink from murder as such (as is clear from the death of Abner and, later, that of Amasa; cf. 2 Sam. 3:22-30; 20:8-10), but 'to leave a soldier deliberately unsupported in battle was the opposite of a soldier deserting his unit; it was the unit deserting one of its men' (1971: 251).

knew that if David's plan were to have some modicum of credibility, no suspicious circumstances should surround Uriah's death. Joab suspected that David, as soon as he would hear of what had happened, would be sure to point out the foolishness of the strategy, for the original plan anticipated no such carnage; the king would not have expected a report of many casualties and would almost certainly be angry that so much blood had been spilled so needlessly. Joab even anticipated the questions that the king, upon learning that his commander had not heeded the most elementary principles of siege tactics, would be sure to raise: 'Why did you go so near the city to fight? Did you not know that they would shoot from the wall? Who killed Abimelech son of Jerubbaal? Did not a woman throw an upper millstone on him from the wall, so that he died at Thebez? Why did you go so near the wall?' (vv. 20b-21a). Lessons from the past should have provided ample warning of the dangers of approaching too close to a city wall in the height of battle;[21] nevertheless, Joab reckoned that once the king realized that Uriah was among the fallen, his anger would be assuaged.

The messengers duly return to the king, and provide a brief account of the battle and, without giving David time to protest the recklessness of the assault, they quickly inform him that Uriah had died.[22] In the event, David is neither angry nor reproachful; on the contrary, his words of consolation in v. 25 are full of understanding and sympathy, and are an implicit admission that Joab's revision of David's orders had been necessary. Joab should not take the loss of lives too personally, for death was simply the inevitable result of the vicissitudes of war. The chapter concludes by stating that Bathsheba mourned for her husband, and it is noticeable that even here Bathsheba is not called by her name but is merely referred to as

---

21. It is possible that the inglorious death of Abimelech, the son of Jerubbaal (cf. Judg. 9:50-55), who was killed by a woman who threw a millstone at him, was regarded as a prime example of recklessness in battle. The fact that in this case the death had been precipitated by a woman and that the weapon deployed was something as unwieldly and unwarlike as a millstone, probably contributed to the ignominy of the episode.

22. At the end of v. 22, the LXX contains a speech from David corresponding almost verbatim to that anticipated by Joab in vv. 20b-21a. This is omitted in the MT, and it is this shorter version that appears in the NRSV. However, the explanation of the messenger in v. 23 reads more naturally if David is represented as complaining in the manner predicted by Joab, and thus the LXX in this instance may preserve the original reading. For a detailed discussion of the divergence between the MT and LXX in 2 Sam. 11:22-25, see Bodner 2005: 112–23.

Uriah's wife (v. 26).[23] The story ends with the narrator's moral evaluation of the events that had occurred: 'the thing that David had done was evil in the sight of the LORD' (v. 27b), an ominous sign that David's action would not go unpunished. The reader, of course, has already been made aware of the events that have transpired, but the narrator now informs us that God is also privy to what had happened. The deity is now introduced into the story and will play a more prominent role in the events that follow.

Since much of the ethical interest of the story is focussed on the characters and how they react to the events with which they are confronted, it seems appropriate at this point to analyse the way in which the narrator and subsequent commentators have contrived to portray the characters of both David and Bathsheba.

The Characterization of David

The Narrator's Evaluation of David's Character

The comment in the opening verse of the chapter to the effect that David remained in Jerusalem during the 'spring of the year, the time when kings go out to battle' is viewed by some commentators as an implicit criticism of David on the part of the narrator: while his soldiers were risking their lives in the national interest, the indolent monarch remained in the city enjoying a leisurely lifestyle, while watching a beautiful woman bathing from the palace roof.[24] 'What is the king doing in his city while the nation is fighting in the field?' asks Sternberg (1985: 194). Was this not a clear abdication of duty on David's part, especially since the very quest for a king was based, at least in part, so that he could 'go out before us and fight our battles' (1 Sam. 8:20)? Surely the king should have been at war, leading his troops, not sitting idly on his rooftop terrace? Had David been in the field of action, directing the course of the war, he would never have seen Bathsheba as he did, and would not have succumbed

---

23. Even in the royal genealogy of Mt. 1, while Tamar (v. 3), Rahab and Ruth (v. 5) are mentioned by name, Bathsheba remains the 'wife of Uriah' (v. 6).

24. Daniel Bodi suggests that the picture of David 'slothfully indulging in a long siesta' while his army was at war suggests a 'sluggish and indolent attitude unbecoming to a warrior' (2010: 41). Philip Esler (2011: 314) views David's remaining in Jerusalem as a breach of the social conventions applicable to kings, and he regards David's action (or, rather, his inaction) as particularly reprehensible in this case, given that the Israelites had such an egregious insult to avenge. Carole Fontaine adds that David's unwillingness to set out from Jerusalem 'foreshadows the less than heroic actions of the king which follow' (1986: 64). See, also, Sternberg 1985: 194–5; R.G. Smith 2009: 121.

to the temptation; consequently, the entire history of the house of David might have been quite different.[25] It seems doubtful, however, whether the narrator was here intending to imply a dereliction of duty on David's part; after all, it is not for his failure to accompany the army to war that David is condemned in the verses that follow, but for what he did at home while his troops were out in the field. There are enough aspersions cast on David's character and egregious conduct in the rest of the chapter without adding indolence as an additional flaw. Moreover, Ken Stone's contention that David's remaining in Jerusalem was an indication of 'weakness and cowardice' on his part[26] fails to take into account the fact that the king had already taken an active role in a previous major expedition (2 Sam. 10:17), and he may well have felt it appropriate to let Joab take charge in the more mundane mopping-up operations.[27]

But even if there is no implicit criticism of David in the opening verse, there are strong undercurrents of disapproval in the narrator's presentation of him in the rest of the chapter, even though the critical tone is somewhat muted (cf. Gunn 1975: 22-3). David emerges as a deeply flawed individual, driven by voracious self-interest, and no attempt is made to draw a veil of decorum over his more disreputable behaviour. Indeed, the narrative leaves the reader in no doubt that it was David's carnal self-indulgence that initiated the whole train of events that was to follow, and the fact that Bathsheba is described at the outset as the 'wife of Uriah the Hittite' (11:3) makes it clear that David knew that in sending for her he was committing an act of adultery. When he hears that Bathsheba is pregnant, his attempts to extricate himself from a potentially embarrassing situation are both crude and cynical. His duplicity is apparent in

---

25. Cf. Polzin 1993: 109. Philip Esler notes that, had David 'done the right thing and led his men to war, he would never have got into the trouble he did' (2011: 314).

26. Stone maintains that 'in a cultural context in which an aggressive and competitive display of masculinity is valued, David's location in Jerusalem casts him in a negative light' (1996: 96).

27. H.P. Smith notes that kings in Israel did not regularly go out to war and were sometimes content just to send their armies; in this case, David probably stayed in Jerusalem because the siege of a walled town would have been too tedious a matter to involve the king. Thus, to argue that 11:1 contains a covert condemnation of David for a dereliction of royal responsibilities seems 'far-fetched' (1899: 317-18). Moshe Garsiel argues that the traumatic deaths of Saul and his sons in battle highlighted the danger of a king's going out to war, and he points out that at the beginning of David's reign he left his general, Joab, to conduct military operations while he remained in the capital (2 Sam. 2:12-32; 3:20-23). He thus concludes that David's preferring to stay in Jerusalem does not imply a failure in his royal duty (1993: 249–50).

the way he affects concern for the welfare of Uriah, for while David's encouragement for him to go home to his wife ostensibly sounds like the act of a gracious king bestowing well-deserved rest on his faithful and loyal soldier, the reader knows that this was just a devious ploy to pass on to Uriah the paternity of his illegitimate child. David's attempt to send Uriah a gift and to get him drunk in order to induce him to enjoy conjugal relations with his wife is a further demonstration of the depths to which he was prepared to sink. Moreover, the calculated way in which he planned to dispose of Uriah, instructing Joab to place him at the forefront of the battle and to leave him without support so that he would be killed by enemy fire, indicates that he was guilty not only of premeditated murder but also of its cunning and cynical concealment. The fact that he even made Uriah carry the letter to Joab that would seal his fate merely adds to the despicableness of his crime. Finally, the way in which David unctuously attributes the death of Uriah and the other soldiers to the vicissitudes of war is a further indication of the narrator's attempt to portray him as a deeply cynical king who was clearly not overly concerned about the unnecessary sacrifice of an entire army unit.

At this point, it seems expedient to consider the role of Uriah in the story, for he clearly appears as a counterfoil to David, exemplifying the very virtues that the king was patently lacking. Indeed, everything he does and says serves to highlight the immorality of David's words and actions. The significance of Uriah's role in this regard has tended to be neglected, partly because much of the scholarly discussion has focussed on whether or not he knew of David's adultery. Meir Sternberg has argued at considerable length that Uriah, upon his arrival in Jerusalem, may well have learned of Bathsheba's infidelity (if not of her pregnancy), since several people would have been in on the secret and could have tipped him off. After all, David had used messengers to summon Bathsheba to him, and Bathsheba did likewise when she informed him of her pregnancy. The adultery, therefore, could scarcely have been a secret within the court and, given the 'ready source of court gossip' (Hertzberg 1964: 310), Uriah may well have had wind of the affair.[28] Some have argued that his suspicions must have been aroused by the fact that he had ostensibly been recalled from the battle just to give a report on the progress of the war, since he would have known that this would have been Joab's responsibility.[29]

---

28. For the view that Uriah may have known or sensed what was going on, possibly having learnt of the affair from the palace guards with whom he spent the night in vv. 9, 13, see Sternberg 1985: 202; Garsiel 1993: 256-9.

29. Cf. Mauchline 1971: 249. Sternberg notes that Uriah 'would not have been summoned to Jerusalem just for a friendly chat' (1985: 200).

Others have suggested that he may well have suspected that David's eagerness to encourage him to go home and 'wash his feet' was far from being a benevolent king's concern and solicitude for the wellbeing of a weary soldier, and his suspicions of the affair may have been further confirmed by the king's generosity in sending him a gift as an inducement to sleep with his wife.[30] Uriah's refusal to accede to David's instructions is consequently viewed as a deliberate attempt on his part to foil the king's designs, and his actions are regarded as representing a protest against the injustice that had been perpetrated against him. Instead of hurling accusations against the king, Uriah opted for a more effective and impressive response, that of 'an obstinate, proud silence' (Sternberg 1985: 206). Uriah's actions thus represented his revenge, but it was a revenge that would eventually cost him his life. Based on such arguments, Sternberg concludes that the conjecture that Uriah knew of the affair has a good deal to recommend it, and he argues that the witting cuckold is a far more alluring and complex character than the unwitting idealist.

There must be a lingering suspicion, however, that Sternberg reads into the text what is not there to be read, and that he pays too much attention to the character's inner world.[31] Indeed, not content with surmising what Uriah may have known, Sternberg goes on to consider whether David knew that Uriah was aware of the affair. But the protracted discussion of what Uriah is thought to have known, and what David may have surmised that Uriah knew, has tended to overshadow the narrator's purpose in his depiction of Uriah's character. Indeed, Sternberg's argument that Uriah knew of the affair and was playing a dangerous game with David (as David was with him) merely serves to blur the moral distinction between the two characters, and undermines the sharp contrast between the honourable, principled, dutiful soldier and the deceitful and duplicitous king.[32] Uriah's

---

30. Sternberg argues that if Uriah did not know of the affair his refusal to go home and sleep with his wife seems unrealistic and '*too* heroic to be true'; moreover, if he did not know, it is strange that he elected to sleep in such close proximity to his home (a fact established by David's being able to see Bathsheba bathing). As Sternberg observes, 'he spends three nights at the entrance to the king's house, when a few more steps would bring him to his own' (1985: 206).

31. Sternberg 1985: 201–13. Gale Yee's contention that the question which is 'uppermost' in the reader's mind is whether or not Uriah knew of the affair is unconvincing (1988: 243–4). Mieke Bal (1987: 27–8) is rightly critical of Sternberg for pontificating at such length as to who knew what, arguing that this is not a question that imposes itself on the reader at all.

32. As Adele Berlin notes, 'everything that Uriah says and does points up the immorality of David's words and deeds. Ironically, it is the innocent Uriah who

dignified stance in v. 11 was probably intended as an implicit indictment of David: 'The ark and Israel and Judah remain in booths;[33] and my lord Joab and the servants of my lord are camping in the open field; shall I then go to my house, to eat and to drink, and to lie with my wife? As you live, and as your soul lives, I will not do such a thing.' Uriah's speech neatly encapsulates the moral aspect of the story: his words show him to be a loyal subject, characterized by courage and self-sacrifice, who chooses the privations of war out of solidarity with his comrades.[34] His refusal to sleep with his wife, keenly aware of the obligations that the war had imposed upon him, merely highlights the culpability of David's behaviour who had slept with another man's wife while her husband was risking his life in battle.[35] Moreover, Uriah would not be bribed by a gift, and his sense of propriety was not affected by the drink with which David had plied him. Indeed, David's attempt to get Uriah drunk in order to make him more pliant and to quell his inhibitions is a crass and cynical manoeuvre,

pays with his life while the life of the guilty David is spared' (1994: 40). Gale Yee notes that many scholars view Uriah as an example of the 'moral superiority of the duty-bound soldier' who provides 'a counter-foil to the king's abuse of power while his troops are away' (1988: 243-4). Leo G. Perdue similarly emphasizes the contrast between the deception and treachery of the lustful David and the total loyalty of Uriah to king, nation and fellow warriors, 'a loyalty that ironically comes from a Hittite mercenary' (1984: 76). Jan Fokkelman observes that the distinction between the king and his subject in this story is 'quite striking and tragic' (1981: 55), and he notes that 'with his piety and fidelity Uriah forms a stark contrast with the cunning despot' (1981: 93).

33. Yigael Yadin (1955: 344-7) proposed that the Hebrew word for 'booths' (*sukkôt*) should be read as a proper noun, and that the reference is to Succoth in Transjordan (so, also, McCarter 1984: 287), but this suggestion has not generally commended itself to commentators. For the problems inherent in Yadin's suggestion, see Homan 1999.

34. Mieke Bal (1987: 31) comments that Uriah's words in v. 11 must have been painful for David to hear, for the honourable soldier holds a mirror up to the king, showing him what real solidarity is and how much the king lacks it. Richard Smith (2009: 125) believes that 'the narrator has made Uriah the mouthpiece for his own sentiments'.

35. The stark contrast between the two characters is neatly summarized by Gale Yee, who observes that the narrator 'sets in opposition David who has sex with Bathsheba (who is not his wife) while the troops are out in the battlefield (11:1, 4) and Uriah who refuses to have sex with Bathsheba (who is his wife) while the troops are out in the battlefield (11:11)'. Yee goes on to note that the ultimate irony is that it is Uriah who will die for not sleeping with his wife, while David, who *has* slept with her, stays alive (1988: 246).

and is an indication, in Peter Ackroyd's oft-quoted words, that 'Uriah drunk is more pious than David sober' (1977: 102). However, as Walter Brueggemann has observed, David had miscalculated Uriah's loyalty and uprightness, and he could 'no more control the principled Uriah than he could manage the pregnancy of Uriah's wife' (1990: 276). Ironically, it is Uriah, the Hittite, the quintessence of loyalty and fidelity, the man of noble spirit and uncompromising conscience, who emerges from the story with honour, and the repeated emphasis on his Hittite origins (vv. 3, 6, 17, 24) merely serves to indicate that whereas the king of Israel was completely lacking in principle, the same could not be said of the foreigner.[36]

The narrator's own evaluation of the events recorded is deliberately left until the end of the story, by which time, of course, readers will inevitably have come to their own conclusions regarding David's behaviour. When we are informed that 'the thing that David had done was evil in the sight of the LORD' (v. 27b)[37] it will hardly come as a surprise, for as Gale Yee has pointed out, the 'author's judgment mostly confirms what the reader has already decided' (1988: 252). No other verdict was possible, given the transparency of David's guilt. But while the laconic comment in v. 27b ostensibly appears to be quite clear and unambiguous, the narrator's evaluation is, in fact, encoded in rather enigmatic terms, for it is uncertain whether 'the thing' refers to David's adultery with Bathsheba or to his murder of Uriah. Some suggest that the narrator intended to draw attention to murder rather than adultery as the essential crime, since David's liaison with Bathsheba is reported briefly in vv. 1-5, whereas his elaborate scheme to shift the appearance of paternity to Uriah, and when that fails, to have him killed, is recorded at much greater length (vv. 6-27).[38] Moreover,

---

36. Cf. Gordon 1986: 253–4. Alter suggests that the fact that Uriah had a pious Israelite name ('the Lord is my light') may imply that he was a native or naturalized Israelite of Hittite extraction (1999: 250). On the significance of Uriah's Hittite origins, see Kim 2008: 198–212.

37. This is preferable to the NRSV's rather anodyne 'the thing that David had done displeased the LORD'. Walter Brueggemann has suggested that these words were probably intended as a deliberate contrast to David's words to Joab in v. 25 (lit. 'do not let this matter be evil in your eyes'; NRSV, 'do not let this matter trouble you'), the implication being that the royal perception of morality was hardly in accord with the divine perception (1990: 279). Cf. Yee 1988: 247.

38. Alter (1981: 182) believes that the sheer amount of detail devoted to the murder of Uriah – unusual, given the laconic style of the narrator – favours the view that David's guilt consisted primarily in his involvement with Uriah's death and with the events that led up to it (cf., also, Bar-Efrat 1980: 173). Ken Stone (1996: 98) concurs, noting that the divine displeasure towards David occurs only after the murder, rather than immediately after the sexual encounter.

since both David and Bathsheba were guilty of adultery, one might have expected both to have been the subject of Yahweh's displeasure; the fact that the narrator is quite specific in noting that it was the thing that '*David* did' that evoked the divine verdict suggests that the reference was to the murder of Uriah.[39] On the other hand, the parable uttered by Nathan in the following chapter makes no reference to murder, only to adultery (if the taking of the ewe lamb by the wealthy neighbour was intended as a reference to the taking of Uriah's wife). In the prophet's reproach that follows the parable, David is admittedly condemned for his murder of Uriah (12:9), but the punishment meted out by Yahweh in 12:11-12 seems to be directed at David's adultery with Bathsheba rather than his murder of her husband, for Nathan warns David that God will 'take your wives before your eyes, and give them to your neighbour, and he shall lie with your wives in the sight of this very sun'.

The rather convoluted debate among commentators as to whether adultery or murder was uppermost in the narrator's mind may well be beside the point, for in Nathan's reproach of the king in 12:7-14, David's primary offence seems to have been the contempt that he had displayed towards Yahweh's acts of kindness towards him. Such divine acts of benevolence are listed at length in 12:7-8: God had anointed David as king, had rescued him from the hand of Saul, and had even given 'your master's wives into your bosom'; but instead of showing gratitude, David had acted brazenly, displaying an arrogance and contempt towards the deity who was the source of all that David had received. Thus, although the issues of murder and adultery are not ignored in Nathan's reproach, they may, as Barbara Green has observed, be tangential to the main charge against David, for at the root of his sin was a failure to recognize Yahweh's power and authority, and a blatant 'disregard of the giver by the beneficiary' (2017: 201; cf. Janzen 2012). It was God's role to give and David's to receive, but his scornful arrogance meant that he had usurped God's prerogative and in so doing had 'despised the word of the LORD' (v. 9). It is not without significance that David's sin, while clearly grievous on the human plane, is depicted as ultimately a sin against Yahweh, for in acknowledging his culpability, David confesses that he has 'sinned against the LORD' (v. 13).

---

39. Adele Berlin argues that Bathsheba is not mentioned as participating in David's guilt because she was basically a 'non-person' in the narrative, merely 'the performer of an action necessary to the plot'; she was therefore not 'an equal party to the adultery, but only the means whereby it was achieved' (1994: 27).

Scholarly Evaluations of David's Character

Although David's unseemly behaviour in ch. 11 is described without a word of mitigation in the narrative, and no attempt is made by the narrator to gloss over the king's conduct, there has been no shortage of attempts by commentators, both ancient and modern, to cast David, despite his misdemeanours, in a positive light. Such attempts go back to the period of the rabbis, who were appalled at the very thought that David, Yahweh's anointed, and the supposed author of many of the psalms, could have been guilty of adultery and murder. In order to exonerate him, they maintained that it was the custom at the time for all who went to battle to write a 'bill of divorce' before leaving for the war; thus, Bathsheba was not technically married when David had the affair, and so he could not have been guilty of adultery.[40] They even suggested that Uriah's death was entirely justified, for by flagrantly disobeying David's order to go to his house he was rebelling against royal authority and was therefore guilty of treason.[41] Although modern commentators do not resort to such casuistry in order to defend David, there has been no shortage of attempts to ameliorate the seriousness of his crime. Thus, Uriel Simon insists that 'David was no oriental monarch who resorted to stealing wives from their husband or who sought to do away with husbands in order to gain their wives'; admittedly, he continues, the consciousness that she was a married woman did not deter him, but he did send her home afterwards 'hoping that the affair, for the lack of practical consequences, would, as far as the husband was concerned, be non-existent' (1967: 212). Walter Brueggemann, reflecting on David's behaviour in ch. 11 concedes – with something of an

---

40. Rabbi Shmuel bar Nakhmani, for example, claimed that, as a soldier on active duty, Uriah would have divorced his wife before going out to battle: 'Whoever says that David sinned is totally mistaken... How could he fall into sin while the Divine Presence rested upon him?... Under the house of David, whoever went forth into battle would give his wife a letter of divorce' (*Shab.* 56a; cf. McCarter 1984: 288; Bach 1997: 140 n. 14). For a detailed discussion of the so-called divorce letter (*gêṭ piṭṭûrîn*) mentioned in rabbinic tradition, see Bodi 2010: 212–24. Bodi compares the practice to a similar provision found in Middle Assyrian Laws in which the wife of an Assyrian prisoner is given 'a tablet as (for) a widow', allowing her to legitimately take another husband should the wife find herself abandoned by the death or capture of her warrior husband. The aim of both the Hebrew 'divorce letter' and the Assyrian 'widow's tablet' was to prevent the abandoned woman from being accused of adultery if she remarried.

41. *B. Sanh.* 107a. Of course, such casuistry on the part of the rabbis fails to account for Nathan's rebuke and David's confession of guilt (2 Sam. 12:13).

understatement – that there is 'not much to celebrate about David in this narrative', but he points out that David does confess his guilt, an action which entailed 'a considerable degree of moral courage and sensitivity' on his part (1990: 282), and despite his cynical and self-serving behaviour 'there is a powerful grandeur about him' (1990: 283). But, among modern commentators, the prize for the feeblest attempt to come to David's rescue must surely go to William McKane, who sought to plead David's cause by suggesting that the circumstances of war altered the normal conventions of human behaviour: 'We may suppose that he was missing the company of his soldiers who were campaigning against Ammon and that he felt at a loose end in Jerusalem. He was in the dangerous condition of searching for something with which to divert himself and then one sin led to another' (1963: 228).

At this point it seems salutary to consider David Clines's overview of the way in which biblical commentators have sought to portray David (1995a: 212–43). Clines argues that male biblical scholars have depicted him in a uniformly positive light, and one of the most striking aspects of their response to the figure of David in the biblical narrative is the strong note of approval that is encountered. Biblical scholars, he claims, have 'unanimously' defended David (p. 234), highlighting his positive qualities, and have glossed over or minimized any negative traits or faults in his character. David is regarded in the scholarly literature as a shrewd politician, a talented administrator, and a loyal and diplomatic leader of his people; even the 'sin' which he commits in ch. 11 is given a positive gloss by commentators, who emphasize that no sooner has he committed his crime than he is represented as repenting.[42] Clines considers one possible explanation for this positive portrayal, namely, that scholars have been unduly influenced by the tone of the biblical narrator, who is remarkably reticent to pronounce judgment upon his characters.[43] But Clines appears to dismiss such a view, maintaining, rather, that there is a more deep-rooted psychological explanation for acquiescing in the narrator's strong note of approval: male commentators subconsciously respond to David's perceived masculinity, and their image of him has been shaped

---

42. Clines claims that David's sin is, as it were, swallowed up in his repentance, so that his 'success in repentance becomes more important than his failure in sin, so even his failure becomes an arena of his success' (1995a: 237). The story has been linked since ancient times with the great penitential Ps. 51; cf. Johnson 2009: 28–39.

43. 2 Sam. 11:27b is an exception, but this is regarded by Clines as merely a 'motivating sentence for the succeeding narrative of the death of the child of Bathsheba and David' (1995a: 234 n. 48).

by their own cultural norms.[44] David was a warrior, a mighty man of valour, and according to Clines's calculation, taking all the references in 1 Samuel 16–1 Kings 2 into account, he was responsible for the deaths of 140,000 men, including 15 whose deaths he was personally responsible for outside the context of battle. Male commentators have chosen to focus on the positive image of masculinity that these stories of David's exploits promote; consequently, they never say a word against David's acts of aggression, appearing at times to condone, if not approve, of his acts of indiscriminate killings (pp. 234-8). Put simply, discussions of David's character by male commentators provide an example of 'gender-based hero-worship' (p. 235): scholars identify their own desires with those of David, and they excuse his faults and misdemeanours because he is a man after their own heart.

Now, Clines's argument must be subjected to serious criticism. In the first place, by emphasizing the narrative's 'strong note of approval', he underplays the decidedly unflattering portrait of David encountered in the text. Quite apart from the negative authorial comment expressed in 11:27b, the narrator can hardly be accused of regarding David as an example of moral rectitude or as a paragon of virtue; indeed, as James A. Wharton has observed, the ruthless candour of 2 Samuel 11 suggests that it was written by someone 'determined to vilify David for all future generations' (1981: 343). Secondly, the claim that male biblical scholars have instinctively responded to David's perceived masculinity is open to question, for, as Cheryl Kirk-Duggan has demonstrated, the narratives concerning David in 1 and 2 Samuel do not always portray him as the stereotypical macho male, and she regards it as significant that his pledge of undying love is made not to Bathsheba or the other women in his life but to a male, Jonathan (2003: 53). Thirdly, the view that male scholars 'unanimously' defend David and gloss over his faults is completely misleading. In this regard, Clines simply cites five dictionary articles (pp. 234-8) as though

---

44. Although not mentioned by Clines, H.H. Cohen (1965) similarly seeks to delve into the psychological motivation for David's conduct. According to Cohen, David by this time was too old to accompany his army into battle, and his mid-life crisis was a blow to his self-esteem and masculinity. He thus had to reassure himself of his virility, strength and power, and the affair with Bathsheba was born of the need to reassert his flagging manhood. The problem with this interpretation is that there is no indication at all in the narrative that David, at the time of his affair, was an old man. As Daniel Bodi amusingly observes, 'a man who can see a naked woman bathing in the dark at some distance and be gripped by a potent desire for her does not appear to be afflicted either by failing eye-sight or impotence' (2010: 43).

these were somehow representative of modern critical scholarship. It is true that he makes passing reference to the commentaries by A.R.S. Kennedy, Peter R. Ackroyd and William McKane, but he is content to focus on that by Kyle McCarter, letting him 'speak for commentators everywhere' (p. 240). But even a quick perusal of the relevant literature on David should have alerted him to the fact that biblical scholars are far from letting the king off the hook.[45] Although, as we have seen, some scholars have been anxious to mitigate the seriousness of David's moral failures, many are quite prepared to condemn his behaviour in no uncertain terms. Thus, he is variously viewed as an 'evil genius' (Whybray 1968: 27), as 'predatory and unscrupulous' (Auld 2011: 454), as a 'brute' who was also 'a liar, deceiver and traitor' (Powis Smith 1933: 10–11), and as a king who acts 'like an oriental potentate wielding absolute authority and treating subjects as subservient to his ends and purposes' (Mauchline 1971: 252).[46] In conclusion, scholarly evaluations of David's conduct are by no means as uniform as Clines suggests, for on the whole, scholars give as much prominence to his weaknesses and vulnerability as to his strengths and accomplishments.

The Characterization of Bathsheba

Apart from the brief note at the end of ch. 11 to the effect that Bathsheba lamented the death of her husband and, after the period of mourning was over, became David's wife (vv. 26-27), her role in the story is limited to a mere five verses at the beginning of the chapter. The opening scene of the story describes David assuming the role of a 'peeping-Tom', watching Bathsheba bathe as he strolled on the palace roof (v. 2). The episode is one that, perhaps inevitably, has fascinated storytellers, artists, filmmakers, and biblical commentators alike. Part of its fascination arises from the fact that the incident is described in deliberately vague and ambiguous

---

45. John Kessler points to numerous recent scholars who have underlined the narrative's criticism of David for his ruthless political ambition and his ineptitude in family relationships (2000: 409).

46. In a similar vein, Jan Fokkelman describes David, walking on the roof of his palace, as a 'despot who is able to survey and choose as he pleases' (1981: 51). Carole Fontaine similarly sees in his behaviour that of a 'potentate who unwisely assumes that his power places him above the Torah' (1986: 64). Daniel Bodi claims that 'David adopts the behavior of an Oriental despot and tyrant' (2010: 34), while Thomas Preston regards David's remaining in Jerusalem and his seduction and seizure of Bathsheba as 'primarily the act of an oriental despot' (1982: 40–1).

terms, and the gaps in the narrative mean that much is left to the imagination of the reader. Bathsheba is denied a voice both before and during the sexual encounter, and her feelings, intentions and motivations remain a closed book; indeed, the only words she utters in the entire narrative are the fateful 'I am pregnant' (v. 5).[47] This deliberately cultivated ambiguity inevitably raises many questions in the reader's mind. Should Bathsheba be viewed as the archetypal scheming temptress, determined to seduce David by purposefully bathing in public view, or should she be regarded as the innocent victim of male lust and as the passive object of the king's voyeuristic gaze? Was she complicit in the sexual encounter, obeying David's summons eagerly, or was she responding under duress to a royal command that could hardly be ignored? Was David guilty of the offence of adultery or rape? Much must remain in the realm of speculation, for we are not told of Bathsheba's reaction to being sent, or whether any blandishments, inducements or threats motivated her to lie with David.

Despite the ambiguity, numerous (predominantly male) scholars have contrived to place the blame for the episode – at least partly – on Bathsheba's shoulders. H.W. Hertzberg, for example, wonders whether Bathsheba did not count on the possibility of being seen (1964: 309), while Edwin M. Good (1965: 36) surmises that 'Bathsheba may not have been unaware of David's whereabouts'.[48] That Bathsheba indulged in some form of exhibitionism is also suggested by George G. Nicol, who claims that the action of bathing in public and so close to the king's residence was, to say the least, provocative, and he suggests that the provocation may well have been deliberate; even if it was not, her actions 'can hardly indicate less than a contributory negligence on her part' (1988: 360). Joseph Blenkinsopp opines that Bathsheba 'was not as blameless as a first reading of the text might suggest' and that she 'took the risk of being observed' (1966: 52). Meir Sternberg, while conceding

---

47. Adele Berlin suggests that Bathsheba is not even regarded as a character in her own right in this account: 'The plot in 2 Sam. 11 calls for adultery, and adultery requires a married woman. Bathsheba fills that function. Nothing about her which does not pertain to that function is allowed to intrude into the story' (1994: 27). Berlin notes, however, that the Bathsheba of 1 Kgs 1–2, by contrast, is a strong and fully fledged character, seizing the throne from her son and playing an important role in affairs of state (pp. 27–30).

48. Craig Ho draws parallels between the story of David and Bathsheba and that of Judah and Tamar (Gen. 38), and argues that both liaisons 'begin with seduction from the female side'; the only difference being that Tamar dressed like a prostitute whereas 'Bathsheba would rather be seen with nothing on' (1999: 517).

that it is impossible to determine Bathsheba's attitude, adds that 'one would not imagine that she showed much resistance' (1985: 526 n. 10). Some scholars have compared Bathsheba's reaction with that of Tamar, who protested vehemently against the sexual advances of Amnon (2 Sam. 13:12); the fact that Bathsheba is *not* portrayed as protesting implies that she must have been a willing participant (Würthwein 1974: 27–8). Randall Bailey observes that the verbs used in connection with Bathsheba are not in the *hiphil* (which would suggest that Bathsheba had been compelled to act) but in the *qal*: she 'comes' and 'returns', evidently of her own accord, and she must therefore be regarded as 'a willing and equal partner to the events which transpire'.[49] David Daube concurs with such a view, noting that 'there is no reluctance – not even a show if it – on Bathsheba's part when summoned to the palace' (1982: 277), and the fact that there is no indication in v. 5 of distress on Bathsheba's part when she discovers that she is pregnant supports the view that she was complicit in the sexual encounter (cf. Bailey 1990: 88).[50]

Indeed, some commentators even suggest that Bathsheba was privy to the plan to fob off paternity on Uriah (cf. Daube 1982: 277). Jan Fokkelman, for example, observes that the reference in v. 21a to the death of Abimelech at the hands of a woman 'gives rise to the question as to whether a woman also plays a central role in Uriah's death' (1981: 69),[51] and while we do not know if Bathsheba ever learned of the circumstances surrounding her husband's fate, the fact that he died shortly after she mentioned her pregnancy to David 'can hardly be attributed by her to coincidence' (p. 70).[52] Similarly, Robert Gordon, while conceding that we

---

49. Bailey 1990: 88; 1995: 230 n. 56. A similar view is advocated by Nicol, who argues that there is no evidence that Bathsheba 'is ever less than a willing participant in their adultery' (1997: 50). Cheryl Exum comments that the verbs 'came' and 'returned' are 'not what one would expect if resistance were involved' (2016: 137).

50. Of course, this is simply an argument from silence, for there is no indication in the narrative that she was particularly happy about the pregnancy either. As Antony Campbell amusingly observes, there are two ways of reading Bathsheba's announcement 'I am pregnant': '"I am pregnant, my darling" or "I am pregnant, you bastard"' (2005: 115). Cf. Kim and Nyengele 2003: 101.

51. A similar view is held by Robert Alter, who claims that one suspects 'that Joab's emphasis on a woman's dealing death to the warrior...points back to Bathsheba as the ultimate source of this chain of disasters' (1999: 254). See, also, Auld 2011: 458–9; Bal 1987: 33.

52. A different view, however, is advocated by Jerry M. Landay, who suggests that 'few, not even Bathsheba, accepted Uriah's death at the gates of Rabbah as anything other than the fate of a brave soldier in combat' (1998: 116).

are not told what Bathsheba thought of David's nefarious scheme, insists that 'a degree of complicity might reasonably be inferred' (1986: 253).⁵³ This has led him to wonder whether her mourning for her dead husband was a genuine sign of her affection for him or was simply a case of performing the formalities expected of a widow.⁵⁴ But perhaps the most critical view of Bathsheba comes from Norman Whybray, who castigates her not only for succumbing to the adulterous king but for her foolishness and naivety as well. He briefly considers Bathsheba's appearance in 2 Samuel 11 and 1 Kings 1–2, and comes to the following startling conclusion: 'We thus have a consistent and thoroughly credible picture of Bathsheba as a good-natured, rather stupid woman who was a natural prey both to more passionate and to cleverer men'; indeed, the portrait of her in 11:4 may be viewed as an 'intentional reflexion on the amorality of women' such as the adulteress encountered in Prov. 30:20, who 'eats, and wipes her mouth, and says, "I have done no wrong"' (1968: 40, 86).⁵⁵

One of the most detailed attempts to argue in favour of Bathsheba's complicity in the affair has been provided by Lillian Klein (2003: 55-71). Klein argues that Bathsheba shared responsibility with David for the sexual encounter, since she had an ulterior motive for her involvement, namely, her desire to become a mother.⁵⁶ Klein notes that we do not know how long Bathsheba had been married without conceiving, yet no sooner does she have sexual intercourse with David than she knew herself to be

---

53. Hyun Chul Kim and M. Fulgence Nyengele (2003) set out, in forensic manner, the case for and against Bathsheba being an accomplice in the conspiracy of Uriah's murder. They conclude that the fact that she mourned and lamented Uriah's death (11:26-27) was perhaps intended to suggest that she had no part in David's plan to kill her husband.

54. Gordon maintains that, although Bathsheba dutifully observed the customary period of mourning for her husband (seven days), it is 'impossible to tell how much affection she had felt for him before or since her infidelity' (1986: 255). Adele Berlin suggests that her mourning was performed in a perfunctory way 'as if it were done out of respect for decency rather than from the need to mourn' (1994: 27; 1982: 73). Ken Stone, on the other hand, claims that, in mourning for her husband, there seems to be 'no reason to doubt her sincerity' (1996: 101).

55. Whybray's judgment ill accords with the description of Bathsheba in 1 Kgs 1, where she is regarded as a woman who is both calculating and clever, and who shows considerable resourcefulness in securing the succession of Solomon to David's throne; cf. Nicol 1988.

56. A similar view is held by Randall Bailey, who maintains that Bathsheba knew only too well of the probable consequence of the affair, and that, from her perspective, pregnancy was the desired outcome (1990: 88).

pregnant. If she was married to an infertile man, she may have found it necessary to mate with another male 'to fulfill her biological and social function as a woman' (pp. 59–60). Her failure to conceive would have been of great concern to her; yet she could not fulfil her capacity for reproduction outside of the marital bond. But if the king commanded her, she would have the pretext of excuse. By bathing within sight of the royal palace, she presented the king with 'a subtle opportunity for enticement' (p. 61), and her aim was to seduce David into seducing her.[57] Such a view of Bathsheba, claims Klein, coheres with the portrait of her in 1 Kings 1, where she appears as a resourceful and determined woman whose decisive intervention ensures that the dynastic succession passed to her son, Solomon.[58] But although Bathsheba was complicit in the sexual encounter, Klein argues that she must not be regarded as entirely blameworthy, for she had been faced with an unenviable choice: accepting the honour associated with motherhood (albeit by the most unorthodox means) or facing social discrimination as a barren woman. Viewed in this light, Bathsheba was merely following in the footsteps of Tamar (Gen. 38) and Ruth (Ruth 3) as the initiator of sexual encounter, and such narratives may suggest that female-instigated seduction could be regarded as morally acceptable if the action served a noble cause, namely, procreation (pp. 62–5).

57. Klein 2003: 60. The rabbis similarly argued that it was Bathsheba who seduced the king, which was why she bathed naked in sight of the royal palace; cf. Sternberg 1985: 526 n. 10. However, John Kessler regards it as highly unlikely that a woman in the culture of ancient Israel would have deliberately engaged in public nudity (2000: 419 n. 44). H.W. Hertzberg argues that Bathsheba's consciousness of the danger into which adultery was leading her 'must have been outweighed by her realization of the honour of having attracted the king' (1964: 310). Jerry Landay comes to a similar conclusion when he states that Bathsheba 'did not feel shocked but rather flattered to be desired by the most renowned figure of Israel, a man so revered, so honored, so beloved of the people' (1998: 113). Criticizing such remarks, Bruce Birch comments that 'it is troubling that coercive use of power for the sake of royal lust is so easily transmuted into an honor' (1998: 1285 n. 279)

58. Klein 2003: 65–8. Alter similarly claims that Bathsheba's later behaviour in the matter of her son's succession to the throne in 1 Kgs 1–2 'suggests a woman who has her eye on the main chance, and it is possible that opportunism, not merely passive submission, explains her behavior here as well' (1999: 251). Such a view has rightly been criticized by April Westbrook, who notes that the idea that Bathsheba 'either knew that David would decide to get out of bed one evening and walk on his roof, or that she went outside the presumed privacy of her own home and washed every night until he actually did, is nothing short of ludicrous. If she is that conniving, then she is too intelligent to depend on such an unreliable scheme to achieve her objective' (2015: 122).

As many commentators have observed, whether Bathsheba was coerced or was complicit in the adulterous affair has implications for the degree of guilt incurred by David. If she was coerced, then his sexual relation with Bathsheba was a blatant expression of royal power and was a case of rape rather than adultery.[59] This is the view taken, for example, by David Clines, who regards the David–Bathsheba story as 'a narrative of aggressive masculinity that began with the rape of Bathsheba and continued with the cynical disposal of her husband' (1995a: 230). Cheryl Exum comes to a similar conclusion, noting that when David's children re-enact his crimes as part of his punishment, David's adultery is replayed as rape – twice: following closely on this incident, Amnon rapes his sister Tamar (who, like Bathsheba, is said to be 'beautiful'; 13:1), and Absalom rapes ten of David's wives in a tent pitched for him on the roof, a reminder – if one were needed – of where David's misdemeanour began (2 Sam. 16:21-22).[60] Some have argued that the use of the verb 'lie with' in 11:4 suggests an element of force on the part of David,[61] while others contend that David's supposed 'rape' of Bathsheba arises not so much from what the text of 2 Sam. 11:4 says but from the impression one gains concerning the character of David in 1 and 2 Samuel generally.[62]

59. Many scholars deploy the term 'rape' (at least, tentatively) in connection with the present narrative (cf. Bal 1987: 11; Yee 1988: 243), but the terminology is problematic because no legal or technical word for 'rape' exists in biblical Hebrew that corresponds precisely to the contemporary understanding of the word. See the discussion by Sandie Gravett (2004). That a distinction was drawn between consensual and non-consensual sex in the Hebrew Bible, however, is evident from Deut. 22:23-27, which dictates that if sexual intercourse occurs in a city (i.e. in a public place where people would be nearby), the girl could cry out for help; if she did not do so, it was assumed that she had consented to intercourse. See Abasili 2011: 5–6.

60. Exum 2016: 140. Thomas R. Preston (1982: 41) similarly regards Amnon's rape of Tamar as a recapitulation of David's rape of Bathsheba. James S. Ackerman (1990: 48–9) sees the rape of Tamar and the murder of Amnon in ch. 13 as mirroring David's taking of Bathsheba and the murder of Uriah in ch. 11.

61. Jennifer Andruska, for example, has argued that when one compares the specific syntactical construction used in 11:4 to that encountered in other biblical passages (notably Gen. 34:2; Deut. 22:25), the text of 11:4 signals, quite explicitly, that this was a case of rape (2017). However, 11:4 does not necessarily imply David's use of force or violence, and it is noticeable that the language of physical domination recorded in Amnon's rape of Tamar in ch. 13 is absent here. Cf. Abasili 2011.

62. Cf. the conclusion of K.L. Noll: 'David's rape of Bathsheba (and certainly it must be labelled for what it is) might have been foreseen, given that David has been presented as an ambitious, woman-taking opportunist, who is not shy about manipulating those around him, including the deity' (1997: 59–60).

In fact, much of the speculation concerning Bathsheba's involvement is beside the point, for the narrative is not concerned with assessing the degree of her guilt;[63] it is David's behaviour that is at issue, and any conclusions drawn regarding Bathsheba's participation cannot be regarded as mitigating factors.[64] Whether Bathsheba was resistant to David's advances or compliant cannot be decided based on the text; nor can it be decided whether David was guilty only of adultery or also of the more serious crime of rape. As Antony Campbell has observed, the phrase 'David sent messengers to get her, and she came to him, and he lay with her' (11:4) is sufficiently vague 'to keep a modern court of law in lengthy session' (2005: 115).

The attempt to place the blame for the incident on Bathsheba's shoulders simply illustrates the way in which the episode is often viewed through the lens of male perception. Of course, not all male commentators regard Bathsheba as blameworthy. Many rightly point out that the narrative does not imply culpability on Bathsheba's part and that there is no indication in the text that she deliberately exposed herself or that there was an element of indiscretion or immodesty in her behaviour. Thus, it cannot be concluded that she was responsible for what transpired. The ambiguity present in the text must similarly warn against coming to the opposite conclusion, for one must view with an equal degree of scepticism the overly confident assertion by Graeme Auld, who claims that 'David alone is to blame for what has been done', for 'there has been no consent on the part of Uriah's wife' (2011: 459).

The above discussion has demonstrated that, due to the range of ambiguities in this episode, the story is open to various interpretations at once, each claiming to be supported by the text. The story has effectively invited readers to fill in the gaps that the narrative has left open; but it is clear that some – predominantly male – commentators have given free rein to their somewhat overheated imagination, reading more into the

---

63. As Jan Fokkelman correctly observes, the text is 'not at all interested in her possibly having shared the responsibility' (1981: 53). Hyun Chul Kim and M. Fulgence Nyengele emphasize that, given that biblical writers in the male-oriented world of the Hebrew Bible were only too ready to blame the woman (Gen. 3:12; Hos. 1–2; Job 2:9-10), the fact that there is no condemnation of Bathsheba in the narrative must be regarded as significant (2003: 108).

64. As John Mauchline rightly comments, whether Bathsheba was resistant or compliant, 'no condemnation of her can in the least exonerate David' (1971: 252). Even H.W. Hertzberg concedes that the 'possible element of feminine flirtation' is no excuse for David's conduct (1964: 309).

text than what it specifically says.⁶⁵ In brief, there is too much illegitimate gap-filling which arises, as often as not, from the commentator's subjective concerns rather than from the text's own directions. This has proved to be the case particularly regarding the role played by Bathsheba. Attempts to blame her for David's lack of self-control merely demonstrates that the syndrome of 'blaming the victim' for the vile acts of the perpetrator is alive and well in biblical scholarship.⁶⁶ If Bathsheba were a real person (as opposed to a literary construct), and if she were alive today, she would almost certainly sue for defamation of character! It says much that in a story of a powerful man's lust, passion and crime, it is the woman who ends up on trial in the court of biblical scholarship.

Before concluding our assessment of scholarly interpretations of the role of Bathsheba in the narrative, it seems appropriate to examine in more detail Cheryl Exum's interpretation of the David–Bathsheba story, since her assessment of Bathsheba's role, and scholarly approaches to her role, has exercised considerable influence, particularly among feminist biblical scholars (1996: 19–53; 2016: 135–62). Exum refuses to be drawn into the argument as to whether Bathsheba was raped by David, observing, quite rightly, that the issue of force versus consent is not raised in the story; besides, she argues that it is inappropriate to subject a literary text to forensic examination. Her main concern is to emphasize that Bathsheba's violation occurs not *in* the story but *by means of* the story. The fault, she

---

65. For example, Alter claims that David looked at the 'naked Bathsheba bathing' (1999: 250), and Athalya Brenner rightly criticizes those who fantasize that Bathsheba bathed in the nude (2000: 15). As David Gunn has pointed out, although it is commonly assumed that David was gazing at a naked Bathsheba, 'the text does not say she is naked; and the association of bathing, nakedness and privacy is certainly a modern North European construction and cannot be assumed for the social world of this ancient text' (1997: 564).

66. Attempts to shift the blame for the adulterous affair on to Bathsheba is by no means limited to biblical scholars. In Joseph Heller's novel, *God Knows*, based on the story of David and Bathsheba, she is represented as saying: 'I made up my mind to meet you. A king and all that too – who could resist? So I began bathing on my roof every evening to attract you.' In the 1985 film, 'King David', Bathsheba reveals to David that Uriah had proved to be an abusive husband, thus giving David a noble motive for the act of murder to rescue an abused woman. In the earlier 1951 film, 'David and Bathsheba', Uriah is portrayed as a soldier who had little interest in his wife, and Bathsheba emerges as the neglected spouse who finds true love in David (cf. Bach 1997: 159–60). For the reference to Heller's novel and the two films, see Birch 1998: 1288–9.

claims, lies partly with the biblical narrator who refrained from indicating Bathsheba's feelings or point of view and thereby left her vulnerable and open to the charge that she set out deliberately to seduce David. The narrator's 'crime' (to use Exum's loaded term) has been replicated by subsequent readers who offer their own versions of, or commentary upon, the story. According to Exum, it is the androcentric narrator (rather than David) who 'rapes' Bathsheba, albeit metaphorically, and generations of artists, film-makers and biblical commentators have been only too happy to follow suit.

Now, in referring to biblical commentators, Exum clearly has within her sights predominantly male commentators, for, ultimately, this is a story 'written by men for men' (1996: 27). By introducing Bathsheba to us through David's eyes, the narrator has put us, male readers, in the position of voyeurs, for the text invites a voyeuristic gaze at the female body.[67] As readers, we find that 'we cannot look away from the bathing beauty' (1996: 25–6), and we are encouraged to invade her privacy, undressing her mentally as we envision her naked or partially clothed body. There is a kind of voyeuristic complicity between the narrator and his assumed or ideal readers, and the intimate description of Bathsheba's bathing accentuates her naked body's vulnerability to David's – and our – shared gaze. Male readers are 'aroused by watching a woman touch herself', and since she is purifying herself after her menstrual period, 'we can guess where she is touching' (2016: 139).

However, Exum's interpretation of the narrative, and her critique of biblical commentators' response to the narrative, seems deeply flawed. In the first place, the story of the affair seems to have been deliberately eroticized by Exum in order to censure the biblical narrative and subsequent male readers' interpretation of the narrative.[68] One of the most striking

---

67. Exum 2016: 138. Alice Bach also notes how the bathing scene 'invites the reader to assume the voyeuristic perspective of a spectator squinting at a keyhole' (1993: 70). Since George Nicol is one of the commentators accused by Exum of perpetuating the narrator's crime, he quite rightly mounts a robust defence of his position: 'It is one thing to be charged with mistaken exegesis; any exegete who cannot live with that is playing the wrong game. But to be charged with perpetuating a crime, albeit a crime committed by the pen, is much more serious… One wonders what kind of criticism considers ambiguity in the portrayal of character a crime, or the recognition of that ambiguity as an "assault", a complicity in the crime' (1997: 44–5).

68. Alice Bach is equally guilty of eroticizing the episode involving Bathsheba by suggesting that the narrator effectively here performs the function of a filmmaker 'slowly panning over…the length of her entire naked body at her bath' (1993: 74–5). Anne Létourneau also regards the episode as erotic and claims that the narrative

features of the description of the affair in vv. 2-5 is that it is recorded in a surprisingly matter-of-fact way, with a stringent economy of words (the entire episode recounted in just four verses), and it can hardly be said to be imbued with erotic innuendo.[69] The sexual encounter is over as quickly as it began, and no attention is given to sexual details in the account. Indeed, most readers, without a feminist axe to grind, would surely recognize that there is nothing in the least erotic or lubricious in the story.[70] As George G. Nicol has observed, it is 'difficult to imagine a narrative that could depict such a scene more decorously or with greater reserve' (1997: 47);

depicts Bathsheba in a promiscuous light and views her as sexually vulnerable and sexually available (2018). Jerry Landay clearly lets his imagination take flight as he provides his own account of the incident: 'With natural modesty, the woman bathed her face, then raised the hem of her robe above her knees and began washing her feet and limbs. The sculpted outlines of her leg and thigh shone ivory against the darkening shadows. With a naturalness more provocative to David than any studied gesture, she loosened the upper portion of her robe, brushed it from her shoulders, and gathered it in folds at her waist. David saw the strong but delicate lines of her back, the roundness of her breasts as she turned to bathe her neck, her bosom, each arm. Then a gentle satisfied toss of her head, and she was finished. She let the breeze caress her body to dry her' (1998: 112).

69. Sternberg notes that biblical narratives generally are notorious for their sparsity of detail, but 2 Sam. 11 'is frugal to excess even relative to the biblical norm' (1985: 191).

70. Walter Brueggemann also plays down the erotic element in the incident, claiming that it was probably little more than 'an afternoon's lark' (1985: 56). Randall Bailey (1990: 83–4, 169–70 n. 4) similarly emphasizes that the narrator does not describe the scene in lustful terms, and contrasts it with the sexually suggestive descriptions encountered in passages such as 2 Sam. 13:1-2, 8. He further suggests that David was more concerned with Bathsheba's political rather than marital status, and that the story is not one of sexual lust gone awry but one of political intrigue in which the sexual encounter was merely the tool to satisfy David's overweening political ambition. According to Bailey, once Bathsheba had notified him that she was pregnant, he set in motion plans to kill Uriah, not to conceal paternity of the child, but so that she could be free to marry him, which is precisely what she does as soon as her period of mourning for her husband had passed (v. 27; 1990: 84–101). However, there is no evidence in the text to suggest that David had originally wanted Bathsheba as his wife; on the contrary, the text implies that David would rather have Uriah assume paternity of the child and presumably continue his marriage to Bathsheba as before if only he could extricate himself from the sexual scandal (cf. Exum 1996: 20; Abasili 2011: 13–14). In fact, the entire narrative suggests the actions of one who regrets his involvement with Bathsheba, and who tries by the most surreptitious means to evade the consequences of his adultery and to free himself from an awkward and embarrassing situation.

he further notes that the irony of Exum's explication of the story is 'that it succeeds in being far more voyeuristic than either the biblical text or the critics she takes to task' (1997: 47 n. 12). It is Exum, not the biblical narrator, who continually refers to Bathsheba as 'naked' (1996: 26, 49, 50, 52–3; 2016: 139, 158) and who insists on referring to David's 'erotic involvement' with Bathsheba, and depicting the affair as one of 'unbridled lust' (1996: 20). It is she, not the biblical narrator, who is intent on portraying Bathsheba as a 'woman who enflames male lust' (p. 27) and as 'the paragon of sensuality' (p. 19). It is she, not the biblical narrator, who depicts Bathsheba as guilty of 'arousing male desire' (p. 49). Similarly, it is her representation of the text, rather than the text itself, that invites our 'collusion in voyeurism' (p. 53). Exum concedes that 'we *can* read the text without visualizing the naked woman' (p. 46), but she fails to recognize that most male readers probably *do* read the text without fantasizing about the naked Bathsheba. Exum claims to be distinctly uncomfortable at being put in the position of the voyeur, without realizing that it is she who has placed herself in such a position. She maintains that Bathsheba's bathing is 'sexually suggestive in our story' (p. 49), but that is only because her retelling of the narrative has made it so! For example, the description of Bathsheba's post-menstrual bathing was intended by the narrator not to excite the sexual titillation of the reader, but simply to leave no doubt in the reader's mind that David was the father of the child. Moreover, far from being invited to view Bathsheba 'through David's eyes', as Exum maintains (2016: 138), Bathsheba's beauty is presented impartially, as a fact, not from David's point of view or in terms of his reaction upon seeing her.[71] In brief, Exum's sexualized portrait of Bathsheba is not how most male readers view the text; it is simply how Exum wrongly *imagines* how male readers view the text.

Furthermore, although Exum claims to refrain from subjecting the text to forensic cross-examination, her interpretation of the story leaves little doubt as to which character should shoulder the blame. It is clear where her sympathies lie when she claims that Tamar's rape by Amnon was 'more explicitly brutal' than the sexual encounter between David and Bathsheba, the implication being that David's treatment of Uriah's wife was brutal,

---

71. Meir Sternberg notes that it is the narrator who passes aesthetic judgment on Bathsheba, observing that Bathsheba's beauty is presented in the narrator's impersonal style (1985: 197). Greger Andersson concurs that Bathsheba's beauty 'is not presented as David's perspective but as a fact in the narrative' (2009: 91). Joel Rosenberg adopts a mediating position and contends that the depiction of Bathsheba's beauty is not communicated completely in the voice of the narrator or completely out of David's thoughts (1989: 107).

but that the rape of Tamar was more explicitly so. Exum points to the fact that the story takes place against the background of military aggression and violence (the war against the Ammonites) and suggests that the embeddedness of the narrative in such a context might itself hint that force was used.[72] Significantly, Exum's discussion of the David–Bathsheba affair takes place in a chapter which deals with 'violence against women as it takes place in biblical narrative' (2016: 135), and at one point she can state quite categorically that it is David, not Bathsheba, who is the offender (p. 138). Even Exum's pusillanimous attempt to exonerate David of the charge of rape is by no means equivocal, for while she concedes that there is no rape in the narrative, she adds as an afterthought, 'at least, not one we can be sure of' (p. 161).[73] Exum's interpretation of 1 Kings 1–2 is also telling in this regard, for she argues that here 'Bathsheba gets her literary revenge against David for taking advantage of her' (p. 160). The important point to note here is that this is just as much a reading into the text as the interpretation proposed by the scholars who try to exonerate David of any blame. Commentators, such as Hertzberg, are criticized by Exum for implying that it was partly Bathsheba's fault, but presumably she expects to be excused for implying that it was completely David's fault!

Finally, Exum's criticism of the biblical narrator for portraying Bathsheba in such an ambiguous way as to leave her open to the charge of seduction seems strange, for it is unclear what exactly she would have the narrator do when recounting such a story as that encountered in 11:2-5. Would she have the narrator state in clear and categorical terms that Bathsheba had been brought to David against her will and that she had sexual intercourse with him under duress? Admittedly, such a statement would avoid all ambiguity, but as George Nicol has observed, such ambiguity is the very spice of biblical narrative, and without it this episode 'would be cut, dried and most certainly insipid' (1997: 44). It is the very ambivalence that draws the reader into the fictive world of

---

72. Exum 1996: 21; 2016: 137. Richard G. Smith similarly claims that the broader context of the war portends what comes in the remainder of ch. 11, implying that David's 'public military aggression abroad will set the stage for his aggressive sexual appetite at home' (2009: 121).

73. Exum wonders whether male biblical commentators are reticent to describe David's encounter as 'rape' because 'most commentators are men, and men are uneasy accusing other men of rape, even in an ancient text' (2016: 137). Such a remark is not only blatantly sexist but unpardonably naïve since it does not seem to have occurred to her that the reason male commentators do not charge David with rape is because there is nothing in the text to justify such an accusation.

the characters, inviting us to become participants in the drama of human experience, and it is precisely the lack of details that engages us to make moral judgments.

Before concluding our discussion of the David–Bathsheba episode, there is one further issue that merits consideration, namely, how it was that the anointed of Yahweh and the one singled out by him as the founder of an enduring dynasty could be depicted as acting in such a base and perverse manner.

Why Was the Story Preserved?

The story of David's adultery with Bathsheba and the murderous intrigue that followed is one that has fascinated readers over the centuries, for a single act of adultery leads to all kinds of complications and unanticipated consequences. Yet, the story raises an interesting question that has seldom been discussed in the scholarly literature, namely, why, given the later idealization of David, was such an unsavoury episode in his life told and preserved?[74] It is easy to understand why the Chronicler should have omitted an account that appeared to sully the posthumous reputation of Israel's most venerated king; it is far more difficult to comprehend why the editors of 2 Samuel should have decided to retain a story that was so harmful and detrimental to David's character. Why was it necessary to depict David, a man 'after God's own heart' (1 Sam. 13:14), in such opprobrious terms, and falling to such depths of depravity?[75]

Although the answer to this question must remain speculative, it is probable that, in the first instance, there were quite pragmatic reasons why the narrative should have been recorded. The damaging circumstances surrounding David's adultery with Bathsheba and his involvement in the subsequent death of Uriah may have been so well-known in court circles that the events could not simply be ignored. It is likely that a wide range of traditions concerning David, some favourable, others unfavourable, existed side by side, and those that reflected badly on him could not simply be erased from the record. That this particular episode in David's life was still remembered centuries later is suggested by the Deuteronomistic qualification in 1 Kgs 15:5 to the effect that David did 'what was right in the sight of the LORD, and did not turn aside from

---

74. The issue is discussed, albeit briefly, by Greger Andersson (2009: 99–103).

75. Walter Brueggemann wonders 'what made this terrible disclosure necessary' and suggests that we might wish that this story about David could be 'untold' and that the memory of the incident could be 'unwritten' (1990: 272).

anything that he commanded him all the days of his life, except in the matter of Uriah the Hittite'. But although the incident could not simply be expunged from the tradition, it was possible to put a positive gloss on it by indicating that David readily acknowledged his sin and did so without excuse or prevarication (2 Sam. 12:13).[76] Moreover, by indicating that the child born of the adulterous union with Bathsheba had died but that Yahweh had given his approval of the second child born of the union with her (12:24-25), the narrator was able to counter any lingering suspicion that the Davidic dynasty was the result of an illicit and immoral liaison. In this regard, the story provided an excellent example of what Keith Whitelam has called 'the defensive nature of court apologetic' (1984: 70). The artful way in which a sordid tale was transmuted into one focussed on the redeeming qualities of the protagonist must be admired, for to expose the terrible flaws of the monarchy while accepting its divinely authorized legitimacy must have proved a difficult and delicate balancing act.

But, in addition to such pragmatic reasons, it seems probable that the narrator intended to communicate certain moral truths by means of the story, for the account of David's fall from grace and ultimate redemption provided a source of sober reflection on human behaviour. It conveyed to its readers the basic truth that human choices matter, and that acting impetuously without weighing up the consequences of one's action can lead to repercussions that were neither intended nor anticipated. In this case, the taking of a man's wife resulted in the murder of a loyal servant of the king and the annihilation of an entire army unit. The story also served as a warning of the corrosive effects of sin and guilt, and that attempts at concealment cannot succeed, for the all-seeing eye of the omnipotent deity will ensure that moral failures will not go unpunished. There was no immunity from God's judgment even for Israel's most venerated king. Moreover, as David was warned by Nathan (2 Sam. 12:10-12), the consequences of his sin would have a long and enduring afterlife, for as a result of his adultery with Bathsheba and his disposal of her husband, David's house would be a place of endless strife, forever plagued by the sword. Thus, attempts to view the story as a simple moral tale about the

---

76. A.A. Anderson states that the story, detrimental as it was to David's reputation, could not be disregarded but it could be re-told in a less critical manner by the addition of David's repentance, Yahweh's forgiveness, and the punishment imposed (1989: 166). By indicating that David had already been judged, and had repented, and was to suffer the consequences of his sin through the tragedies that were to afflict his family, the narrator was able to imply that his dynasty could continue free from the taint that blighted David's life (cf. Birch 1998: 1291–2).

wickedness of adultery and murder is to do the narrative less than justice, for it was almost certainly designed to make its original readers ponder on the broader truths concerning actions and their inevitable consequences. Perhaps the intention was also to demonstrate that even David's anointing and consecration as king did not make him into a being of a different order from ordinary mortals; rather, he appears as a reassuringly fallible character who, like all hearers and readers of the story, was subject to human passions and temptations.

Conclusion

Just when David had garnered Yahweh's unquestioning approval and it seemed that he could do no wrong, we are introduced to a story of his illicit liaison with the wife of one of his loyal soldiers. It is a story clearly designed to stimulate the imagination, and readers are invited to speculate why the characters act as they do. As we have seen, the depiction of the protagonists in the story is ambiguous and, not surprisingly, quite different evaluations of the various characters have emerged, depending on the interpreter's account of the motives underlying their words and actions. The narrator's own evaluation of David's behaviour is left to the very end of the chapter; yet, what David says and does in the course of the story is just as significant as the unqualified note of condemnation in 11:27b. The words and actions ascribed to him constitute an indirect means of narratorial judgment even in what may ostensibly appear to be a neutral and objective account.

Despite the negative undercurrents in the portrait of David, we have seen that some scholars have been only too anxious to come to his defence and attempt to mitigate the seriousness of his moral failure. The main ploy adopted in order to achieve this was to cast Bathsheba as the archetypal scheming temptress exploiting her sexual allure by purposefully bathing on the roof to attract David's attention. However, attempts to deflect some of the blame to Bathsheba seem wide of the mark. There is certainly no suggestion in the text that she was being deliberately promiscuous by bathing in full view of the royal palace, or that she was a willing partner in the sexual encounter. In fact, it is made abundantly clear in the narrative that it was David who does the watching, and there is no suggestion that she knew that she was being observed or that she intended to be seen. After all, it is what 'David had done' that was 'evil in the sight of the LORD', and it is against David that Nathan announces God's judgment in the following chapter.

The role of Uriah in the story is significant in that it highlights the stark contrast between his honourable behaviour and the callousness and duplicity of the king, for Uriah represents the unmistakable embodiment of the higher values that the king has betrayed. The behaviour of Uriah in the narrative has not escaped the scrutiny of biblical commentators, but too much scholarly attention has been focussed on what the text does not say rather than what is explicitly and unambiguously stated. The seemingly interminable debate as to whether Uriah knew of David's infidelity and whether David was aware that Uriah knew, has merely served to detract attention from the importance of the role of Uriah in enabling the reader to arrive at a moral evaluation of David's conduct. Readers of the story are invited to contemplate the glaring disparity between Uriah's probity, valour, and unflinching sense of loyalty on the one hand, and the baseness, duplicity, and despicableness of David's behaviour, on the other. The narrator's aim seems to have been to contrast the dutiful Uriah with the manipulative David, the soldier of extraordinary devotion with the treacherous and duplicitous king who clearly lacked moral scruples.

Finally, some consideration has been given to the reason as to why such a tawdry story of royal lust should have been chronicled, preserved and passed on in the tradition. It is most improbable that it was intended merely as a cautionary tale to underline the wickedness of adultery and murder, for such a bland interpretation of the narrative does less than justice to its richness and its ethical complexity. The temptation to force the text into such a narrow moral straight-jacket, neglecting the various truths it was intended to convey, must be resisted. It is a story about human lust, desire, ambition, deception, loyalty, and the deadly spiral of violence that can escalate from a single sinful act. Through his failures and follies, David provided readers of the narrative with an image of the fallible state of human nature, for the story was intended to elicit in them an acknowledgment of their own flaws and imperfections. While previous stories focussed on David's strengths and accomplishments, this episode highlighted his weakness and vulnerability. Thus, when the narrator states explicitly at the end of the story that 'the thing that David had done was evil in the sight of the LORD' (v. 27b), the conclusion merely reaffirms our own moral perception regarding his abusive behaviour. But despite the divine disapproval, and despite our instinctive negative judgment of David, it will be argued in the following chapter that our appraisal of his conduct may need to be somewhat revised as we consider his reaction to Nathan's rebuke and as we encounter the grief that he experiences at the loss of the child born to Bathsheba.

Chapter 4

NATHAN AND DAVID
(2 SAMUEL 12:1-25)

Although 11:1-27, from the *literary* point of view, represents a fairly self-contained narrative, the story, as it stands, is hardly satisfactory from the *moral* point of view, for it ends without David having to confront the despicable nature of his act or even being made aware of the divine judgment on his behaviour. Hence, it seems appropriate at this juncture to consider Nathan's parable and the prophet's sharp rebuke of the king which occurs in 12:1-15a, and the punishment inflicted upon David by God in 12:15b-25. Indeed, the full ramifications of the David–Bathsheba affair and its aftermath can only be properly appreciated when due account is taken of the events recorded in ch. 12.[1]

1. Some scholars view ch. 12 as a later secondary addition to ch. 11 (cf. Bailey 1990: 101–13); however, in its extant form, chs. 11 and 12 are clearly to be read together (cf. McCarter 1984: 305–6). The prologue in 11:1, describing the campaign against Rabbah, and the epilogue in 12:26-31, describing the victorious resolution of the military campaign, form an *inclusio* and provide the framework for both chapters. Moreover, both are connected by the use of similar terminology, such as the repetition of the key word, *šālaḥ*, 'send' (11:1, 4, 6, 14; 12:1, 25; cf. Alter 1999: 257). Verses 1-15a are usually divided into three parts: Nathan's parable and David's reaction (12:1-7a), the oracular threat (vv. 7b-12), and David's admission of guilt and Yahweh's response (vv. 13-15a). However, the unity of the section has been much discussed. Some regard vv. 7b-12 as a subsequent addition to the chapter, and the parable itself is regarded as having reached its climax with Nathan's stark pronouncement, 'You are the man!' (v. 7a); this would originally have been followed by David's admission of guilt in v. 13a and Nathan's response in vv. 13b-15a (cf. Hertzberg 1964: 313–14). According to this view, Nathan's assurance in v. 13 ('you shall not die') constituted a nullification of the death sentence that David had unwittingly pronounced upon himself in v. 5. However, there is no reason to suppose that the divine retribution predicated in vv. 7b-12 could not have been a part of the original prophetic invective, rather than a later amplification based on subsequent events in

Nathan's Parable and its Sequel

This chapter opens with the appearance of Nathan, the prophet, who has been sent by Yahweh to confront David with a message of condemnation and judgment. The parable which he utters in the king's presence is simply and succinctly told.[2] It concerns two men who lived in a certain city, one rich and the other poor. While the wealthy man had 'very many flocks and herds' (v. 2), the poor man had nothing except a little ewe lamb that he had purchased, and that he subsequently came to regard as his most treasured possession. The animal had been adopted by the poor man as a pet, nurtured with care, and had even been allowed to 'eat of his meagre fare, and drink from his cup, and lie in his bosom'; indeed, to all intents and purposes, the lamb had been 'like a daughter to him' (v. 3). A traveller came to visit the wealthy man who, mindful of the obligation of hospitality owed to his guest (cf. Gen. 19:1-8; 24:28-33; Judg. 19:16-21), decided to prepare a meal for him. However, since he was unwilling to provide his visitor with anything from his own ample resources, he resolved to take the poor man's lamb 'and prepared that for the guest who had come to him' (v. 4). Upon hearing of the incident, David was immediately appalled and outraged at the rich man's crass behaviour, and declared that the culprit was worthy of death: 'As the LORD lives, the man who has done this deserves to die' (v. 5).[3] Moreover, some form

---

David's life (cf. Bodi 2010: 78). Questions have also been raised concerning the unity of vv. 1-7a and the relationship between the parable in vv. 1-4 and David's response in vv. 5-6. But since the point of relating a fictional tale was to obtain a ruling from the king and to apply the consequences of the ruling to his own case, there is much to be said for maintaining the unity of vv. 1-7a.

2. Jan Fokkelman comments on the 'stylistic compactness' of the parable which consists, in Hebrew, of just 61 words (1981: 76). The parable has been described by Graeme Auld as 'brilliantly crafted' (2011: 465). Whether the term 'parable' is an apt description of the story related by Nathan in vv. 1-4 is discussed below.

3. The MT reads, literally, 'son of death', but this is usually rendered 'deserved to die', as in 1 Sam. 20:31 and 26:16 (cf. REB; NIV; NRSV; Phillips 1966: 243–4). Some commentators have wondered why David should have pronounced the death sentence in this instance when, according to the law, the only penalty demanded was one of restitution (Exod. 22:1; cf. Lk. 19:8). A.A. Anderson (1989: 162) suggests that this should be understood as David's spontaneous emotional outburst rather than his considered legal judgment (just as one might say, in exaggerated terms, 'he ought to be shot!'). Cf., also, Campbell 2005: 116–17; Seebass 1974: 204–5. Pietro Bovati notes that the oath deployed here ('as the LORD lives') often accompanies a royal judgment, possibly to prevent the king from going back on his own decision (1994: 357 n. 34).

of reparation was required, and David pronounced that the wealthy man must recompense his poor neighbour fourfold for his loss 'because he did this thing, and because he had no pity' (v. 6).[4]

At this point, Nathan delivered his punchline and, addressing the king directly, made his dramatic announcement: 'You are the man!' (v. 7).[5] Nathan followed this declaration with a word of judgment couched in the form of a prophetic oracle, with the usual introductory formula, 'thus says the LORD'. Nathan proceeded to recount Yahweh's previous acts of kindness towards David:[6] he had appointed him king over Israel, and protected him when his life was in danger (v. 7); he had enabled him to live in the royal palace, with Saul's harem at his disposal ('I gave you your master's house, and your master's wives into your bosom');[7] and he had allowed his dynasty to succeed that of Saul ('and gave you the house of Israel and of Judah'; v. 8a). If all this were not enough, David need only

---

4. The MT reads 'fourfold' (followed by Vulgate, Peshitta and Targum), and this clearly refers to the law in respect of compensation reflected in Exod. 22:1. The Talmud (*Yoma* 22b) suggests that the fourfold retribution refers to the untimely death or violent fate suffered by four of David's offspring – Bathsheba's child, Tamar, Amnon, and Absalom (cf. Levenson 1978: 21–3). The LXX here reads 'sevenfold' (*heptaplasiona*), and this is preferred by some (Carlson 1964: 152–7; McCarter 1984: 299; Coxon 1981: 249–50) and taken as representing David's spontaneous, angry reaction, which is regarded as more apt in the circumstance than a considered statement of the precise legal requirement. S.R. Driver (1890: 224–5) suggests that the text may have been altered subsequently to 'fourfold' to have David render a judgment in line with the law. It is interesting to observe that the LXX reading has a parallel in Prov. 6:31, and some have surmised, based on this text, that sevenfold had become the established penalty for theft in later times. It seems preferable to retain the reading of MT and to regard the LXX as representing a later interpretation based on a recollection of the proverbial saying.

5. As Hugh Pyper notes, Nathan's words have taken on a life of their own outside the text and have become a byword for the moment of shocked recognition when someone is confronted with their own behaviour (1996: 5).

6. Robert Alter (1999: 259) notes that there are ironic echoes in what follows of David's prayer in 2 Sam. 7, where he thanks God for all his benefactions, and professes himself to be unworthy of them.

7. There is no mention elsewhere of David having taken his predecessor's consorts, though it is known that such a practice is well attested in both Ugarit and Mari, and was regarded as symbolic of the transfer of power from one king to another (cf. Bodi 2010: 82–4). On a ruler's requisitioning of his predecessor's harem to bolster the legitimacy of his own rule, see Tsevat 1958: 241–2. David is here said to have done what Absalom was about to do with David's concubines on usurping power (2 Sam. 16:21-22), and Hertzberg suggests that the fact that Absalom acted in this way was due to a precedent set by his father (1964: 313).

have said so, and Yahweh would have given him even more (v. 8b). In response, David had treated God's word with contempt by doing 'what is evil in his sight' (v. 9). He had 'struck down Uriah the Hittite with the sword' and married his widow;[8] as a result, Yahweh's punishment would be far-reaching in its scope. The king is warned that 'the sword shall never depart from your house',[9] and that his wives will commit adultery in public (v. 11).[10]

Having been confronted with his crime, David unconditionally admitted his guilt: 'I have sinned against the LORD' (v. 13).[11] David's contrition was duly rewarded, for although the king had adjudicated the villain in the parable as deserving death (v. 5), Nathan reassured him that no such penalty would be exacted by Yahweh: 'Now the LORD has put away your sin; you shall not die' (v. 13).[12] God's forgiveness, however, did not mean that David would be completely exempt from punishment, and Nathan announced that the son born of the adulterous union with Bathsheba would not live: 'because by this deed you have utterly scorned the LORD, the child that is born to you shall die' (v. 14).[13]

---

8. According to 2 Sam. 11:24, Uriah fell by an arrow; the reference to a 'sword' here must therefore be understood figuratively, as in 11:25.

9. This is generally taken as a reference to the violent deaths of David's sons, Amnon (2 Sam. 13:28-29), Absalom (2 Sam. 18:9-15), and Adonijah (1 Kgs 2:13-25). Regina M. Schwartz (1991: 44) notes an element of irony in Nathan's words, for the very prophet who had guaranteed that the Davidic dynasty would be forever secure now prophesies that the sword will destroy his house.

10. This is usually connected with the subsequent rebellion of Absalom and his appropriation of David's concubines; cf. 2 Sam. 16:21-22. Job 31:9-11 expresses a similar belief in the retribution principle in respect of adultery, for Job expects God to punish him for adultery by delivering his wife to others for sexual abuse. Daniel Bodi (2010: 88) points out that a similar notion is encountered in Middle Assyrian Law, dating from the twelfth century BCE, which states that if a man rapes a virgin, the girl's father may take the rapist's wife and hand her over to others for sexual abuse.

11. Bodi (2010: 89) notes that in the ancient Near East, adultery was viewed as an offence not only against the husband but against the deity and must be visited with divine punishment.

12. The law prescribed the death penalty for adultery, although it is by no means certain whether the penalty was ever carried out in practice. Henry McKeating (1979) notes that there are no recorded instances of its application in the Hebrew Bible, which leads him to conclude that the penalty was probably not resorted to very often.

13. The MT reads 'the enemies of the LORD' here, but most commentators regard 'the enemies of' as a pious interpolation into the text made on religious grounds – an attempt to absolve David, the chosen king, from having scorned Yahweh (cf. Mauchline 1971: 255). Although some commentators prefer to retain the phrase

Nathan's Parable and the Story of David and Bathsheba

Several scholars have drawn attention to the apparent incongruity between the parable uttered by Nathan and the events to which it supposedly refers. The parable is concerned with a case of theft to satisfy the demands of hospitality and seems to have nothing to do with the issues of adultery and murder highlighted in the previous chapter.[14] Moreover, it is unclear who the various characters in the parable are supposed to represent. Most commentators assume that the rich man corresponds to David, while the poor man corresponds to Uriah, and the ewe lamb represents Bathsheba. However, the rich man in the parable is not responsible for the death of the poor man (as David was ultimately responsible for Uriah's death) and, unlike the lamb that was slaughtered to provide food for the rich man's guest, Bathsheba was not harmed and was certainly not killed.[15] Furthermore, there is nothing in ch. 11 that corresponds to the visit of the traveller in the parable.[16]

(cf. Hertzberg 1964: 315; Fokkelman 1981: 87–8), the NRSV is probably correct in consigning 'the enemies of' to the footnote.

14. David Daube claims that, when viewed in connection with the story of David and Bathsheba, the parable seems to be a glaring misfit, and if the writer had intended the parable to refer to the David–Bathsheba affair, one would have to attribute to him 'an extraordinary degree of ineptitude' (1982: 275).

15. L. Delekat (1967: 33) seeks to overcome this difficulty by suggesting a different identification for the characters in the parable. He maintains that the ewe lamb was supposed to represent Uriah, the visiting guest represented David, the poor man referred to Bathsheba, while the rich man represented Yahweh. Viewed in this light, Delekat claims that the parable fits the story of ch. 11 much better. This suggestion, however, must be regarded as improbable, for it would effectively render Yahweh as the culprit, whereas Nathan's response in v. 7a clearly indicates that the culprit was David; besides, in the verses that follow, both Nathan and David agree that David is to be identified with the rich man (cf. Pyper 1996: 99). Jeremy Schipper (2007) provides an alternative identification of the characters in the parable by suggesting that David understood Nathan's tale as a parable (rather than as a legal case) but that he misunderstood its significance by assuming that the rich man represented Joab, the ewe lamb referred to Uriah, the poor man was Bathsheba, while David himself was represented by the traveller. This explanation, however, seems unduly convoluted and has not generally been accepted.

16. Randall Bailey (1990: 106) raises the further problem that the parable evokes our sympathy with the ewe lamb, whereas in the narrative of ch. 11 Bathsheba evokes little sympathy, since she (unlike the lamb) is hardly a helpless victim but was, in all probability, complicit in the adulterous affair. This, however, raises the complicated question of whether Bathsheba was a willing participant in the affair or was acting under duress; see the discussion above, pp. 76–83.

The gulf between the essential details of the parable and the crimes attributed to David in the previous chapter has led some scholars to the conclusion that the case presented by Nathan in 12:1-4 was originally unconnected with the story recounted in ch. 11. Indeed, it has been argued that the parable belonged initially to a stock of folktales and was only later placed in the present context.[17] Such a conclusion, however, seems unsatisfactory, for the ominous ending of ch. 11 points forward to the reproof and discipline of David in ch. 12. The king was answerable to Yahweh's moral governance, and without Nathan's parable and the prophet's subsequent indictment, the story of David and Bathsheba would end with an unrepentant David and without any divine judgment on his behaviour.[18] Moreover, attempts to separate the parable from the events encountered in 11:1-27 ignore the fact that some subtle links are discernible between the parable and the account related in the previous chapter. In the parable, the lamb is said to 'eat' from the poor man's food, to 'drink' from his cup, and to 'lie' in his bosom (12:3), and this echoes Uriah's refusal to 'eat', 'drink' and 'lie' with his wife (11:11).[19] Furthermore, the lamb is said to have been like a 'daughter' (Heb. *bat*) to the poor man, and some have suggested that this was a deliberate play on the first element of Bathsheba's name (Heb. *bat-šebaʿ*).[20] A further echo is seen in the fact that David 'sends' on four occasions in ch. 11 (vv. 1, 4, 6, 14), and ch. 12 begins with Yahweh 'sending' Nathan to David.[21] Based on such subtle points of comparison, David Gunn was able to conclude that Nathan's parable clearly 'encapsulates the essence of David's dealing with Bathsheba' (1978: 97). While

---

17. Cf. Gunkel 1987: 55. R.A. Carlson (1964: 152–62) went so far as to argue that 12:1-15a in its entirety is a later insertion by a Deuteronomistic editor and that 12:15b is a logical continuation of 11:27b.

18. Cf. A.A. Anderson 1989: 152. Kyle McCarter argues in favour of the internal unity of the narrative in 11:2–12:24 on the basis that the Nathan–David confrontation in 2 Sam. 12:1-15 was necessary to resolve the moral ambiguity of the David–Bathsheba story in the previous chapter (1984: 304–6).

19. Peter Coxon suggests that an ancient audience would have appreciated the irony in the parable's use of similar terminology (1981: 248–9; cf. Vorster 1985: 111–12).

20. Cf. Gordon 1986: 257; Auld 2011: 465; Fokkelman 1981: 79. Antony Campbell wonders if Nathan was here deliberately giving David a clue as to whom the 'lamb' represented; he concludes, however, that 'as signals go, it is so small David can hardly be blamed for missing it' (2005: 116).

21. Based on such correspondences, Keith Bodner (2005: 71) argues that the episode reveals Nathan to be a '*creative purveyor of fiction*' (his italics). On the network of correspondences between Nathan's parable and the preceding story of David's adultery with Bathsheba and murder of Uriah, see Polzin 1993: 120–6.

Gunn's view may, perhaps, be regarded as something of an overstatement, there do seem to be strong reasons for viewing Nathan's parable in 12:1-4 alongside the incidents recorded of David in the previous chapter.[22]

A different solution to the lack of correspondence between Nathan's parable and the events recorded in ch. 11 has been proposed by Uriel Simon (1967). Simon argues that Nathan's story represents 'a typical example of a well-defined category of biblical parables', which he terms the 'juridical parable', other examples of which he claims to find in 2 Sam. 14:1-20; 1 Kgs 20:35-43; Isa. 5:1-7; and Jer. 3:1-5.[23] The point of such parables was to relate a realistic story about the violation of the law to someone who had committed a similar offence with the purpose of leading the unsuspecting hearer to pass judgment on him/herself. Offenders would only be caught in the trap set for them if they did not detect prematurely the similarity between the offence committed in the story and the offence of which they themselves were guilty (pp. 220–1). The parallel must not be too conspicuous to betray the connection between the two cases, for it must 'strike a careful balance between getting too close to the parable's application and being too remote from it'.[24] According to Simon, therefore, it is the element of concealment, which was integral to the very functioning of the parable, that accounts for why the story presented by Nathan does not correspond in detail to the account related in ch. 11. Only if the connection between the story and David's offence was obscured would the parable succeed in ensuring that the king would unwittingly condemn his own actions.

While Simon's argument has been accepted by some scholars, albeit with some modifications,[25] others have expressed doubts as to whether

---

22. So Brueggemann 1985: 64–5. Harry Hagan (1979: 303–8) suggests that Nathan's deception of David in 12:1-4 provides a kind of counter-deception to that perpetrated by David against Uriah in ch. 11.

23. Simon 1967: 208. The juridical parables are said to follow a similar structure: the introduction (12:1a) is followed by the hypothetical legal case (vv. 1b-4) and the judgment that is elicited (vv. 5-6); finally, the judgment is reapplied to the actual culprit himself (v. 7a). In Isa. 5:3-4 there is an explicit appeal for judgment, as there is in the Greek Lucianic text of the present chapter (12:1), which prefaces Nathan's parable with the words: 'Give me a ruling on this'.

24. Simon 1967: 221. Claudia V. Camp notes the same phenomenon in the parable uttered by the wise woman of Tekoa in 2 Sam. 14, which similarly exhibits the ploy of 'distancing and of re-involvement' which was 'necessary for a person blinded by proximity to a problem to achieve a new perspective on it' (1981: 21).

25. Some have suggested, for example, that the term 'judgment-eliciting parable' would be a more appropriate designation for this genre; cf. A.A. Anderson 1989: 160; Gunn 1976: 217–22; 1978: 40–3; McCarter 1984: 304; Gordon 1986: 256.

2 Sam. 14:1-20; 1 Kgs 20:35-43; Isa. 5:1-7; and Jer. 3:1-5 can all be regarded as belonging to the same genre.[26] Indeed, some have questioned whether the term 'parable' is an appropriate category for classifying such texts.[27] The most serious flaw in Simon's argument, however, is his assumption that those listening to such parables must believe that the case reported to them 'actually happened'; indeed, he argues that it is the realistic nature of the story that conceals the fact that it *is* a parable (p. 221).[28] He thus claims that, in the present narrative, David is represented as construing Nathan's words as a 'real-life' case, involving some petitioner for whom the prophet was speaking.[29] But whether David believed he was being asked to adjudicate a real-life case seems most improbable, for if such a case were being described, one would have expected the two parties in the dispute to have been named, and the location where the event took place to have been disclosed; moreover, the typical features of a legal process (such as the presence of witnesses and testimony) are notably absent.[30] Furthermore, the supposed realistic nature of the case is further undermined by the fact that a simple case of theft

26. For reservations concerning the functional similarity between Isa. 5:1-7 and 2 Sam. 12:1-4 from a form-critical perspective, see Yee 1981: 33–7.

27. Von Rad, for example, classified 2 Sam. 12:1-4 as a 'fable' (1972: 43–4), a view accepted by George Coats, who claims that 2 Sam. 12:1-4 bears comparison with such fables as those encountered in Judg. 9:7-15; 2 Kgs 14:9; and Num. 22:21-35 (1981, 1986).

28. The realistic nature of the story undermines Coats's argument that we are here dealing with a fable. As Daniel Bodi has noted, 'the genre of a juridical parable implies that the story is life-like and is removed from the fantasy world of the fable' (2010: 72).

29. Barbara Green observes that, given that the king in Israel was the arbiter of justice, it was not unreasonable for David to have believed that he was listening to a real-life case brought to him for adjudication: 'For readers – better informed, less involved, and more familiar with genre than is David – the matter seems obvious, but that may not be the case in a story featuring a king charged with doing justice' (2017: 200).

30. Cf. A.A. Anderson 1989: 161; Birch 1998: 1292. On the typical features of the judicial process in ancient Israel, see E.W. Davies 2019. Scholars differ markedly as to whether David believed he was listening to a genuine case or to a fictional account. On the one hand, Meir Sternberg claims that 'the king labors under the illusion…that he is dealing with a genuine legal case, utterly divorced from his own affairs' (1985: 429; cf. Fokkelman 1981: 72); on the other hand, Peter Ackroyd comes to the opposite conclusion, and states quite categorically that 'David, and with him the reader, hears a fictional case and it is not to be supposed that he for one moment thinks that he is dealing with actuality' (1977: 109; cf. Lategan 1985: 81).

would, in all probability, have been settled by the lower courts and would hardly have called for a royal verdict.[31] Thus, Simon's supposition that the parable recorded in 12:1-4 was intended to report 'a realistic story about a violation of the law' (p. 220) must be regarded as highly questionable.[32] Moreover, if Simon is contending that the literary genre that he claims to have discerned reflected actual legal situations that occurred in ancient Israel, with the king himself or a judge in the dock, then, as David Gunn has observed, the so-called juridical parable can 'hardly have enjoyed much of a vogue' (1978: 41), for cases in which a litigant would have the temerity to bring a legal case against the king by a deliberate deception must have been rare indeed, given the considerable risk involved.

A further weakness of Simon's position is his assumption that not only was the case presented by Nathan real but that the encounter between the prophet and the king reflects an historical occurrence in the life of the monarch. Even those who hold the case presented by Nathan to be fictitious tend to regard the incident as one which (in some sense) happened to the 'real', historical David. This, however, seems most unlikely, for had the king been rebuked in such a fashion, he could have dismissed Nathan's interpretation, and refused to acquiesce with the prophet's application of the parable to his own situation. As Chaya Halberstam wryly observed, 'David could have avoided the whole scene by thanking Nathan for his entertaining story and sending him on his way'.[33] It seems preferable to accept that the account of David listening to Nathan's parable and its explanation is just as much a fiction as the parable itself.

The view taken here is that the parable was intended to suggest a general point of comparison with the events depicted in the previous

---

31. Cf. Keith Whitelam, who notes that there 'seems to be no easily apparent explanation as to why such a case would have been submitted to royal legal jurisdiction' (1979: 124).

32. As Robert Alter observes, the very beginning of Nathan's parable ('there were two men in a certain city') makes clear that the events recorded were no more than a 'traditional tale and a poetic construction', for such tales in the Hebrew Bible often begin with the formula 'there was a man' (cf. the beginning of the book of Job). One might compare the familiar 'once upon a time' in traditional English tales. Alter thus concludes that the 'patently literary character' of Nathan's tale would have been 'transparent to anyone native to ancient Hebrew culture' (1999: 257).

33. Halberstam 2007: 351. A similar point is made by David Gunn: 'If the addressee were to give the wrong answer to the parable (for example, if David had said to Nathan, "Well, I'm sorry for the poor man, but there may be more to this than meets the eye – take the case to the local examining magistrate") the parable would have been ludicrously pointless' (1978: 41).

chapter, and attempts to seek in the story of 11:1-27 a counterpart to all the incidents and characters in the parable are misguided.[34] Indeed, attempts to insist on such a rigid correspondence have often resulted in the parable being overinterpreted. For example, the fact that the ewe lamb is taken to refer to Bathsheba has been viewed by some as an indication that women were regarded as the 'property' of their husbands, and that the parable implies that David was guilty of 'property theft'.[35] Instead of seeking a rigid correspondence between ch. 11 and the parable, and forcing every detail in the latter to match the narrative concerning David and Bathsheba, it is preferable to accept that there is sufficient correspondence between the two texts to serve Nathan's purpose. Both exemplify instances of flagrant injustice and a blatant abuse of power (cf. Seebass 1974: 205–6; Hertzberg 1964: 312). The rich man took advantage of his position to exploit his poor neighbour; in a similar way, the king misused his own authority and status vis-à-vis Bathsheba. Of course, Nathan could have rebuked the king outright for his crime, but an oblique analogy such as the one presented by the prophet was likely to prove more effective than a direct frontal attack on David for his wrongdoing.[36] The point of the parable was not to evince David's judicial ability; indeed, his judicial ability was conspicuously lacking, for

34. Cf. C.H. Dodd, who claims that the typical parable presents one single point of comparison and that the individual details 'are not intended to have independent significance' (1943: 19). A similar point is made by Hugh Pyper, who argues that it is inappropriate to look for a strict equivalence between the characters in Nathan's parable and the wider story in ch. 11: 'The more general themes of murder, deprivation and the severance of a loving bond are what matters, rather than a mechanical transformation of one narrative into another' (1996: 100).

35. Regina M. Schwartz, for example, claims that the 'polluting' of Bathsheba is analogous to the slaughter of the ewe lamb, and that the point of Nathan's parable is that 'the king's adultery is a violation of a property right' (1991: 47). Mary Mills similarly maintains that the emphasis in the parable is on man's right to own his property; the implication is that David 'has seized an innocent creature and devoured her', and the crime of which he was guilty was against another male, Uriah, 'whose property has been stolen' (2001: 66–7). Cheryl Exum also observes that the biblical text condemns David, 'but only because the woman is another man's property' (1996: 27).

36. As John Barton observes, 'Uriah has been treated as a nonperson who can be elbowed out of the way with impunity, but it takes the construction of a moral case about a wholly different set of events to bring this home to David' (2003: 5). Usually, however, a more direct denunciation is more typical of the prophets in the Hebrew Bible (as in Elijah's accusation against Ahab in 1 Kgs 21:18-24), rather than the more oblique parabolic approach favoured by Nathan.

the theft of a ewe lamb would hardly necessitate the application of the death penalty.[37] The point, rather, was to appeal to David's innate sense of justice, which is why such emphasis is placed on the stark contrast between the poor man's meagre provisions (he had 'nothing but one little ewe lamb') and the rich man's ample resources (having possession of 'very many flocks and herds'). Moreover, as John Barton has observed, the detailed description of the lamb which was 'like a daughter' to the poor man was not intended merely as a literary flourish; on the contrary, it was an essential part of the moral case being made. By indicating that the lamb was not just the poor man's rightful possession but one that was dear to him, the parable suggests that possession was not merely a matter of legal entitlement but one of emotional attachment.[38] The rich man was condemned not just because of theft – if, indeed, the lamb *had* been stolen[39] – but because 'he had no pity'. The fact that the one who had everything was prepared to take away the treasured possession of the one who had nothing betrayed not simply a disregard for the demands of the law but a distinct lack of compassion and a failure to appreciate the way humans ought to relate to one another.

There can be little doubt that original readers or hearers of the story would have appreciated the irony: David appoints himself to the role of the just judge who will redress the balance between the rich and poor only to be told that the role he really plays is that of the unscrupulous oppressor. The very man appointed to maintain the law and administer 'justice and equity to all his people' (2 Sam. 8:15) had violated the very

37. Cf. Jan Fokkelman (1981: 76), who observes that David here 'reacts as a judge, but without exercising the sobriety and patient discrimination prerequisite for the practice of such an eminent profession'. Horst Seebass points to the incongruity of the sentence applied to a straightforward case of theft (1974: 203–4). Anthony Phillips suggests that David's emotional outburst was intended to highlight the limitation of the law, for the punitive damages provided for cases of theft would have been little deterrent for the rich, even if his poor neighbour had the financial resources to seek redress at law (1966: 242–4).

38. Barton 2003: 4–5. Hugh Pyper comments that 'by its exaggerated and slightly ludicrous insistence on the emotional implications of a minor incident of sheep-rustling, it calls attention to the disproportion of David's own actions and his disregard for the emotional lives of others' (1996: 128).

39. Keith Whitelam makes the interesting point that there is no explicit reference to the fact that the lamb had been stolen (since the verb for 'to steal', *gānab*, does not occur in the text); the passage merely states that the rich man 'took' (*lāqah*) the lamb in order to entertain an unexpected guest; the lamb may have been taken as a pledge for a loan or for some other reason (1979: 125–6, 254 n. 9).

law he was supposed to uphold. As Hugh Pyper has succinctly put it, Nathan's 'You are the man!' identifies David 'not with the restorer of order but its disrupter' (1996: 89).

The Death of Bathsheba's Child (12:15b-25)

The fulfilment of Nathan's prophecy that the child born to David and Bathsheba would die is here recounted in considerable detail. Yahweh 'struck the child' so that it became extremely ill, and David pleads with God that the child be saved. During the child's illness, David behaves as if he was already in mourning: he fasts, lays down all night on the ground and, despite the urging of his servants, he refuses to rise or to eat any food (vv. 16-17).[40] On the seventh day, the child dies, and David's servants are afraid to tell him, since 'he may do himself some harm' (v. 18).[41] Upon hearing the servants whispering together, David senses that the child had died, and as soon as he obtains confirmation of the fact, he gets up from the ground, washes, and anoints himself, before going to worship in the 'house of the LORD'[42] and partaking of a meal that his servants had prepared (vv. 19-20). David's actions, however, seemed strange and incomprehensible to his servants (as, no doubt, to contemporary readers), for he appeared to have reversed the conventional procedures in such circumstances. He had behaved like a mourner while the child was ill, but now that the child had died, he seemed to have disregarded the rites of mourning and dispensed with all outward signs of grief, electing instead to resume, without delay, the activities of normal life. His servants ask, not unreasonably, 'What is this thing that you have done? You fasted and wept for the child while it was alive; but when the child died, you rose and ate food' (v. 21).[43] David responds by saying that he had done what

---

40. Robert Alter (1999: 261) notes that David's acts here pointedly replicate those of the man he had murdered, who refused to go home and eat but instead spent the night lying on the ground with the palace guard (11:11).

41. T. Veijola (1979: 242) suggests that the 'seventh day' is to be reckoned from the time when the child became ill, not from the day of its birth; hence the age of the child at the time of death is unknown.

42. The expression 'house of the LORD' usually refers to the temple, but since there was no temple in Jerusalem before the time of Solomon, some assume that in the present context it must refer to the tent which sheltered the ark of the covenant (so, e.g., A.A. Anderson 1989: 164).

43. Alter regards the puzzlement of the servants as a manifestation of the 'human capacity for surprise, and for paradoxical behavior, that is one of the hallmarks of the great biblical characters' (1999: 261).

he could to influence Yahweh to spare the child's life while there was still hope, but now there was nothing more he could do, for the child could not be brought back from the dead. The section ends on a positive note: David consoles Bathsheba, lies with her, and she bears him a son, whom she names Solomon.[44] The second child of their union was clearly destined to enjoy divine favour ('the LORD loved him'; v. 24). The child was given a second name, Jedidiah ('beloved of the LORD'), and this provided further assurance of Yahweh's changed attitude towards Bathsheba's second child.[45]

A Nussbaumian Reading of the Story

It will be recalled that Martha Nussbaum has argued that the most enduring truths of fiction cannot be grasped by intellectual activity alone, since powerful emotions have an irreducibly important cognitive role to play as we contemplate a narrative (see above, pp. 25–6). Indeed, she believes that reliance on the powers of the intellect alone can become an impediment to our ethical appreciation of a story by stifling our instinctive, compassionate response.[46] This observation seems particularly pertinent to our discussion of the story of David in chs. 11–12, for this is

---

44. The NRSV follows the *Ketib*, 'he called', and attributes the naming of the child to David, whilst the *Qerē*, with the support of some manuscripts, the Syriac and the Targum, reads 'she called', thus attributing the naming to Bathsheba. Since it was customary in Israel for the mother to name her child (cf. Gen. 4:25; 16:11; 19:37-38; Exod. 2:22), the feminine form of the verb is to be preferred here. The name Solomon is usually connected with the Hebrew *šālôm*, 'peace', as in the Chronicler's play on the name in 1 Chron. 22:9, where Yahweh foretold the name to David as an indication that Israel would enjoy 'peace' during Solomon's reign. Some scholars, however, connect the name with the root *šlm* which is used in the Pi'el to mean 'to replace' or 'to substitute'; hence, the name Solomon is taken to mean 'his replacement' or 'his substitute'. That the name was intended to refer to Solomon as the substitute for Bathsheba's dead husband, Uriah (so, e.g., Veijola 1979: 235–7), seems most improbable; it seems far more likely that the child was regarded as a substitute for the lost child. See the discussion in Jones 1990: 111–13.

45. The name Jedidiah appears nowhere else in the Hebrew Bible. It might seem odd that the child should be given two names, one by his mother (or father) and the other by God through his prophet, Nathan. Some suggest that Solomon may have been his personal or private name, whilst Jedidiah was his official throne name (so Honeyman 1948: 22–3).

46. It was for this reason that Nussbaum was able to claim that 'the intellect is not only not all-sufficient; it is a dangerous master' (1990: 81).

clearly a narrative that is suffused with emotion: we are made aware of David's sexual desire upon seeing Bathsheba, his frustration when his plan concerning Uriah fails to work, his anger upon hearing Nathan's tale, and his grief and mourning over the illness and death of his son.[47] Inevitably, then, this story, perhaps more than any other in 1 and 2 Samuel, engages the emotional involvement of the reader, and invites us, in our empathetic imaginings, to ponder the tangled complexities of David's life.

In ch. 11 we, as readers, are naturally appalled at the nature of David's transgression, and outraged at his despicable behaviour, but when we read in the following chapter of his instinctive response to Nathan's parable ('the man who has done this deserves to die!') we find that – temporarily, at least – our moral judgment is placed on hold, for his spontaneous reaction mirrors our own innate feelings about the callous nature of the rich man.[48] As the story progresses, and we read the emotionally charged description of David fasting and pleading with God to spare his child's life, we begin to feel the depth of his anguish for ourselves, an anguish that was made all the more palpable for him by the recognition that his own guilt had been transferred to his new-born son (12:14). When we read of David's realization that nothing will detract from the inevitability of the divine judgment, and that the child must die, our sympathy for him inevitably increases. And then, when we become aware of David's reaction after hearing of the death of his child, and the way he was able briskly to resume his normal activities, stoically refusing to be sublimated by his grief, and accepting the ineluctable finality of death, we almost begin to admire him for his resilience in the face of adversity.[49]

---

47. Walter Brueggemann (1985: 47) argues that it is the depiction of David's emotional response that lends depth and credibility to the narrative, and ensures its continued relevance and appeal: 'If there had been no interiority to David, if there were only public events, the narrative would scarcely attract us'. By contrast, little is said of Bathsheba's emotional response upon hearing of the death of either her husband or her child. Adele Berlin's comment on 11:26-27a seems particularly apposite: 'One and a half cold, terse verses to sum up the condition of a woman who has had an adulterous affair, become pregnant, lost her husband, married her lover, the king of Israel, and borne his child!' (1994: 26). Berlin argues that the narrator has ignored Bathsheba's feelings completely, because she was merely an 'agent', an Aristotelian term which describes 'the performer of an action necessary to the plot' (p. 27).

48. As John Barton (2003: 5) has observed, the parable expects not just the king but all right-minded people to be outraged by someone who has all that he needs and yet exploits the poor and vulnerable to his own advantage.

49. David's resilience, exhibited in vv. 15b-25, is explored at length by David A. Bosworth (2011). David Gunn cites David's reaction upon hearing of the death

The end of ch. 12 elicits as much heartfelt sympathy for David in his vulnerability as ch. 11 elicits revulsion on account of his treachery, for we are made to appreciate that even an adulterer and murderer can have some redeeming features.

Thus, we sense that David, in the course of two chapters, has become a changed man, the arrogant, presumptuous king having been metamorphosed into the anguished, bereaved father, and the ruthless manipulator having been transmuted into a man consumed with concern for the innocent victim of his sin.[50] Perhaps nowhere is this more evident than in his contrasting reaction to the death of Uriah and that of his new-born son. Upon hearing of the loss of his most loyal soldier, David appears to be unmoved, cold and emotionless, and his dismissive reaction to Joab's concern betrays a cynical indifference to Uriah's death (11:25); on the other hand, the death of his own son is felt personally and with deep emotion, and becomes an event that forces him to contemplate his own mortality (12:23). Nothing could have prepared us for this revelation of a humbled and chastened David, the scornful arrogance having given way to an unconditional acknowledgment of his guilt before Yahweh.

Once we allow ourselves to be emotionally and imaginatively seized by the story, entering into its world and into the personal struggles of its protagonist, we realize that our moral evaluation of David's character is by no means clear-cut, for we cannot condemn the self-serving opportunist and unscrupulous king without at the same time feeling sympathy for the anguished, grieving and distraught father, bleakly aware of the immutability of death as he mourns for his new-born son. It is precisely because David is not depicted in black and white terms that we, as readers, are prevented from vilifying him or from valorising him. Despite the words of the wise woman of Tekoa, we realize that David was not a man 'like the angel of God' in his ability to discern good and evil (2 Sam. 14:17, 20); on the contrary, he appears as a reassuringly fallible character who, like all hearers and readers of the story, was subject to human

---

of Absalom (2 Sam. 18:33; 19:1-4) as providing a further instance of a narrative that elicits the emotional response of the reader, since it invites 'our identification with the king as man at his most elemental' (1975: 25).

50. Bosworth argues that it may have been precisely because the narrator wanted to convey the contrast in David's character that the detailed description of his behaviour during the illness of his child and after his child's death is reported, for the storyteller could simply have narrated the death of the child and the birth of Solomon without the intervening section about David's behaviour. He concludes that the episode in vv. 16-23 was included specifically because 'it shows us something about David that the narrator wants us to see' (2011: 696–7).

passions and temptations, and beset by human infirmities.[51] As Mary Mills has observed, David in this narrative provides an image of the 'pitiable state of fallible human nature' (2001: 52). It is the story of one who acted egregiously and who, in Walter Brueggemann's words, 'set himself against the whole moral tradition of his people' (1990: 278); but it is also the story of a man who could acknowledge his shortcomings and who was able to accept the prophet's rebuke without demur and without a word of self-justification or casuistry.

Conclusion

In this chapter we have considered the significance of Nathan's parable and the prophet's subsequent rebuke of the king, together with David's response. As many have observed, the parable uttered by Nathan hardly corresponds to David's crimes in the previous chapter, since there is no mention of either adultery or murder. But we have argued that the point of the parable was simply to emphasize the disjunction between rich and poor, between justice and injustice, between possession and loss. The story of the rich man's callous behaviour was designed to illustrate a gross abuse of power, and it was precisely such abuse that had been manifested in David's behaviour towards Bathsheba and Uriah. The self-indicting parable uttered by Nathan was a clever ruse designed to let David draw his own conclusions, thereby ensuring that the king unwittingly convicted himself.

The fact that David dispenses summary justice upon the rich man not simply because of his theft of the ewe lamb but because 'he had no pity' invites us to contemplate the emotional impact of the narrative, an aspect that comes particularly into prominence in the account of the grief and mourning of David over the illness and death of his child. Once we allow ourselves to become emotionally involved with David's dire predicament, we recognize that our evaluation of David's character is not so straightforward and clear-cut as we might initially have supposed. Our critical view of David's conduct in ch. 11 is modified by his response to Nathan's indictment, and his confession ('I have sinned against the LORD') serves to reinstate him, at least in part, in our estimation, as we realize that this is not only a story of human infidelity and betrayal, of lust and deceit; it is also a story of guilt and remorse, of grief and despair.

51. Steven McKenzie observes that we, as readers, tend to find that David's faults attract our attention more than his virtues: 'We admire the fearless and pious young hero, but we cannot identify with him. The adulterer who gets caught in a cover-up, on the other hand, is one of us' (2000: 154).

Chapter 5

THE RAPE OF TAMAR
(2 SAMUEL 13)

The tale of woe that is to bedevil David and his family continues in ch. 13, which recounts the rape of Tamar, his daughter, and the murder of Amnon, her rapist, by his brother, Absalom. The chapter describes how Amnon, David's firstborn son and heir to the throne, becomes infatuated with his beautiful half-sister, Tamar, and desires to have sex with her. On the advice of his friend Jonadab (David's brother's son), Amnon pretends to be ill and persuades David to instruct his daughter to go to Amnon's house in order to prepare food for him. Tamar obeys, but after she bakes some cakes for him, Amnon refuses to eat anything; instead, he sends the servants away and tries to persuade Tamar to submit voluntarily to his advances ('come, lie with me, my sister'; v. 11). When Tamar protests, Amnon seeks to force her, whereupon she warns him of the potential disgrace both would suffer. Amnon, however, disregards her plea, and as soon as he rapes her, he callously commands his servants to evict her from his house. When David hears of the incident he becomes 'very angry' but does nothing to console Tamar or to reprimand Amnon 'because he loved him, for he was his firstborn' (v. 21). Absalom, on the other hand, was determined to avenge his sister's violation. He waits for two years and prepares a feast for his sheep-shearers, inviting his family to attend the occasion. During the feast, when Amnon is drunk, Absalom commands his servants to kill him. David's other sons, no doubt sensing a danger to their own lives, flee from the scene. News reaches David that Absalom had killed 'all the king's sons' (v. 30), but Jonadab reassures him that only Amnon had died. For his part, Absalom is forced to flee the country and remain in exile for three years before he eventually returns and is reconciled with his father.

Viewed in the broader context of 2 Samuel 11–20, the events depicted in this chapter clearly have political repercussions, for they impinge on issues of succession to David's throne.¹ Having introduced David's eventual successor with the assurance that Yahweh's favour rests upon him (12:24), the story proceeds to tell how the other potential candidates disqualified themselves from appointment to the high office to which they aspired. But the story clearly has resonance on a more personal level, for it features rape, fratricide, and possibly incest, within a single dysfunctional family.² As such, it remains one of the most disturbing narratives in Scripture and, not surprisingly, it features as one of the four 'texts of terror' which Phyllis Trible (1984: 37–63) has analysed in the Hebrew Bible. Perhaps inevitably, some have compared the story narrated in ch. 13 to the account of David and Bathsheba in ch. 11, and have discerned in the action of Amnon echoes of David's own sexual aberration.³ In both stories, murder results from a sexual offence, and in both the murder is executed by servants of the protagonists.⁴ However, the similarities

1. 2 Sam. 13 is usually regarded as part of a larger unit, though there is some dispute as to whether that unit consists of chs. 13–20 (so Conroy 1978: 5–6; A.A. Anderson 1989: 176; McCarter 1981: 362–3), chs. 13–19 (Ackroyd 1977: 117, 119; 1981: 385–6), or chs. 13–14 (Carlson 1964: 164–7). The following chapters make clear that, although Tamar's dishonour is avenged and her assailant killed, harmony is far from being restored, for this incident is merely the precursor to further tragic events, including the rebellion and death of Absalom and civil war.

2. H.W. Hertzberg rightly recognizes the consummate skill of the narrator who has deftly managed to weave together the political and personal elements within a single narrative; however, he tends to focus on the political aspects of the story to the detriment of the personal. Thus, he views Tamar as a tragic but subsidiary figure in the narrative, whose fate is important only for the light it sheds on the struggle between the two older princes and the consequences of that struggle for the subsequent history of David's kingdom (1964: 322).

3. Norman Whybray suggests that the rape of Tamar and the murder of Amnon by Absalom 'show clearly how the sons had inherited the vices of their father', for in their actions they reflect 'the passionate and the calculating sides of David's nature' (1968: 37). Jan Fokkelman (1981: 125) describes Amnon and Absalom as 'chips off the old block', and Mark Gray regards David and Amnon as 'birds of a feather', since they both share a similar lustful disposition (1998: 39). Regina Schwartz claims that Amnon's rape of Tamar has echoes of David's 'forcible taking of Bathsheba' (1991: 49), and William Propp states that 'in many respects the children of David re-enact their father's crime' (1993: 40 n. 4). Cf., also, Mauchline 1971: 259; Hertzberg 1964: 322; Gros Louis 1977: 30–1.

4. Hertzberg argues that the parallels 'were surely intended by the author and would have been understood by the first audience' (1964: 326). David Gunn similarly contends that we are meant to see ch. 13 as a recapitulation of what had transpired in ch. 11, since David finds 'coming to expression within his own family the elements of his own earlier experience' (1978: 99). Richard Smith claims the narrative of

between the two accounts should not be overemphasized, for although both David and Amnon are determined to satiate their frustrated desire for a 'beautiful' woman, the violent attack on Tamar is far more horrifying than the sexual encounter depicted in ch. 11, for Amnon's action is one of unmitigated brutality and a blatant use of physical force and abuse of power.[5] Moreover, whereas David's love for Bathsheba continued after the adulterous affair, Amnon's unbridled lust is followed by a deep loathing towards his victim.

Nevertheless, as was the case with ch. 11, the story of Amnon and Tamar raises profound moral (and, in this case, legal) issues which resonate far beyond the immediate scope of the narrative. Was Amnon's crime deserving of death and, if so, did Absalom have the right to take the law into his own hands? Was his revenge an act of justifiable homicide or was it a case of premeditated murder? And was his action intended solely to vindicate his sister's honour or did he have an ulterior motive, for Amnon's death meant that he became heir to the throne? And what of David's action – or lack of action – in the story? His uncritical paternal indulgence evidently prevented him from punishing or even reprimanding his son; had he acted decisively instead of turning a blind eye to the incident, he may have been able to prevent a case of fratricide. Was the king so tainted by his own immoral behaviour that he was reluctant to pass moral judgment on others? And from the narrator's point of view, was David's reticence to act in the face of a blatant case of injustice intended to raise questions about the nature, competence and judgment of the monarchy? After all, if the virgin daughter of the king could be raped within the royal household with impunity, what hope was there for other victims who suffered similar abuse?[6] Furthermore, if the story of Tamar is viewed as the first in a chain of events that constituted the

---

ch. 13 presents Amnon's crime as a 'heightened version' of the sin perpetrated by David (2009: 148–9). Other scholars have also viewed Amnon's crime against Tamar as paralleling his father's crime against Bathsheba; see Fokkelman 1981: 124–5; Bar-Efrat 1989: 281–2.

5. Philip Esler (2011: 330) notes the differences between David and Amnon over against commentators who emphasize the commonality between them. Cf., also, Gray 1998: 40.

6. April Westbrook (2015: 154–5, 164–5) has suggested that such a negative description of the way in which the monarchy functioned may have been intended to encourage the reader to evaluate the ethical failures of such a system of government; after all, the safety of the people and the ability to maintain justice were among the main motivations for their desire to have a king in the first place (1 Sam. 8:1-4). It

punishment of David foretold by Nathan, another ethical imponderable must be considered: to what extent are the characters responsible for their own actions? Do they bear culpability for their misdemeanours or were they merely puppets of Yahweh, who was manipulating events behind the scene as part of the divine punishment for David's affair with Bathsheba?[7]

Although this is widely regarded as one of the most disturbing and harrowing stories in the Hebrew Bible, it is striking that it contains no explicit editorial comment or evaluation. But while the omniscient narrator eschews any temptation to pass judgment directly, the protagonists in the story are characterized by what they say and do (or fail to do in David's case). Thus, the labelling of Amnon's crime by Tamar as 'vile' (v. 12), and the callous way in which Amnon banishes her from his house after the rape (v. 17), are clearly intended to shape the reader's reaction and suggest where the sympathies of the narrator lay. As A.A. Anderson has observed, 'the pleading of Tamar (vv. 12-13, 16) is a more effective judgment on Amnon's actions than any editorial remarks or moralizing could have been'.[8] The lack of explicit authorial moralizing may therefore have been a deliberate part of the storyteller's technique: in effect, the narrator invites readers to draw their own conclusions regarding the culpability or otherwise of the characters. Before examining the ethical implications of the narrative, however, it will first be necessary to outline the story in more detail.

The Rape of Tamar

The opening verse serves to link this story to the previous chapter ('some time passed') while at the same time introducing us to all the main characters who will appear in the ensuing narrative. These included

---

was clear that even a king 'after God's own heart' had done little to improve societal problems, since even when there was no king in Israel, violent murder and rape were rampant (cf. Judg. 19).

7. Westbrook (2015: 154) notes that both David and the reader may be wondering whether Tamar's experience was part of Yahweh's retributive justice. William Propp (1993: 53) argues that if the events were merely the working out of the divine punishment predicted in ch. 12, the reader may be inclined to sympathize not only with Tamar but even with Amnon and Absalom, despite the horrific nature of their actions.

8. A.A. Anderson 1989: 177. A similar observation is made by Charles Conroy, who notes that the 'rarity of explicit judgments by the narrator should not obscure the fact that a good narrative can convey a very definite attitude without making explicit statements at all' (1978: 23 n. 16).

Amnon, David's son, his half-brother Absalom, and Absalom's sister, Tamar.[9] Tamar is described as 'beautiful', and Amnon is said to have fallen in love with her; indeed, his infatuation with her was such that he 'made himself ill because of his sister, Tamar' (v. 2). But although Amnon was – quite literally – 'lovesick', he was unable to satisfy his intense desire for her because she was a 'virgin'[10] and would therefore presumably have been carefully guarded and chaperoned within the protected environment of the royal house.[11] Her circumstances were such that 'it seemed impossible to Amnon to do anything to her' (v. 2), which perhaps suggests, rather ominously, the carnal nature of his desire, and that the love mentioned in the previous verse was, in fact, more akin to an 'erotic obsession' (Alter 1999: 265).

Amnon's lust may never have found gratification were it not for a shrewd plan devised by his resourceful 'friend'[12] and cousin, Jonadab, the son of David's brother. Jonadab, depicted as a very wise man (v. 3; NRSV 'crafty'), suggests a scheme to have Tamar legitimately called from her

---

9. Apparently, Absalom and Tamar were children of David by Maacah, daughter of King Talmai of Geshur (2 Sam. 3:3), while Amnon was the son of David by a different mother (3:2).

10. Gordon Wenham has argued that the Hebrew term *bĕtûlāh* means 'a girl of marriageable age' who may or may not have been a virgin; he claims that in the present chapter the term simply describes 'a girl who is probably in her teens' (1972: 340). For the view that the term refers to a phase of a young woman's life between the onset of puberty and either marriage or the birth of her first child, see Day 1989: 59. Frymer-Kensky argues that the meaning of the word must be determined by the context, since in some cases it clearly designates a 'virgin' (e.g. Gen. 24:16; Lev. 21:13; Deut. 22:14; Judg. 19:39; 21:12), whereas in other cases, such as Joel 1:8 (which refers to the *bĕtûlāh* mourning 'for the husband of her youth'), it cannot mean 'virgin'. She suggests that the ambiguity and variability of the term arise from the basic cultural assumption that a young woman of marriageable age would be a virgin (1998: 79–81). In the present context, the balance of probability is that the term should be rendered 'virgin' since, after the rape, Tamar is depicted as tearing her robe (a special long robe with sleeves, which was how 'the virgin daughters of the king were clothed in earlier times'; v. 18), an action which symbolized the loss of her virginity. See, further, the detailed discussion by Stone 1996: 107–12.

11. That this was the reason that Tamar was inaccessible to Amnon is assumed by both medieval Jewish commentators and some modern scholars (cf. Bar-Efrat 1989: 243; Ackroyd 1977: 121; A.A. Anderson 1989: 174; Gordon 1986: 262). Graeme Auld wonders whether, if Tamar had been married, she would have been more rather than less available (2011: 477).

12. Alter (1999: 265) maintains that the word *rē'a* (rendered 'friend' in NRSV) in royal contexts may also be used as a title of someone who played an official role as the king's or prince's companion or counsellor (cf. Ackroyd 1977: 121). In this context,

quarters to Amnon's house.[13] He advises Amnon to feign illness and to ask the king to send Tamar to prepare some food for him. Jonadab had already observed that Amnon had looked 'haggard' (v. 4), and he encouraged Amnon to make the most of his situation by pretending that he was ill and in need of special ministration from his sister. Such a ploy would provide the very opportunity Amnon had been seeking by getting Tamar within his reach ('that I may see [the food] and eat it from her hand'; v. 5), and it would even ensure that her presence in Amnon's bedchamber had been approved by express permission of the king. No sooner is the advice given than it is swiftly taken up and put into effect by Amnon. He pretends to be ill and requests his father to permit Tamar to visit him 'and make a couple of cakes in my sight' (v. 6).[14] Jonadab's scheme works effectively, for Tamar is dispatched by David to Amnon's house and is instructed to prepare food for him. Thus, David unwittingly seals his daughter's fate and, as Robert Alter rather indelicately puts it, he 'inadvertently acts as Amnon's pimp for his own daughter' (1999: 267).

The narrative proceeds to describe Tamar visiting Amnon's house and, in accordance with her father's command, preparing food for him. The narrator lingers over the details of the preparation of the food, thus slowing down the pace of the story and injecting an element of suspense into the account ('she took dough, kneaded it, made cakes in his sight, and baked the cakes; then she took the pan and set them out before him'; vv. 8-9a).[15] Amnon, however, refuses to eat the cakes that Tamar

---

however, Jonadab was probably one friend among others and did not have an official function; as Kyle McCarter suggests, he may simply have routinely served Amnon as 'matchmaker and adviser in affairs of the heart' (1984: 321).

13. Norman Whybray questions whether the wisdom attributed to Jonadab should be taken at face value, for 'it was superficially "wise" in that it ingeniously enabled Amnon to gain his immediate purpose, but entirely lacking in true wisdom in that it failed to point out the dangerous consequences of success' (1974: 91). Charles Conroy also wonders why, if Jonadab was so shrewd, his first words were effectively an admission of ignorance, since he had to ask Amnon why he appeared so poorly; he concludes that the narrator may be insinuating a pejorative judgment on the quality of Jonadab's astuteness (1978: 28).

14. As Philip Esler (2011: 339) has observed, the instruction is carefully worded, for by asking David to order Tamar to make the cakes 'in his sight' (vv. 5-6), the possibility is avoided that David might ask her to make the cakes but have someone else to dispatch them to Amnon. See, also, Bar-Efrat 1989: 253.

15. As Bar-Efrat has observed, since Amnon had no interest in the food and had no intention of eating it, there is a certain irony in the narrator's long and detailed account of the various stages of its preparation (1989: 256).

had prepared,[16] and issues a command for everyone except his sister to leave, thus ensuring that there were no witnesses to what was about to occur. Amnon instructs Tamar to bring the food into his chamber 'so that I may eat from your hand' (v. 10). When she does so, Amnon seizes the opportunity to take hold of her and invite her to lie with him. Tamar is outraged that Amnon should be prepared to flout the moral conventions of her people ('such a thing is not done in Israel'; v. 12), and she implores him not to 'do anything so vile'.[17] Her repulsion of Amnon's advances shows clear thinking on her part, for she discerns at once what the consequences of illicit sexual intercourse would be both for him and for herself: she would forever have to live with the shame,[18] while Amnon would be exposed for all time as a 'wanton fool'.[19] Realizing that her remonstrance

16. The term *lĕbîbôt*, which occurs only here in the Hebrew Bible, is usually rendered 'cakes', but Kyle McCarter (1984: 322) suggests that they were, rather, 'dumplings' or 'puddings', since the verb used in Hebrew, *bāšal*, means 'to boil' rather than 'to bake'. While 'cakes' certainly sounds more romantic, given the context, 'dumplings' seems more appropriate for the culinary process described (cf. A.A. Anderson 1989: 174). By derivation, the term *lĕbîbôt* may suggest that they were 'heart-shaped' confections (cf. Hebrew *lēbāb*, 'heart'), which might be appropriate in the present context (cf. Alter 1992: 66). As Phyllis Trible observes, the 'pun fits the occasion' (1984: 42). McCarter also draws attention to the denominative verb *libbēb*, 'enhearten', 'give strength, vigour', and he suggests that Tamar was to prepare traditional food for the sick because of its nourishing quality; David would thus have understood the request as one for invigorating food. He further notes that such a request from a person who was ill would have seemed eminently reasonable, though, of course, in Amnon's case, the 'patient' was 'privately anticipating more than the restoration of his health' (1984: 322). Peter Ackroyd adds that food prepared in a sick man's presence and administered to him by a young woman (perhaps especially if she was a virgin) was believed to have special curative or therapeutic qualities (1977: 121; cf., also, A.A. Anderson 1989: 174).

17. Bar-Efrat notes that whenever the phrase *'āśâ nĕbālâ bĕyiśrā'ēl* occurs in the Hebrew Bible (Gen. 34:7; Deut. 22:21; Judg. 20:6, 10; Jer. 29:23), except for one instance (Josh. 7:15), the reference is to a sexual crime, and in all instances the culprit pays with his life. In the present context, it defines the deed Amnon intends to commit as 'an appalling crime with the gravest consequences' (1989: 262). Wolfgang Roth argues that the term *nĕbālâ* originally referred in a general way to a breach of the laws and customs of Israel, but that it later came to refer to the infringement of one particular law and custom, namely, treating an Israelite woman 'like a harlot' (1960: 406).

18. Danna Nolan Fewell and David Gunn discern a contemporary ring in the notion of Tamar's feeling 'shame', noting that 'the history of patriarchy is replete with societies where a sexually violated woman is conditioned to be ashamed' (1993: 32).

19. The word *nĕbālâ* (rendered 'scoundrel' in NRSV) is usually translated 'fool' (cf. KJV; RSV), but Anthony Phillips (1975: 237–42) and Wolfgang Roth (1960) have

was going unheeded and that her appeal to Amnon's compassion was to no avail, she suggests a way to extricate herself from the situation: if he would just speak to 'the king' – the familial language now giving way to a more formal address – and ask for his permission to marry her, he could fulfil his desire within the context of lawful marriage. Her words, however, fall on deaf ears and, unable to resist Amnon's superior strength, she is raped by her half-brother (v. 14). As soon as the rape had been committed, Amnon's desire for Tamar turns to hatred. With remarkable psychological insight, the narrator shows how Amnon's self-gratification was followed by a feeling of deep revulsion at the act for which he was responsible.[20] The reason for Amnon's abrupt *volte face* is not explained, but, given the fact that Tamar had turned out to be a bitterly resistant woman, perhaps the experience had 'hardly been the fulfilment he dreamed of' (Alter 1999: 269).[21] At any rate, as Walter Brueggemann has observed, Amnon's appalling behaviour indicates that, contrary to what was implied in v. 1, his feeling towards Tamar constituted 'nothing that might remotely be called love' (1990: 288).

Amnon now resolves to banish Tamar from his presence as soon as possible with the brusque command, 'Get out!' (v. 15b). As in v. 12, Tamar appears thoughtful, articulate and clear-sighted, and she will no more heed Amnon's order of dismissal than she consented to his demand for sexual intercourse; instead, she tells Amnon that his abandonment of her was a greater affront than his initial act of brutality: 'No, my brother; for this wrong in sending me away is greater than the other that you did to me'

argued that such a translation is inadequate and misleading. Elsewhere, the *něbālâ* is a person who has scant regard for the proprieties of human conduct, and thus could be described as 'brutish' or as a 'beast' (cf. Ps. 73:22 in REB). See, also, Ackroyd 1977: 122. The collocation of 'shame' and 'folly' occurs elsewhere in the Hebrew Bible; cf. Pss. 39:8; 74:22; 1 Sam. 25:39 (cf. Bar-Efrat 1989: 263).

20. Many commentators suggest that the observation that Amnon loathed his half-sister with an intensity that exceeded his earlier passion for her represents a remarkable and acute psychological reflection on the part of the narrator, who seemed only too aware of the irrationality of sexual attraction and revulsion (cf. Gordon 1986: 263; Alter 1999: 269; Brueggemann 1990: 287–8). Jan Fokkelman suggests that the narrator's profound insight is 'psychologically so accurate and so brilliantly formulated that it forms the story's culmination' (1981: 107). Bar-Efrat notes that this emphasis on the emotions and internal state of mind of the protagonists is an unusual feature in biblical narrative and gives this account a special character (1989: 275–6).

21. Fokkelman suggests that the hatred results from Amnon's realization that every subsequent meeting with Tamar would be 'a repeated, extremely shameful unmasking and intolerable confrontation with his own shortcomings as a person' (1981: 108).

(v. 16).²² Tamar evidently realized that being banished was even worse than being raped, for as a violated virgin, abandoned by her assailant, she would have to endure a pariah status in the community and would be condemned to a lifetime of desolation in her brother's house. Amnon, however, refuses to listen to her, and Tamar's appeals to his humanity and self-esteem are ignored. Indeed, Amnon now acts with utter callousness, commanding his servant to 'put this woman out of my presence and bolt the door after her' (v. 17),²³ thus giving the impression that Tamar was 'a bothersome, stubborn and repulsive creature against whom every measure must be taken to ensure that she does not re-enter the house' (Bar-Efrat 1989: 269). The servant obeys and Tamar departs, adopting the conventional public gesture of mourning ('put ashes on her head'), and crying aloud as she went (v. 19). The narrator breaks the thread of the narrative in v. 18 to note that Tamar was wearing a long robe with sleeves, which was the customary garment worn by virgin daughters of the king;²⁴ Tamar, however, tears the robe, thus making the scandal visible for all to see, and giving public and prominent expression to her despair.²⁵ If Amnon had entertained hopes that the matter would remain hidden from public notice, Tamar's overt demonstration of sorrow was a clear indication that she would have no part in such a cover-up.

With the rape and dismissal of Tamar concluded, the plot now moves to the aftermath, and it is Absalom who now emerges as the central character in the story. He immediately identifies the cause of his sister's

---

22. The text of v. 16 is somewhat confused and it may be that an originally longer text has been accidentally curtailed (cf. Ackroyd 1977: 122). However, the general intent is clear, and the NRSV, following the LXX and Vulgate, provides a reasonably coherent translation. For a discussion of the various possibilities to emend the text based on the Versions, see Driver 1890: 231.

23. Most modern translations (which tend to read 'this woman') fail to catch the full force of Amnon's blunt and contemptuous dismissal, for the Hebrew just has the feminine single demonstrative pronoun (lit. 'take this out of my presence'), a further indication, if any were needed, that he regarded Tamar merely as a disposable object that was no longer required (cf. Trible 1984: 48). As Robert Alter observes, Amnon's politeness towards the servant (using the customary particle of entreaty, *n'ā*, 'pray') contrasts sharply with the brusque words addressed to the daughter of the king (1999: 270; cf. Bar-Efrat 1989: 268). S.R. Driver (1890: 231) notes that the Hebrew word translated 'out of my presence' (*mē'ālay*) is used of dismissing a menial (as in v. 9) or one whose presence was considered obnoxious (cf. Exod. 10:28).

24. On the textual problem in v. 18, see Driver 1890: 231–2; Gunn 1978: 32–3.

25. As Shimon Bar-Efrat notes, the tearing of the robe in this instance indicates not merely the conventional expression of grief but a symbolic expression of the deterioration in Tamar's status, having now been robbed of her virginity (1989: 270).

distress, and the person responsible for it, thus implying that perhaps this was not the first time that Amnon had behaved in such a way: 'Has Amnon your brother been with you?' (v. 20).[26] His reference to Amnon as '*your* brother' suggests a reluctance on his part to admit his fraternal connection. The next words that Absalom utters to Tamar ostensibly seem to be unfeeling and unsympathetic, almost as if he were intent on minimizing the gravity of the incident: 'Be quiet for now, my sister; he is your brother; do not take this to heart' (v. 20). It is unclear whether he wished Tamar to maintain a discreet and dignified silence in order to prevent the royal household from being sullied by the scandal, thus sparing Tamar the misery and humiliation that would inevitably follow, or whether, as Walter Brueggemann suggests, he wanted to relieve Tamar 'of the burden of rage and resentment' (1990: 288), in the full knowledge that he would eventually take the law into his own hands and avenge the rape of his sister. For her part, Tamar takes up residence in Absalom's house, as a desolate widow, a perpetual reminder to her brother of her unavenged violation.[27] When David hears what had happened, he becomes very angry but refuses to reprimand or punish Amnon for his behaviour 'because he loved him, for he was his firstborn' (v. 21).[28] Absalom takes no action immediately but is filled with hatred towards Amnon 'because he had raped his sister Tamar' (v. 22).

Absalom waits two full years before settling the score with Amnon. The occasion was provided by a sheep-shearing celebration, normally a grand occasion for feasting and rejoicing. Absalom invites all the royal princes to the event, an invitation extended also to the king himself, though the latter declined, while at the same time giving his blessing to the occasion (vv. 24-25). Absalom then makes a special plea for Amnon to attend the celebration in place of David; as the eldest son, Amnon would probably have been regarded as the king's representative and would presumably

---

26. Alter notes that Absalom was here exercising 'a kind of delicacy of feeling in using this oblique euphemism for rape' (1999: 270).

27. The narrative contains no specification of time for Tamar's dwelling in Absalom's house, but the implication is that her desolation was prolonged and indefinite (cf. Conroy 1978: 35).

28. The words 'but he would not punish his son Amnon because he loved him, for he was his firstborn' are absent from the received text, but most commentators follow the Vulgate, and some Greek MSS and 4QSam^a in including these words as an explanation of David's reaction: as the indulgent father, Amnon had a special place in his affection, for he was his firstborn and presumptive heir to the throne. The addition looks suspiciously like an explanatory gloss, a later attempt to put a positive spin on David's reticence to punish his son.

have needed his special permission to attend. David is initially dubious ('why should he go with you?'; v. 26), but then relents and consents to Amnon joining his brothers at the celebration. Absalom waits until Amnon is drunk and then issues an order for his servants to kill him. The joyful sheep-shearing thus becomes the setting for a cold-blooded murder. Since the penalty for killing the crown prince would have been severe, Absalom reassures his servants that they were merely obeying his command and that they should be 'courageous and valiant' (v. 28). The execution of Absalom's order is not described, and the narrator is content simply to note that the servants did as Absalom had commanded.[29] In the aftermath of the killing, all the members of the royal party, fearing that their own lives might be in danger, take flight.

A garbled version of the event reaches David and, believing (mistakenly) that all his sons had perished, he observes the customary mourning rites: overwhelmed with grief, he tears his garments and prostrates himself on the ground (v. 31). At this point, Jonadab reappears on the scene and, with characteristic sharpness, surmises (correctly) that Absalom had taken the opportunity to avenge Amnon for his crime against Tamar; the king should therefore discount the rumours he had heard, for only Amnon had been killed (v. 32). Echoing virtually the same words that Absalom had used to console Tamar after her rape, Jonadab tells David 'do not let my lord the king take it to heart' (v. 33).[30] The veracity of Jonadab's claim is confirmed when the royal entourage return to the city (v. 35).

Absalom, no doubt realizing that his own life was now in jeopardy, flees to Geshur, where he remains for three years, after which time David's grief over Amnon's death has been assuaged and he begins to long for reconciliation with his son, Absalom. Despite the formal reconciliation, however, Absalom's estrangement from his father would eventually embroil the kingdom in a civil war, as becomes evident in the following chapters. As a kind of postscript to the story, 14:27 relates that Absalom had three sons and one daughter, whose name was Tamar and, like her namesake, is said to be 'beautiful'. Phyllis Trible suggests that by naming his daughter Tamar, Absalom had created 'a living memorial for his sister' (1984: 55).

---

29. We hear nothing about the fate of the assassins, but it is clear from the narrative that responsibility lay entirely with the one who had given the command, as Absalom himself recognized.

30. Barbara Green (2017: 208) refers to Jonadab's words to David as 'crass consolation', for having just informed him of his son's death, how could David *not* take such a thing to heart?

The Legal Aspects

As part of her elaborate protestations against Amnon's behaviour, Tamar begs her half-brother to speak to the king, assuring him that 'he will not withhold me from you' (v. 13). Her words are interpreted to mean that David, if asked, would permit Amnon to marry her, thus avoiding any negative repercussions that would inevitably follow from his actions. However, the legal enactments in the Hebrew Bible suggest that such a marriage would have been impossible, for sexual intercourse between siblings is expressly forbidden in both Deuteronomic and Priestly law (Deut. 27:22; Lev. 18:9, 11; 20:17). Inevitably, commentators have been forced to consider how the discrepancy between what the law seems to forbid, and what the narrative seems to permit, is to be explained.

Some scholars have suggested that Tamar's words were merely an attempt on her part to prevaricate in order to stall Amnon's advances; her words are interpreted as a tactic designed to thwart her sexual assailant and were not intended as a genuine possibility (cf. Kalmanofsky 2014: 108; Alter 1999: 268; Gray 1998: 49–50). This suggestion, however, seems most improbable, for her words must have had some plausibility and some bearing in fact to carry conviction (both for Amnon and for readers of the story).[31] It seems far more probable that marriage between half-brothers and half-sisters was permitted, at least during some period in Israel's history, and the relation between Abraham and Sarah is sometimes cited as further evidence that marriage between half-siblings was allowed (Gen. 20:12).[32]

---

31. As William Propp has remarked, if the union between Tamar and Amnon had been forbidden, her suggestion that David would approve a marriage between them 'would have been too ludicrous to be believable' (1993: 45 n. 22). In a similar vein, Ken Stone observes that Tamar's attempt to reason with Amnon 'could only have made sense in a context in which liaisons between siblings were at least conceivable' (1996: 114). Medieval Jewish commentators generally concur that marriage between Amnon and Tamar would have been permissible at this time (cf. Rosenberg 1986: 245 n. 57).

32. Cf. H.P. Smith 1899: 329; Hertzberg 1964: 322–3; Mauchline 1971: 260. It is worth noting that marriages between half-brothers and half-sisters were well-known outside Israel (cf. Schwartz 1997: 99; Goody 1969: 13–38). William Propp observes that Egyptian and Phoenician kings married their full- or half-sister, and he contends that such a practice may not have been unthinkable in Israel, especially if there was some indirect Egyptian or Phoenician influence on David's court (1993: 44). For the influence of Egyptian culture on the courts of David and Solomon, see Whybray

The apparent discrepancy between the present narrative and the legal injunctions of the Hebrew Bible is usually resolved by suggesting that the prohibition of such marriages was a later development in Israel's history and that such enactments were not in existence in David's time.[33] The fact that the present narrative makes no direct reference to any legal formulation governing sexual relations may be viewed as supporting the argument that such legal provisions were a later innovation in Israel's history. Another possibility is that the laws may have been in force during David's reign but that such rules were deemed not to apply in royal circles, in which case their existence or non-existence during David's reign would be an irrelevance.[34] But if sibling marriages were permitted in David's day it remains to be explained why Amnon, given his obsession with Tamar, did not pursue this option? If he could have taken Tamar as his wife, why did he not take advantage of the possibility, since he could have fulfilled his desire within the context of lawful marriage?[35] Indeed, such a marriage may well have served his political interest, consolidating his position as putative heir to the throne.[36] But it may be that Amnon did not instigate the marriage because he knew that Absalom would object, since a marriage between Tamar and his brother would strengthen the latter's position at his expense (cf. Stiebert 2016: 192).

1968: 1–6, 96–116. Joel Rosenberg similarly comments that Tamar's plea to Amnon to marry her comes 'in a context seemingly well used to such ingrown alliances' (1986: 145).

33. Cf. Ackroyd 1977: 122. This view was strongly advocated by David Daube, who claimed that 'the evolution from a regime under which marriage with the sister from the same father is allowed to one under which it is forbidden is an almost universal phenomenon' (1947: 78–9).

34. So, e.g., Alter 1999: 268. Roland de Vaux suggests that consanguinity was originally thought to exist only with children of one's mother, so that marriage with the son or daughter of one's father may have been permissible in David's time (1961: 19–20).

35. This point has forcefully been made by Pamela Tamarkin Reis, who asks: 'If he [Amnon] *could* marry her, as most commentators posit, why does he not do so? Men were allowed multiple wives; what difference would one more make?' (2002: 177).

36. William Propp remarks that 'were Amnon the slave of ambition rather than passion, he could declare and fortify his right to the succession by marrying Tamar' (1993: 46). As Reis (2002: 177 n. 11) observes, the fact that marriage to the king's daughter was an advantage to the succession is shown by Saul's retraction of Michal (1 Sam. 25:44) and by David's insistence on regaining her (2 Sam. 3:13-14).

The issue of the permissibility of marriage between half-siblings has a bearing on the nature of the offence committed by Amnon. Virtually all commentators agree that Amnon was guilty of the crime of rape,[37] but there is less unanimity among scholars as to whether he was also guilty of incest.[38] If marriage was permitted between half-siblings, then clearly incest was not an issue, and it is striking that nowhere in the narrative is it regarded as at all strange that the object of Amnon's affection should be his half-sister. Indeed, v. 2 implies that it is not Tamar's status as his half-sister that was the factor preventing Amnon from fulfilling his desire; rather, it was her status as an (unattached) virgin that placed her firmly off-limits.[39] Based on such arguments, Jan Fokkelman claims quite categorically that 'the horror of incest is out of the question' (1981: 103; cf. A.A. Anderson 1989: 175). On the other hand, Kyle McCarter is equally adamant that the outrage committed by Amnon was 'incestuous rape' (1984: 328; cf. Keefe 1993: 92), and he argues that the story makes it unmistakably clear that incest was an issue by the extraordinary frequency of sibling terms in

---

37. A notable exception is Reis, who argues that Tamar willingly engaged in sexual intercourse with Amnon (2002: 169–95); however, such a view seems most improbable, and is difficult to sustain based on the text (cf. Stiebert 2016: 187–93). Admittedly, the verb *'innâ*, in its sexual uses, does not necessarily mean 'rape'; however, in the present context, where Tamar is depicted as resisting Amnon's advances and where he is described as overpowering her (v. 14), there can be little doubt that the offence committed was that of rape (cf. Gravett 2004: 280–1). The issue regarding Dinah in Gen. 34, where the same verb is used, is far less clear (cf. Frymer-Kensky 1998: 87; Bechtel 1994). That the verb *'innâ* in 2 Sam. 13:14 does have the connotation of forced sexual intercourse is further confirmed by the phrase *wayyiškab 'ōtāh* which immediately follows (literally, 'he laid her'; cf. Birch 1998: 1304). S.R. Driver (1890: 230) observes that when *šākab* is used of illicit sexual intercourse, the pronoun with *'ēt* is regularly pointed by the Masoretes as though it were the object of the verb in the accusative (Gen. 34:2; Lev. 15:18, 24; Num. 5:13, 19; Ezek. 23:8).

38. The laws of Lev. 18:9, 11; 20:17 specifically prohibit sexual relations between siblings and between half-siblings. Of course, it is important to recognize that what may not be regarded as incest today (such as sexual relations between a daughter-in-law and father-in-law; cf. Gen. 38) *would* have been regarded as incest in biblical times (cf. Lev. 18:15). See Kalmanofsky 2014: 103.

39. This point is forcefully made by Fokkelien van Dijk-Hemmes, who comments that, although 'only her virginity is put forward here as an impediment', it was not the fact of virginity *per se* that constituted the problem but that, as a virgin, she would have been under her brother's protection, and the only one who could remove that obstacle was David, as Jonadab rightly perceived (1989: 139–40). See, also, Stone 1996: 107.

vv. 1-14 ('brother' and 'sister' occurring six times each). Other scholars are similarly of the view that the many references to the brother–sister relationship in the narrative was intended to highlight the incestuous nature of the offence (cf. R.G. Smith 2009: 149–50; Flanagan 1972: 180). However, it is just as likely that the frequent references to the brother/sister relationship was intended to highlight the callous disregard of filial loyalty and lack of fraternal feelings on the part of Amnon (cf. Birch 1998: 1304; A.A. Anderson 1989: 174). Furthermore, as Shimon Bar-Efrat has observed, among the arguments deployed by Tamar to dissuade Amnon from raping her, no mention is made of the family relationship between them; if sexual intercourse had been forbidden on grounds of incest, she would certainly have referred to it (1989: 264).

Although rape was not regarded with the same degree of opprobrium as incest or adultery, it was nevertheless viewed as a serious offence that merited punishment.[40] The law stated that a man who had raped an unattached virgin was required to pay the bride-price to her father and to marry his victim (Deut. 22:28-29). Such punishment was presumably designed to relieve the father of the financial burden of having to support a daughter whom nobody else would have wished to marry on account of the loss of her virginity. Esther Fuchs has argued that, from the raped woman's point of view, such a law must have appeared offensive and obnoxious in the extreme, adding insult to injury, for presumably the last thing she would have wanted would have been to marry her assailant (2000: 216).[41] However, the law may have been viewed quite differently by women in ancient Israelite society, who would have been only too aware that rape would have denied them any hope of a future

---

40. Johanna Stiebert notes that the rape of an unattached virgin was not regarded as a 'crime' as such: 'within the parameters of social acceptability and legality reflected in this story, Amnon has exploited his power and behaved badly – but he has not committed a crime'. In other words, although Amnon had committed an act of which Absalom disapproved, it was 'not something illegal' (2016: 191). Stiebert argues that this was why Absalom urged Tamar to 'be quiet for now' (v. 20), for he knew that there was no legal recourse available to her: as a royal prince there would have been no barrier to Amnon's taking a woman as long as she was not betrothed or married to another.

41. Fuchs argues that 'rape according to the Bible is a crime that stigmatizes the victim, not the victimizer' (2000: 215). Frymer-Kensky attempts to find some redeeming feature in the law from a feminist perspective; she notes that the rapist would have to support his victim financially, and she suggests, no doubt more in hope than expectation, that 'perhaps the law assumes that an angry wife could make his life miserable' (1998: 94).

family life. In such circumstances, marriage to the rapist may have been regarded as preferable to the prospect of remaining an outcast in society and condemned to a lifetime of desolation.[42] It is in this context that we must understand Tamar's complaint in v. 16 that her callous dismissal by Amnon after the rape was a greater wrong than the rape itself: the latter deed could at least partly be compensated by marriage whereas her rejection would have been regarded as the ultimate dishonour.

In her attempt to resist Amnon's advances, Tamar makes no reference to the legal statutes governing sexual relations, observing instead that 'such a thing is not done in Israel' (v. 12).[43] Tamar's appeal was not to the law but to the accepted standards of right conduct within the community. That the kind of behaviour exhibited by Amnon 'was not done in Israel' explains why David had no qualms in instructing Tamar to visit her supposedly sick brother, and why the servants were content to withdraw and leave her unsupervised (v. 9; cf. Stiebert 2016: 191). The very idea of a brother raping his own sister was so contrary to acceptable norms of behaviour in ancient Israel as to be 'almost unimaginable' (Green 2017: 206). Amnon's outlandish behaviour meant that boundaries had been crossed, social mores had been ignored, and rules of decorum and decency had been flouted. Significantly, Tamar labels Amnon's behaviour as 'vile' (*nĕbālāh*), a term used to denote an act that threatened the very fabric of an ordered society.[44] Moreover, existing law did not take into account such factors as injured family honour and pride; from Tamar's perspective,

---

42. Cf. Stone 1996: 115–16. The rapist was not only obliged to marry the victim but was prevented from subsequently divorcing her, though her father could refuse to allow him to marry his daughter in the first place, in which case the rapist must pay him compensation (cf. Exod. 22:17). Of course, if the woman was betrothed or married, the situation would have been quite different, for the rapist would be put to death as an adulterer as, indeed, would the woman, if she was suspected of complicity (Deut. 22:23-24). Cf. Propp 1993: 41.

43. The statement that such practices were not done 'in Israel' is regarded by some as an indication that Israel drew a clear distinction between itself and its Canaanite environment, 'especially in the realm of sexual conduct' (Zimmerli 1978: 55). Cf. Brueggemann 1990: 287; Gordon 1986: 263; H.P. Smith 1899: 329.

44. The word *nĕbālāh*, sometimes translated as 'disgrace' or 'folly' (cf. BDB 615), is often used in the Hebrew Bible to describe the consequences or effects of acts of sexual violence within the social order. In Judges it refers both to the threat of homosexual rape ('but against this man, do not do such a vile thing'; 19:24b), and to the gang rape of a woman ('they have committed a vile outrage in Israel'; 20:6). In Gen. 34:7 Shechem is said to have committed 'an outrage' (*nĕbālāh*) in Israel by lying with Jacob's daughter. In such cases the term seems to be used to describe

Amnon had broken a code of conduct based on honour and shame, and her concern was to preserve her own and her brother's reputation untarnished, lest she be forced to carry her shame and he be regarded as 'one of the scoundrels in Israel' (v. 13).

The nature of Amnon's offence has implications, in turn, for Absalom's redress of the outrage committed against his sister. Was the elimination of Amnon a case of justifiable homicide or premeditated murder? Was his death a just and lawful response to the offence that he had committed? Certainly, if Amnon is deemed to have been guilty of incestuous rape, the death penalty could easily be defended on the basis of biblical law, though whether Absalom was a legitimate agent to carry out the execution (through his servants) must remain a moot point (cf. R.G. Smith 2009: 153–6). On the other hand, if, as was argued above, Amnon was guilty of rape, his death at the hands of Absalom would be difficult to justify, for he was not, in law, guilty of a capital offence, and despite his outlandish behaviour he would not have deserved the death penalty.[45] Yet, there is no indication on the part of the narrator that Absalom had committed a heinous crime by killing the crown prince. It seems probable that the narrator had scant interest in the legal niceties involved, and whether Amnon's death was a case of legal execution or fratricide was not a matter of great concern. It was enough that such a deed as that committed by Amnon was 'not committed in Israel' (v. 12) and that the incident depicted was a violation of the deeply held principles that governed the Israelite social order.

It is clear from the above discussion that the story of the rape of Tamar raises a plethora of questions which biblical scholars have been at pains to resolve. Was marriage between two siblings considered legal? Did Amnon's offence fall into the category of rape or incest? Was Absalom's execution of his half-brother within the bounds of legality? Attempts to answer such questions have not always proved to be particularly convincing, and the story of the rape of Tamar provides a particularly good example of the difficulties that arise whenever one seeks to examine the relationship between law and narrative in the

---

'extreme acts of disorder or unruliness' (Phillips 1975: 238) that not only rendered the perpetrators outcast but resulted in a dangerous breakdown in the order of social relationships. See, also, the discussion by Wolfgang Roth (1960).

45. While it is true that in Gen. 34 Simeon and Levi, Dinah's brothers, kill the rapist (and, indeed all the other men of Shechem), Jacob's mortified response supports the position of the law, namely, that execution was not a legitimate punishment for rape. Cf. Propp 1993: 41–2.

Hebrew Bible. On the one hand, Tamar's words to the effect that David would consent to her marrying Amnon (v. 13) are difficult to reconcile with the laws enshrined in Lev. 18:9, 11; 20:17; Deut. 27:22; on the other hand, Tamar's suggestion that Amnon's abandonment of her after the rape was worse than the rape itself *does* seem to cohere with the law of Deut. 22:28-29, which states that the rapist was obliged to marry his victim.[46] As Richard Smith has pointed out, attempts to make the biblical narrative correspond to biblical law (and vice versa) fail 'to appreciate the ethical grounds upon which the narrator makes his moral appeal' (2009: 148). The important factor for the narrator of the present story was not the breach of the divine law but the wilful undermining of the collective conscience of the community.

The Characters in the Story

At this point, consideration may be given to the way in which the actions and conduct of the characters are evaluated, both by the narrator and by subsequent commentators.[47] A superficial reading of the story might suggest that Amnon is the villain, Tamar the innocent victim of her brother's lust, Absalom the hero and righteous avenger of his sister's rape, David the indulgent father who refuses to reprimand his son, and Jonadab the evil genius behind Amnon's chicanery. Such a bland appraisal of the characters, however, is overly simplistic, and does less than justice to this richly nuanced and carefully crafted story.[48] In what follows, an attempt will be made to consider each character in turn, and how their actions might be evaluated from the ethical point of view.

---

46. Ken Stone rightly observes that 'assumptions about sexual practice which underlie biblical narratives are not always compatible with those underlying biblical laws, so that the critic cannot simply use, without reflection, the one to explain the other' (1996: 114).

47. Ken Stone claims that this story provides some of the most interesting instances of characterization to be found in the Hebrew Bible (1996: 106).

48. This is particularly emphasized by Charles Conroy, who observes: 'One would miss the point...if one took the pericope primarily as a gallery of moralizing character sketches: Amnon the type of violent and passionate man, David the type of the weak and indulgent father, Tamar the type of injured innocence and beauty, and Absalom the type of the cold-blooded calculating avenger. While these aspects do come through with greater or less clarity, they are not the narrator's main purpose' (1978: 22).

Tamar

Tamar seems to be presented by the narrator in a sympathetic light. At the beginning of the story she appears as the dutiful daughter who obeys her father's command, and by the end of the story she emerges as a vulnerable and blameless figure who was the victim of forces beyond her control and exploited by the very person who should have been her custodian and protector.[49] In contrast to the men of the story, who are implicitly criticized and censured (Amnon for his depraved violence and David for his lack of paternal care and protection), Tamar is viewed in positive terms.[50] Even when being raped by her brother, she appears to be shrewd and discerning, realizing immediately that the consequences for both would be serious and long-lasting. After the rape, we hear nothing further about her, save that she remained desolate in her brother's house, resigned to the unhappy fate that awaited her. As the story progresses, the reader's empathy towards Tamar (and resentment towards Amnon) increases, for the woman who appears at the beginning of the story as a beautiful princess ends up as a lonely, abused and rejected outcast, with one brother who is a rapist and another who is a murderer.

In view of this seemingly positive appraisal of Tamar by the narrator, it seems all the more surprising that some biblical scholars view her in a decidedly negative light. Pamela Tamarkin Reis, for example, has argued that Tamar, far from being the vulnerable victim, was, from the outset, complicit in arranging the private meeting with Amnon, and that the subsequent sexual encounter between them was entirely consensual.[51] Had Tamar been raped by her brother, her natural inclination would surely have been to cover it up, knowing that were the loss of her virginity to

---

49. Philip Esler describes her as 'the very picture of desolation' (2011: 349).

50. Cf. Stiebert 2013: 64. Antony Campbell claims that 'Tamar is the only figure portrayed with any nobility' (2005: 127).

51. Reis contends that the verb *'innâ* in the Hebrew Bible does not have the connotation of forced sexual intercourse but merely denotes the type of sexual intercourse of which the biblical writers did not approve. Hence, she concludes that in v. 12 Tamar is resisting seduction, not rape (2002: 171, 186 n. 47). Reis finds further confirmation for her argument in the fact that Tamar did not 'cry out' as the rape law of Deut. 22:24 demanded of a woman assaulted in the town (where, presumably, she would be heard); failure to call out was legally valid proof of consent according to the Deuteronomic law. The fact that the present narrative records no outcry from Tamar 'conclusively compromises her virtue, confirming complicity' (2002: 186–7 n. 51). However, since the Deuteronomic law refers specifically to women who were engaged to be married, it is difficult to see how it could have been relevant to Tamar's situation.

become public knowledge, her marriage prospects would have been scuppered; by making the incident public, her aim was to pressurize Amnon to take her in marriage, in accordance with the law of Deut. 22:19 (2002: 191). Reis contends that Tamar's insistence on making 'heart cakes' (believed to have aphrodisiac qualities; cf. Fokkelman 1981: 105–6; Dijk-Hemmes 1989: 140), rather than the therapeutic 'food' (Heb. *biryāh*) that her father had ordered (vv. 7-8), suggests that she was intent upon arousing Amnon's desire with her 'libidinous confections' (p. 182). Moreover, by baking the cakes in Amnon's sight (v. 8), Tamar was being deliberately provocative, and her flirtatious behaviour was designed to ensnare the heir apparent so that she would one day become queen. That Amnon's love turned to hate so quickly after the sexual encounter merely shows that she was 'the archetype of the virgin who gives in to immoral suasion and is not respected in the morning' (p. 187). The narrative thus implies that Tamar was ultimately responsible for her own violation, and by deliberately acting in such an unconventional manner in order to arouse Amnon's sexual appetite, she had only herself to blame when she became the victim of male sexual passion. Yet, although such ostensibly clever manoeuvrings on the part of Tamar might suggest a woman who was shrewd, wily and manipulative, Reis insists that she was, in fact, rather dense, tactless and stupid, since she engaged willingly in an act of incest while evidently oblivious to the social opprobrium with which her incestuous act would have been viewed.[52]

Reis's argument, however, has been heavily criticized by scholars, and not without reason.[53] Her suggestion that Tamar was complicit in the sexual encounter with Amnon seems to run counter to the plain meaning

---

52. In a similar vein, Graeme Auld, while not accusing Tamar of complicity in the sexual encounter, believes that she was quite 'as foolish as the fool who rapes her' (2011: 484). His argument is based on the fact that Tamar failed to appeal to a divine sanction as she sought to repel her brother's advances, relying instead on her father to do the right thing by consenting to their marriage, even though he had hardly acted appropriately in the matter of Bathsheba and Uriah. However, Auld overlooks the fact that Tamar appeals to a far more fundamental moral principle than any enshrined in the law by claiming that Amnon's action was completely contrary to the accepted moral standards of the nation ('such a thing is not done in Israel'; v. 12).

53. Johanna Stiebert provides a detailed critique of Reis's arguments (2016: 185–93), and concludes that 'hers is a maverick voice, and in some ways profoundly pernicious' (p. 187), since it serves to reinforce the view that women were ultimately responsible for their rape, and inevitably feeds into the 'blame the victim' syndrome so common in our own day.

of the text, which makes it abundantly clear that she did all she could to extricate herself from the situation, but that her valiant efforts were in vain, given the superior strength of her brother. Tamar's repulsion of Amnon's advances could hardly be clearer, and the three transitive verbs in quick succession in v. 14 (he 'overpowered her', 'forced her' and 'laid her') reflect the assertion of male physical aggression, an aggression which Tamar, despite her courageous efforts, was unable to withstand. Moreover, far from being compliant, Tamar is clearly appalled that Amnon should flout the moral conventions of Israel and, far from being foolish, Tamar appears in the story as a woman possessed of insight, discernment and perspicacity, and one who has a clear sense of moral propriety. Indeed, she was sufficiently shrewd to make the scandal visible for all to see, thus forcing the other characters in the narrative to respond to what had happened, and she was sufficiently outspoken to claim that Amnon was the real fool, since he could have married her in the ordinary way, had he just asked for David's permission.

Esther Fuchs provides a further example of one who views Tamar in a decidedly negative light, not because she was in any way complicit in the sexual encounter but because, by her actions, she served to foster and perpetuate patriarchal values and ideals. Indeed, Fuchs regards both the story of Tamar's violation by Amnon and the account of the rape of Dinah in Genesis 34 as providing excellent examples of how male authors of the biblical texts deal with a singularly feminine experience, and how they use the literary devices of plot, dialogue and characterization in the most subtle ways in order to promote their own patriarchal interests. Fuchs maintains that neither woman is permitted by the narrator to participate actively in the plot; rather, both are regarded as passive objects of the rapists' desire and aggression (2000: 202), and in both narratives there is complete silence concerning the women's response to the rape, and a deliberate suppression of their emotional attitude to the rapist. Both characters are portrayed as subservient to the male members of their family, and the offence against national dignity and family honour overrides the suffering of the women (pp. 213–15). Moreover, in both stories it is left to the men of the family to punish the rapist and to restore some semblance of moral order. By enhancing the part played by the male protagonists while subordinating or marginalizing the role of the female, the stories serve to perpetuate the patriarchal ideology of women's impotence and inability to protect themselves, and to promote the notion of male dominance and female subservience. Tamar is even made to speak in defence of patriarchal interests by reminding Amnon of his legal obligation to marry her (cf. Deut. 22:28-29), and she is depicted as more outraged by his refusal to do so than she was by the rape itself (v. 16). Fuchs argues that Tamar's reaction reflects how, from the male narrator's point of view, a woman *ought* to react when she had been raped. As one who unquestioningly obeys her father's command (vv. 7-8) and her brother's wish (v. 10), she appears as the obedient, subservient female, responsive to patriarchal domination and control. In brief, she emerges from the story as the 'perfect rape victim' (2000: 216).

It is beyond the scope of the present chapter to discuss Fuchs's interpretation of the episode concerning Dinah, but there can be little doubt that her characterization of Tamar is hardly borne out by the text. In the first place, it beggars belief to understand how Tamar's elaborate protestation in vv. 12-13 can be considered as 'silence' on her part, and far from being a passive character in the story, she appears to be strong, bold and determined – bold enough to name the deed for what it is (a 'vile' act that was unthinkable in Israel; v. 12), and brave enough to tell the presumptive heir to the throne that he will be viewed as one of the 'scoundrels' of Israel (cf. Westbrook 2015: 156). Tamar is far from being the stereotype of the compliant, submissive female who does not participate actively in the plot (Fuchs 2000: 201–2). Moreover, it is difficult to see how the narrator can be regarded as downplaying her suffering, for, after the rape, she is depicted as a 'desolate' woman, isolated in Absalom's house, without hope of marriage or family. Nor is it clear that the narrator deliberately suppresses Tamar's emotional attitude towards her rapist; on the contrary, as Alice Keefe has observed, the rape scene 'is powerful with the fullness of character and human emotion', and the effect of the narration is to draw one into the tragedy of Tamar's life, 'so that it becomes not merely a narrative fact, a device of the plot, but an experience of a woman's pain shared intimately with the reader' (1993: 91–2). Given Fuchs's unrelenting emphasis elsewhere in her writings on the patriarchal ideology implicit in the Hebrew Bible, one might have expected her to applaud Tamar as a prime example of a woman who sought to undermine male power structures in society and who refused to conform to the traditional image of the dutiful and subservient female. While it is true that she complies obediently with her father's wishes to attend to her supposedly sick brother, it is no less true that she has the resolve and temerity to repel Amnon's instructions, for when he requests her to lie down, she declines, and when he orders her to go away, she again refuses.[54] Having been ejected from his house, she could have remained silent (as Absalom later enjoined her),

---

54. As Fokkelman observes, from Amnon's perspective, Tamar appears to be 'totally unmanageable' (1981: 113).

but, instead, she conspires to make her wronged status public by gestures of mourning and by tearing her garment as a sign of her lost virginity and the shame that had been visited upon her.

Thus, Tamar appears in the narrative as an eloquent and honourable woman, a character of integrity and intelligence who speaks and acts with considerable wisdom and courage. Indeed, she is the only character in the entire narrative to emerge with any dignity. While Tamar clearly appears in the story as a victim, it is arguable that she is doubly victimized by scholars who fail to appreciate her considerable courage and resourcefulness (cf. Birch 1998: 1303).

Jonadab

Jonadab seems to be something of an elusive character in this story, appearing on the scene unheralded and then, at the end of the chapter, disappearing, never to be heard of again. Jonadab is introduced at the beginning of the story as the son of David's brother, and described as a 'very clever man' (*'îš ḥākām mĕ'ōd*; 13:3).[55] The scheme which he devised to enable Amnon to satisfy his desire was undoubtedly shrewd because it ensured not only that Tamar would come to Amnon's house but that she would do so by express permission of the king.[56] A further illustration of Jonadab's shrewdness comes towards the end of the chapter (v. 32), for he was able to discern that Absalom wanted only revenge against Amnon, and he was thus able to provide David with reassurance that only Absalom had been killed and that he could safely discount any rumours to the contrary. The arrival of the royal princes back in Jerusalem (vv. 34-36) confirm that what Jonadab had told David was, indeed, true.

---

55. The word used here, *ḥākām*, is usually rendered 'wise' but, in view of Jonadab's ethically dubious advice to Amnon, some prefer to render the word as 'crafty' (NRSV) or 'shrewd' (REB) in the present context. However, as Norman Whybray has argued, 'wisdom' in the Hebrew Bible is a purely intellectual and morally neutral quality used for achieving specific aims, whether good or bad, admirable or unsavoury; thus, the term 'wise' is perfectly justified in relation to Jonadab. See Whybray 1968: 58; 1974: 89–91. Von Rad similarly contends that the term *ḥākām* does not contain any element of ethical evaluation; it simply means 'competent' or 'skilled' and must be 'completely dissociated from a scale of values' (1972: 20).

56. Philip Esler (2011: 335) suggests that Jonadab wanted to curry favour with a man who was not only his friend and cousin but who, as David's firstborn, would have seemed most likely to succeed to the throne after David's death.

Commentators have tended to view Jonadab in a negative light, for while they concede that he does not share Amnon's culpability, it was nevertheless he who masterminded the plot to bring Tamar within Amnon's reach, thus paving the way for him to rape her.[57] In their appraisal of Jonadab's character, scholars appear to assume that he knew at the outset that Amnon intended to rape his sister. Philip Esler, for example, claims that Jonadab devised a scheme 'that will enable one cousin to rape another' (2011: 333). He admits that Jonadab was not privy to the information possessed by the reader, namely, that Amnon was ill because it seemed impossible for him 'to do anything' to his sister, but he has little doubt that 'both men know exactly what he has in mind' (p. 333). By 'devising the plan for her rape', Amnon's act would have been 'regarded as particularly appalling by an ancient Israelite audience because of his violation of the relationship between two paternal cousins' (p. 335). Antony Campbell wonders why Jonadab is not criticized in the narrative for his nefarious scheme, for he is 'portrayed knowing exactly what was going on and he is never brought to account for it' (2005: 128). Amy Kalmanofsky similarly takes for granted that Jonadab 'plots rape' (2014: 104), and even the normally cautious Johanna Stiebert concludes that Jonadab suggested 'the rape strategy to Amnon' (2016: 192).

The problem with such an appraisal of Jonadab's character, however, is that his scheme is evaluated retrospectively in the light of the events reported in vv. 11-17. As Jan Fokkelman (1981: 109) has observed, Jonadab may have been very clever (v. 3), but he was hardly a clairvoyant able to predict the future and know precisely what Amnon's intentions were. It may be, as Shimon Bar-Efrat suggests, that Jonadab was just 'contriving an innocent assignation at which Amnon could enjoy the proximity of his beloved', and that the idea that Amnon would rape Tamar never occurred to him.[58] Admittedly, Jonadab was guilty of deception in the way he presented his nefarious scheme, but to assume that he foresaw sexual contact between Amnon and Tamar is to read too much into the text and to besmirch his character unnecessarily.

---

57. Von Rad refers to Jonadab as one of those 'intriguers whose presence at court never bodes any good' (1966: 181).

58. Bar-Efrat 1989: 249. He does concede, however, that the advice proffered 'casts a dark shadow over Jonadab's morals' (p. 247). Alter (1999: 266) keeps the options open, stating that it remains ambiguous whether Jonadab has in mind the facilitating of a rape or merely creating the possibility of an intimate encounter between Amnon and Tamar. Brueggemann similarly observes that Jonadab's plot 'only assured Amnon of a private interview with Tamar' (1990: 287).

David

In contrast to chs. 11–12, David occupies a peripheral role in the present narrative; he appears, in Phyllis Trible's words, merely as 'a member of the supporting cast'.[59] He first emerges as the unwitting accomplice to Amnon's scheme, and then as the one who conspicuously fails to provide protection and justice for his own daughter.[60] Unlike the powerful figure of the previous chapters, David appears here as a considerably weakened man, the violent aggressor having morphed into the doting father. On two occasions, David's sons make him complicit in their dubious plans: first, he is manipulated by Amnon into sending Tamar to him, thus providing a situation enabling Amnon to rape his sister; then he is manipulated by Absalom into consenting to Amnon's presence at the sheep-shearing festival, thereby providing Absalom with a suitable opportunity for him to kill his brother.[61] Some have argued that David was naïve in acquiescing to his sons' requests, but this is to do him an injustice, for he no doubt expected proprieties to be observed when Tamar, a virgin, visited her brother,[62] and he surely had no reason to believe that Absalom, having

---

59. Trible 1984: 38. Bar-Efrat (1989: 240–1) draws attention to the fact that both David and Absalom are mentioned before Tamar and Amnon in v. 1 even though it is the latter two characters who dominate the first portion of the narrative. From this, he concludes that the events that transpire between Amnon and Tamar – both of whom disappear from the stage before the end of the chapter – are recounted only because of their significance for the relationship between Absalom and David which features in several of the following chapters. Jan Fokkelman similarly regards the story of Amnon and Tamar as just a 'component of Absalom's history' (1981: 101; cf. Stone 1996: 106).

60. Johanna Stiebert (2013: 63) notes that Tamar is identified in the first instance not in terms of her father but as the sister of David's son, which suggests an implied criticism of David, who had not acted as a father should, having failed in his custodial paternal duty to protect his daughter.

61. As Matthew Newkirk points out, the theme of deception runs through the present chapter: David is deceived into believing that Amnon was sick; Tamar is deceived into visiting his house; and Absalom deceives both his brother and father into believing falsely that he wanted them to celebrate at the sheep-shearing festival when his real intention was to kill Amnon (2015: 109–16; cf., also, Hagan 1979: 308–10).

62. Fokkelien van Dijk-Hemmes has argued that David was fully aware of Amnon's true intention in having Tamar visit his house. She bases her argument on the fact that Jonadab, in presenting his scheme to Amnon, had suggested that Tamar should make some 'healing food' for him, but in Amnon's request to David the 'healing food' has been altered to 'heart cakes'; Amnon thus implicitly lets David

done nothing for two years to avenge Tamar's rape, would take advantage of the sheep-shearing festival in order to wreak vengeance upon his brother.[63]

David's reaction after the rape, however, casts him in an unambiguously negative light, for he is said to have been fully informed of what had happened ('when King David heard all of these things'; v. 21), and was evidently even told the name of the culprit; yet, although he became 'very angry', and recognized that a serious wrong had been committed, he did nothing to rebuke or punish his son.[64] It is not clear from the MT whether his anger was aroused by the fact that Tamar had been raped or because Amnon, his firstborn son, had sunk to such depths of depravity. The reading of the LXX (supported by 4QSam[a]) suggests the latter alternative: David did not punish Amnon because 'he loved him, for he was his firstborn'. Evidently, the affection of the indulgent father for his son was such that he was prepared to overlook even the most serious blemishes in his character.[65] As Phyllis Trible has observed, David's reaction (or, rather,

---

know his real intention and perhaps even obliquely asks for the king's permission (1989: 140–1). Amy Kalmanofsky similarly argues that David was cognizant of Amnon's intention and was therefore co-responsible for the rape of Tamar (2014: 105–6). This interpretation, however, seems most improbable and reads far too much into the text.

63. Some commentators have detected in vv. 26-27 an inkling of suspicion in David's mind as to what Absalom intended to do, for he initially had reservations concerning Amnon's attendance at the sheep-shearing festival ('Why should he go with you?'). Amy Kalmanofsky (2014: 113) suggests that perhaps David senses danger at this point and 'accepts the inevitable act of vengeance' that was to follow. Antony Campbell (2005: 130–1) wonders why, if Jonadab later had the wherewithal to surmise Absalom's intention (vv. 32-33), David would not have been aware of the potential danger that Amnon might incur by attending the festival. But given David's reluctance to punish or even reprimand Amnon for his behaviour, it seems most unlikely that he would have deliberately allowed his son to walk into Absalom's trap.

64. As many commentators have observed, David's passivity contrasts sharply with the man of action depicted in chs. 11–12. In fact, his reaction here is like that of Jacob when he hears of the violation of Dinah, for he, too, does nothing, thereby paving the way for the bloody act of vengeance carried out by his sons, Simeon and Levi (Gen. 34:5).

65. Commentators, however, have not been slow to suggest less charitable explanations for David's pusillanimous reaction. Regina Schwartz (1997: 100) suggests that David was too tainted by his own previous immoral behaviour to enforce punishment on others; given that he had taken the wife of one of his most loyal soldiers,

his lack of reaction) leaves little doubt as to where his sympathies really lay: 'the father identifies with the son; the adulterer supports the rapist; male has joined male to deny justice for the female' (1984: 53-4).

After instructing his servants to kill Amnon, Absalom fled, and David is said to have 'mourned for his son day after day' (v. 37).[66] Commentators have debated whether David was grieving for Amnon, or for Absalom, or for both,[67] but given that Amnon was David's firstborn and had a special place in his affections, it is probable that the intense sorrow expressed by David was over Amnon's death. Absalom remained in exile for three years, during which time David's grief over his son's death had been assuaged ('for he was now consoled over the death of Amnon'; v. 39b), and he began to long for his son, Absalom ('the heart of the king went out, yearning for Absalom'; v. 39a).[68] This would eventually lead to a

---

perhaps he did not feel himself to be on high enough moral ground to rebuke his son (cf. Halpern 2001: 40; Gordon 1986: 264; Brueggemann 1990: 289; Birch 1998: 1305). Fokkelman (1981: 112) explains David's reaction as due to the awkwardness and embarrassment aroused in him by the realization that he had been misled in sending Tamar to visit her brother. A variety of possible reasons for David's refusal to chastise Amnon is contemplated by J.S. Ackerman 1990: 45-6.

66. David's protracted grieving for his son evokes little sympathy from John Mauchline, who comments: 'he had more need to bewail his own inability to rule his own household than to shed tears for Amnon' (1971: 264).

67. Phyllis Trible pointedly remarks that while David mourns, 'we cannot be sure if the object of his grief is Amnon the murdered or Absalom the fugitive', but we 'can be sure that it is not Tamar the violated' (1984: 55).

68. The received text of v. 39 is clearly defective, for the verb *wattĕkal* is feminine though there is no feminine noun in the clause. Given that the second half of the verse (and, indeed, the following chapter) requires that v. 39a should make some reference to the softening of David's attitude towards Absalom, many commentators assume that the word *nepeš* has been accidentally omitted, and they read, with NRSV, 'the heart of the king went out, yearning for Absalom'. Robert Alter, however, argues that such paternal longing ill accords with David's refusal to see his son once he returned to Jerusalem, and he prefers to read the feminine noun *ruaḥ* (with some support from Qumran) as the subject of the verb ('David's impulse to sally forth against Absalom was spent'), on the grounds that an abasement of hostilities against Absalom rather than a longing for him makes more sense in terms of what follows (1999: 274). Barbara Green's comment neatly sums up the ambiguity in the meaning of v. 39: 'It is a most ambiguous and contested verse in a narrative not short on ambiguity. The uncertainties can be somewhat disentangled as follows: Is the king's spirit positively or negatively reaching out to Absalom, exiled? Is David consoled or changed about Amnon because he is dead? In other words, does David want Absalom back or not, and with what feelings would he be welcomed?' (2017: 208).

reconciliation between father and son, and the return to favour of the one who was now able to become the next king.

In retrospect, David's failure to exact punishment on Amnon turned out to be a serious error of judgment on his part; had he acted decisively, as the occasion required, he may have prevented the death of Amnon and the subsequent estrangement between himself and Absalom, an estrangement that would eventually plunge the nation into civil strife.[69] The one responsible for ensuring justice for his people (2 Sam. 15:2-4) had failed even to provide justice for his own daughter. As king, David had the power and authority to resolve the situation by making Amnon accountable for his crime, but the sentimental father had allowed his judgment to be clouded by an uncritical paternal indulgence. Although the narrator seems to be at pains to exonerate David by suggesting that he did not intentionally collaborate with Amnon (vv. 5-7) or, later, with Absalom (vv. 26-27), there can be little doubt that the revered king in this chapter does not appear in a positive light. As Mark Gray has remarked: 'Depending on one's perspective, David is either presented as innocent to the point of gross naivety or blind to a degree that stretches credulity, neither qualities much esteemed in an astute ruler' (1998: 43).

Absalom

The narrative appears to offer a broadly sympathetic portrait of Absalom. While David remains silent in the face of the outrage committed against his daughter, Absalom takes up the cudgels on her behalf.[70] The measure he took to avenge his sister's honour may appear excessive, but such was the callous nature of Amnon's offence that the reader is persuaded that at the very least there was an element of poetic justice in the way in which he exacted vengeance.[71] It is true that he engaged in deception in order

---

69. April Westbrook notes the irony that the one character in the narrative who possesses absolute power does nothing and was prepared to witness 'the bald reality of violation and injustice happening in the very heart of the monarchy' (2015: 164). She believes that the story is deliberately constructed as an implicit indictment of the monarchy, portraying those in power as above the law and abdicating responsibility for their actions.

70. Ken Stone notes that the ability to guard against any threat to a sister's sexual purity and to avenge any sexual misconduct perpetrated against her was often regarded as a badge of masculine honour; hence, readers of the narrative would have assumed that Absalom would, sooner or later, respond to his sister's rape 'in socially approved ways' (1996: 107).

71. Cf. Propp 1993: 47. Irrespective of whether Absalom acted within the law in eliminating his brother and, indeed, whether he was a legitimate agent to carry out the

to manoeuvre Amnon to attend the sheep-shearing festival, but his action was hardly more blameworthy than the deception perpetrated by Amnon to ensure a visit by Tamar to his house. It is also true that his words of consolation to Tamar immediately after the rape ('Be quiet for now, my sister; he is your brother; do not take this to heart'; v. 20) appears to be curiously cold and unsympathetic, but his seemingly blasé attitude and his reticence to betray his true feelings concerning the incident to his brother ('Absalom spoke to Amnon neither good nor bad'; v. 22) were probably designed to allay any suspicions concerning his plan to avenge his sister's rape. For the same reason, Absalom refrained from summary vengeance, preferring instead to bide his time, thus creating a false sense of security for Amnon. Moreover, when the time came to take revenge, Absalom was careful to ensure that only the offender was punished, unlike Dinah's brothers who pillaged an entire village and showed no restraint in their ruthless revenge.

Some commentators, however, have provided a far less positive estimation of Absalom's character. They point out that since he was second in line for the throne (2 Sam. 3:3), Absalom could not hope to become king unless Amnon had been eliminated; hence, suspicions are cast on his motivation for vindicating his sister's honour. David Gunn and Danna N. Fewell, for example, ask whether it was Tamar's honour that was uppermost in Absalom's mind 'or is she displaced by the prospect of royal power?' (1993: 145). Other scholars have come to a similar conclusion, arguing that Absalom's elimination of his brother was motivated by his dynastic ambitions and his designs on the throne rather than by a determination to avenge his sister's rape.[72] However, no such

---

execution (albeit through his servants), many scholars assume that Absalom's killing of Amnon was a just response to the sexual assault on his sister. Walter Brueggemann, for example, while conceding that Absalom's act of vengeance was aggressive and brutal, admits that 'one can understand why he acts as he does' (1990: 290). William McKane argues that, in eliminating Amnon, 'Absalom could plead great provocation in mitigation of his murder of him' (1963: 242). David Gunn expresses the view that Amnon's death 'causes little regret' (1978: 100), and Philip Esler concludes that Amnon is a tragic figure 'whose death would cause no one to shed a tear' (2011: 355).

72. So, e.g., Hertzberg 1964: 326; McKane 1963: 242; H.P. Smith 1899: 331; A.A. Anderson 1989: 173; Gilmour 2011: 219–20. Bruce Birch contends that Absalom's revenge 'seems to be more a matter of restoring family honor and securing his own place in the succession than a matter of solidarity with Tamar' (1998: 1305), while Walter Brueggemann suggests that 'Tamar may have been only the excuse Absalom needed for his assault' (1990: 290). Von Rad (1966: 181) regards Absalom's action as merely a convenient pretext for the removal of the heir to the throne, and, in a similar

ulterior motive is implied in the story itself, for there is no suggestion that Absalom wished to be rid of a rival for succession to the throne.[73] Indeed, Jonadab makes Absalom's motivation clear when he reports Amnon's death to David, informing him that this had 'been determined by Absalom from the day Amnon raped his sister Tamar' (v. 32; cf. Bar-Efrat 1989: 274-5). While it is true that Absalom's desire for power emerges clearly in later chapters, it is questionable whether later events should be interpreted retrospectively to cast aspersions on Absalom's motive in the present story. Absalom did, indeed, become a candidate for the throne by virtue of Amnon's death but, as Charles Conroy has wisely remarked, 'political consequences should not be confused with political motivation' (1978: 103). In brief, the fact that Absalom moved closer to the throne by ensuring the death of the heir-presumptive does not mean that this was why he eliminated his brother.

Esther Fuchs has also come to a negative view of Absalom's character, though for a very different reason. She concedes that Absalom's response ostensibly seems favourably disposed to Tamar, for he is said to have 'hated' Amnon because of the incident, and to have refrained from speaking to him (v. 22). However, when he meets Tamar after the incident, and realizes that she was giving public expression to her despair, he asks her to maintain a discreet silence, anxious to keep the matter secret, aware that to publicize the scandal would harm the reputation of the royal household. Moreover, by telling her not to take the matter to heart (v. 20) he appears to be dismissive and patronising, minimizing the gravity of the offence, and implying that it was a trivial matter that could easily be ignored (2000: 206). Fuchs argues that his reaction was not one that was likely to have given much comfort or solace to his sister. She concedes that Absalom eventually sought revenge for Amnon's outlandish behaviour, but the fact that he expressed no anger during his initial conversation

---

vein, Graeme Auld claims that 'in bidding his men strike down David's eldest son, Absalom is also implicitly asking them to recognize a new political reality' (2011: 484).

73. At the beginning of v. 28, the LXX (supported by 4QSam[a]) has an additional clause 'and Absalom made a feast like the feast of a king', which some commentators regard as hinting at the kingly pretensions that Absalom would later display (cf. Ackroyd 1977: 125; Gordon 1986: 265), although no such hint appears in the story itself. Richard Smith, on the other hand, believes it reflects the narrator's sense of irony and was intended 'as an indication of Absalom's sense of authority and his exhibitionist tendencies (14:26) rather than as a hint of his early designs on the kingship' (2009: 155).

with Tamar, and that he refused to retaliate immediately, meant that his sister was forced to remain desolate for two years, not knowing whether her rape would be avenged, and her rapist punished. Furthermore, Fuchs argues that by demanding the right to avenge his sister, Absalom effectively restricted Tamar's autonomy and freedom to act on her own behalf. If Amnon had robbed Tamar of her virginity, Absalom had managed to rob her of her own voice (2000: 205).

Fuchs argues that, by portraying Absalom as the avenger of Tamar's rape, the narrative simply perpetuates the patriarchal ideology that emphasizes women's impotence and their inability to protect themselves. Such stories were (no doubt, gleefully) recounted to underline the power of the man and the helplessness of the woman, thereby preserving the familiar stereotype of the strong, heroic male and the vulnerable, defenceless female. Having fulfilled her role as the passive rape victim, the narrator removes her from the story in order to allow the brother/hero to ensure justice and to restore some semblance of moral order. By depicting Absalom as avenging his sister's rape, the narrative served an androcentric agenda, effectively perpetuating gender roles and expectations, and fostering the notion of male dominance and female subordination.

It is difficult not to harbour the suspicion that Fuchs is intent on portraying Absalom in an unfavourable light so that she is able to tar all the male characters in the story with the same brush. Her argument that Absalom's consoling words to Tamar in v. 20 are to be viewed as 'a brutal act of suppressing a raped woman's bitter plea for justice' (2000: 203) is surely difficult to sustain, considering Absalom's determination to avenge his sister's rape. The fact that he took no immediate steps to redress the wrong done to his sister was merely a ploy on Absalom's part to catch his half-brother unawares. It is hard to know what Absalom could have done in order to gain Fuchs's approval. Had he not avenged his sister's rape, Fuchs would no doubt have criticized the narrator for letting the rapist off the hook. Ideally, from Fuchs's perspective, the narrator would have permitted Tamar to avenge her own rape (2000: 201), but if the narrative was to ring true to its original readers, it is difficult to know what steps Tamar could have taken within the bounds of the law to ensure justice for her cause. Indeed, Fuchs almost undermines the gravity of Amnon's offence when she states, rather bizarrely, that 'the protection of the sister by her "good" brother is just as harmful as her abuse by her "bad" brother' (p. 205). Fuchs concedes that the narrative 'is unambiguous in its indictment of the rapist and vindication of the avenger' (p. 202); yet, by questioning Absalom's motives and besmirching his character, Fuchs manages to make the hero in the story appear to be almost as bad as the villain.

Amnon

Amnon's behaviour in the narrative is such that it inevitably evokes intense revulsion on the part of the reader, for in the space of 17 verses, he deceives his father, rapes his sister, and then humiliates her by callously evicting her from his house.[74] In contrast to the account of the rape of Dinah in Genesis 34, there is no attempt by the narrator to exonerate the rapist of his responsibility for the offence; on the contrary, the detailed description of Amnon's plot to ensnare Tamar by feigning illness (vv. 5-6) leaves no doubt as to his culpability, and the premeditated nature of the offence merely makes it all the more reprehensible. This was not a momentary, impulsive act committed when an unexpected opportunity presented itself, but part of a carefully calculated plan which the reader sees unfolding stage by stage.[75] Even at the beginning of the story, the narrator implies that Amnon's intentions were not entirely honourable, for he is said to have been tormented by Tamar's beauty, and frustrated because it seemed impossible for him 'to do anything to her' (v. 2).[76] Doubts about his intentions increase when he asks David to command her to make some food that he may 'eat from her hand' (v. 6). The tension is further intensified when Amnon instructs her to bring the food to his chamber and sends everyone else out of the room (vv. 9-10). It thus comes as little surprise to the reader that when Amnon stretches out his hand it is not to seize the food proffered but to seize Tamar herself (v. 11). When his attempt to persuade her to lie with him fails, he proceeds to rape her. In contrast to the violation of Dinah in Genesis 34, where love blossoms after the rape, Amnon's desire turns to hatred; indeed, he is said to have

---

74. Dijk-Hemmes's observation that Amnon's behaviour 'lacks romantic overtones' seems something of an understatement (1989: 139).

75. Bar-Efrat suggests that the reader's assessment of Amnon changes as the narrative proceeds. At the beginning of the story, the reader is merely told that Amnon 'fell in love' with Tamar, and since the word 'love' in the Hebrew Bible usually has positive connotations, there is little reason to suppose that Amnon's feelings towards his sister was little more than a passing desire. Indeed, at this point the reader might initially 'even feel a certain sympathy and compassion for him' (1989: 243). It is only as the story progresses that the reader's feelings of disapproval and disgust emerge, so that by the conclusion of the narrative our attitude towards Amnon is 'indisputably negative' (p. 264).

76. Contrast Bar-Efrat, who suggests that the word 'anything' (*mě'ûmā*) is so general in meaning that no conclusions can be drawn as to Amnon's true purpose. Had the narrator wanted to portray Amnon in a distinctly negative light at the outset of the narrative, the vocabulary used would have been less vague. It is only later, after the rape, that the word 'anything' is filled with content (1989: 244).

loathed his half-sister with an intensity that exceeded his earlier passion for her (v. 15). Clearly, in Amnon's eyes, Tamar was no more than a sex object that could be cast aside once his sexual appetite had been satisfied. Not content with raping her, he shows his complete disdain for Tamar by casting her out in the most degrading and undignified way. Summoning his servant, he instructs him to remove 'this one' (Heb. *zō't*) from his presence and to bolt the door after her (v. 17), giving the impression that it was she who had forced her unwelcome attentions upon him. In order to safeguard his own reputation, the incident is made to appear as the result of enticement on Tamar's part. Thus, Tamar, the daughter of the king, faces the ignominy of being expelled by a servant, who then locks the door as if she were a repulsive creature against whom every measure must be taken to ensure that she did not return to the house (Bar-Efrat 1989: 268–9).

The story of Tamar's rape is not without interest for its political ramifications. Amnon is presented as David's firstborn son and was therefore probably regarded by David (and by himself) as heir to the throne; however, his deplorable behaviour and his scant regard for the proprieties of human conduct reveal him to be totally unworthy of such a responsibility. Since Solomon had already been introduced as David's successor with the assurance that Yahweh's favour rested upon him (12:24-25), the position of Amnon, who would have been higher in line of succession to the throne, had to be clarified. The present chapter thus makes clear that Amnon's behaviour rendered him unsuitable for the throne, and his manipulative machinations were such that he had disqualified himself from the high office of kingship. Indeed, by emphasizing the violence of Amnon's actions ('being stronger than she, he forced her and lay with her'; v. 14),[77] and his failure to heed Tamar's protests, not to mention his cruel rejection of her after the rape, the narrator suggests that the obvious candidate for the throne was not only unworthy of such an office but that his death at the hands of Absalom was entirely justified.[78]

Conclusion

The story of the rape of Tamar has raised a plethora of issues, both as regards the relation of biblical law to biblical narrative, and the way in which the characters have been portrayed, both by the biblical narrator

---

77. H.P. Smith's rather anodyne description of Amnon's actions ('he solicits her to unchastity') hardly does justice to the violent nature of his behaviour.

78. Richard Smith claims that, from the narrator's point of view, Amnon received 'the execution he so justly deserves' (2009: 153).

and by subsequent scholars. Much scholarly discussion has centred on trying to make the narrative compatible with the legal texts of the Hebrew Bible. If marriage between a stepbrother and sister was forbidden, as the laws of Leviticus and Deuteronomy imply, why does Tamar suggest that a marriage between her and Amnon would have been perfectly permissible, provided it received the royal imprimatur (v. 13)? Moreover, from the legal point of view, neither David nor Absalom follow the usual, expected course of action. The legal consequence of Amnon's offence was clear: the rapist should have married his victim, paid the bride-price to her father, and forfeited the right of divorce. Furthermore, it is questionable whether Absalom's execution of his brother was within the bounds of legality, for, despite the despicable nature of Amnon's action, if he had committed only rape (as opposed to incestuous rape) he would not, according to the law, have been deemed guilty of a capital offence. Despite the rather convoluted attempts that have been made, at times, to fit the narrative into a legal straitjacket, the story has continued to baffle commentators, for it raises far more questions than it resolves. What has been insufficiently appreciated is that the narrator probably had little interest in the niceties of legal enactments; it was enough, from this storyteller's point of view, that Amnon had perpetrated an act that 'was not done in Israel' and that he had completely disregarded the accepted moral norms of the community.

The way in which the characters in the story have been portrayed throws an interesting light on the narrator's method of evaluation. The story is emphatic in its implicit indictment of Amnon, for he is depicted as a prey to sexual lust and as one who was prepared to act with utter callousness. The evaluation of his character, however, comes not through the narrator's explicit condemnation, but through Amnon's own heartless words and actions. By describing the deception Amnon used to lure Tamar to his house, his refusal to heed her plea, and his subsequent ejection of her after the rape, the narrator leads us to regard his offence with the utmost repugnance and revulsion. By contrast, Tamar appears as one who has a clear sense of moral propriety, for she valiantly attempts to save both herself and her assailant from the consequences of his unbridled passion. The narrator skilfully enlists the reader's sympathy with her plight: having entered the story as a beautiful virgin princess, she makes a tragic exit, her life henceforth blighted, and denied the possibility of a happily married life which her previous status as a virgin daughter of the king would have offered her.

David plays a relatively peripheral role in the story, but the narrator depicts him as weak and easily duped by the nefarious machinations of his sons. The one responsible for ensuring justice for his people (2 Sam. 15:2-4) had failed to ensure justice even within his own household, and the one with the right and obligation to act is depicted as doing nothing. Indeed, by his silence, he sides with his deceitful and depraved son rather than with his distraught and desolate daughter. It is therefore left to Absalom to assume the role of righteous avenger and defender of justice; however, although the rape is eventually avenged, harmony is far from being restored, for Absalom's execution of his brother was the precursor to further tragic events that would eventually lead to civil war.

This chapter has also highlighted the way in which contemporary scholars have evaluated the characters in the story. Jonadab has been criticized by some scholars because he is deemed to have facilitated the rape, although his plan was probably merely intended to arrange an intimate encounter between Amnon and Tamar. Other scholars have even contrived to view Tamar in a negative light, although attempts to suggest that she was a willing partner in the encounter seems to run counter to the plain meaning of the text. Absalom is similarly viewed with suspicion by many commentators, since it is assumed (without any evidence in the story itself) that his main motivation in having his brother killed was not to avenge his sister's rape but to eliminate the heir to the throne.

Viewed in the light of 2 Samuel 11–12, the story of the rape of Tamar raises some challenging and thought-provoking moral issues, which the narrator is content to leave to the reader to ponder. Was the rape of Tamar part of Yahweh's retributive punishment on the house of David for the sins committed in relation to Bathsheba and Uriah? Should Tamar be viewed as the victim not only of Amnon's lust but of David's sin and Yahweh's judgment? Were the events recorded in 2 Samuel 13 the inevitable fulfilment of Nathan's prophecy in 12:10-11? If so, it is a strange justice that involves the suffering of others as opposed to the perpetrator of the offence. Are the characters entirely responsible for what they do or are they subject to forces beyond their control? If Yahweh is viewed as manoeuvring behind the scenes, it raises the uncomfortable question as to whether the characters should be absolved of their actions. The absence of Yahweh from the story has not gone unnoticed, for while he readily intervened to punish David the adulterer, there is no suggestion of any such divine intervention to punish Amnon the rapist, a fact not lost on Esther Fuchs, who concludes that 'rape does not appear to displease God as much as adultery does' (2000: 223). The role of Yahweh in the story of King David will be the focus of our discussion in the next chapter.

Chapter 6

Ethical Criticism and the Character of Yahweh
(2 Samuel 12:7-25; 24:1-17)

In secular literary criticism the moral evaluation of a work was for a long time taken for granted, and it is only comparatively recently that it has fallen into desuetude. The point is well made by Wayne Booth, who has done more than most to place ethical criticism firmly back on the critic's agenda:

> Before modernism of various kinds broke into our scene, almost every critic agreed that the moral worth of stories must be addressed with rational inquiry and that some inquirers do the job better than others. If one had asked Plato or Sir Philip Sidney or Samuel Johnson or Samuel Taylor Coleridge or Matthew Arnold whether the critic's job included questions about literature's moral worth, they would have scorned the questioner, even if they disagreed in their particular judgments. Every reasonable critic, they assumed, must ask about the moral value of any work addressed.[1]

The aim of the present chapter is to argue that biblical scholars have a similar duty and responsibility to enter into serious ethical engagement with the text and apply to the Hebrew Bible the kind of ethical-ideological probing that scholars such as Wayne Booth (1983, 1988), Terry Eagleton (1978) and Hillis Miller (1987) have applied to secular literature. While biblical commentators have traditionally been quite prepared to question the historical accuracy and reliability of the text, they have tended to shy away from questioning the validity of its moral norms and underlying

---

1. Booth 2006: 242. See, further, Booth's richly nuanced volume *The Company We Keep* (1988), in which he makes a compelling case for the importance of ethical criticism and does so with humour and clarity. Martha Nussbaum provides a sympathetic review of Booth's volume and similarly emphasizes the importance of applying ethical criticism to works of literature (1990: 230–44).

assumptions; they have deployed all the critical tools at their disposal to expound the biblical traditions but have stopped short of passing judgment upon them. As a result, the task of evaluation has all but been evacuated from the realm of biblical scholarship. It is true that some recent scholars have sought to enter into dialogue with the ethical position advanced in the Hebrew Bible, and have occasionally found it necessary to adopt a critical, dissociating position from what the text offers;[2] however, by and large, scholars have been reticent to concede the validity and importance of ethical criticism in relation to the Bible. If such criticism has been recognized at all, it has usually been disguised under labels such as 'reader-response criticism' or 'feminist criticism'; it is high time, however, for ethical criticism to be accepted by biblical scholars as a distinct discipline in its own right and not shunted to the sidelines as an issue of secondary importance.

Ethical Criticism and the Hebrew Bible

Ethical criticism demands that the values inscribed in the biblical text must not be allowed to go unchallenged, for it is not enough to outline the moral vision of the text without asking how valid that vision is. As Schüssler Fiorenza has forcefully argued, scholars must apply a 'hermeneutic of suspicion' to the Hebrew Bible and ask searching questions of the text. Do the biblical narratives exemplify lives that can be imitated and provide readers with a benevolent vision that will inspire them to live a virtuous life? Or do they call for moral indictment? Do the stories celebrate violence and discount its consequences or do they reinforce our abhorrence of gratuitous brutality? Do they contribute to the general well-being of society or do they have a negative, detrimental effect, perhaps by reinforcing the language of oppression and domination? Are they likely to work for good or ill on those who read them? In brief, can the so-called good book be bad for you?[3]

2. Danna N. Fewell and David Gunn are among the few scholars who have been prepared to distance themselves from the position advocated in the biblical text. In discussing the role assigned to women in the biblical narrative, for example, they make no apology if, at times, a note of anger enters their writing, since 'it is difficult to avoid anger and irreverence in the face of the violence against women which permeates these texts' (1993: 19). In a similar vein, both David Clines (1995b: 77–106) and Philip Davies (1995: 164–73) argue that, at times, it may be necessary to question or resist the moral vision embedded in the text.

3. Schüssler Fiorenza 1988: 13–17; 2001: 175–7. She even goes so far as to suggest that all biblical texts should contain the label: 'Caution, could be dangerous to your health and survival!' (1999: 14).

That such questions need to be asked, and asked as a matter of urgency, should be obvious, for it is well known that the Hebrew Bible contains a veritable litany of morally objectionable practices – polygamy, holy war, blood vengeance and slavery, to name but a few – and there can be little doubt that the presence of such customs in the Hebrew Bible has often had a profoundly negative impact on human society.[4] It should never be forgotten that it was on the basis of biblical teaching that slavery was condoned over the centuries (cf. Bright 1967: 49–51), and that male domination and anti-Semitism were justified (Thatcher 2008). It is an indisputable fact – as Plato long ago recognized – that literary works often produce actual, tangible changes in the lives of those who engage with them, and various disciplines, such as feminism, queer studies, and postcolonial studies all agree – if sometimes obliquely – that stories *do* have moral significance and *are* capable of influencing social norms (cf. E.W. Davies 2016). Life does, indeed, imitate art, albeit often unconsciously, for the stories we imbibe are capable of shaping and influencing our behaviour and disposition. Of course, we can always stubbornly refuse to enter imaginatively into the stories we read, carefully anaesthetizing our mind to protect ourselves from their potentially baleful and malign influence. The problem with such a strategy, however, is that we emerge from the reading experience the same person as the one who went in, comfortably unharmed but, in truth, no better off than if we had spent our time playing cards. A far better option is to engage fully with the story, to pause for critical and ethical reflection, and to consider the relationship between narrative experience and human behaviour. As Stanley Fish rightly recognized, the process of reading is not only a matter of discovering what the text means, but what the text *does*, that is, what effect it might have upon those who read it.[5]

In the area of biblical studies, it is primarily feminist critics who have considered the effect that biblical texts have had upon human behaviour. They have demonstrated how the Bible over the centuries has served to reinforce deep-seated sexist beliefs and how it has succeeded to miseducate its male readers by reinforcing their egotism and cheerful willingness

---

4. For a detailed discussion of the morally objectionable passages in the Hebrew Bible, and an examination of some of the proposed solutions, see E.W. Davies 2005, 2010, passim.

5. According to Fish, the literary text was not so much an object to be analysed as an effect to be experienced. Consequently, the fundamental question that should be asked of any text was not 'What does it *mean*?' but 'What does it *do*?', and the task of the critic was to analyse '*the developing responses of the reader in relation to the words as they succeed one another in time*' (1972: 387–8; his italics).

to assume the role of lord and master, while at the same time miseducating its female readers by emphasizing their sense of dependence on, and inferiority to, their male counterparts. They have reminded us that what ostensibly appears quite innocent – the words on the page – are capable of being immensely powerful, and for that reason studying the Bible involves a particularly vigilant type of reading, lest the text lull us into a complicit acceptance of its morality. In practice, this is precisely what has happened when commentators have broached the biblical text: male biblical scholars have tacitly approved misogynistic passages, while white bourgeois critics have been oblivious to the racial undertones of particular texts.[6] It is for this reason that ethical criticism invites us not only to consider the text itself but to reflect upon our interpretative and evaluative habits, and to contemplate our own values and assumptions as we interpret those texts. In this way, the scholar's own ethical standards become the subject of scrutiny. Ethical criticism thus becomes an exercise in self-awareness: in subjecting the Bible to criticism we must allow the Bible to criticize us, otherwise we end up seeking support for moral positions arrived at on other grounds and, as William C. Spohn has rightly reminded us, Scripture then becomes 'not a challenge but an echo' (1995: 9).

Since the application of ethical criticism to the biblical material tends to be either airily dismissed or, at the very least, viewed with considerable suspicion, it may be appropriate at the outset to consider some of the objections usually raised by opponents of this approach. The most common objection is that the application of ethical criticism to the biblical text is irretrievably subjective, since the judgment we pass on the text will simply be an expression of our own personal moral preference. Indeed, even re-reading the same text at a different time may lead to a fresh moral evaluation of a passage and a revision of a previously held judgment. The fact is, however, that individual evaluation need not be entirely personal or subjective because it can always be corrected and improved in discussion with others. In this regard, Stanley Fish's notion of the 'interpretative community' is important, for readers will be constrained in their evaluation by the beliefs and practices of the community to which they belong.[7] If the reader is a biblical specialist, his or her evaluation can be analysed, discussed and adjudicated by the community of scholars of which he

---

6. For an example of the way in which male commentators have condoned the misogynistic aspects of the biblical text, see E.W. Davies 2003a: 104–5; and for a discussion of the way in which scholars have overlooked the racial undertones of biblical passages, see E.W. Davies 2013: 57–60.

7. For a discussion of Stanley Fish's notion of the 'interpretative community', see E.W. Davies 2003b: 27–35; 2013: 20–9.

or she is a part (represented, perhaps, by such illustrious professional bodies as the Society for Old Testament Study or the Society of Biblical Literature); if the readers are members of a church or synagogue, their evaluation will similarly find acceptance or rejection within the religious community of which they are a part. As Wayne Booth has suggested, our evaluation, far from reflecting an unbridled subjectivity, can be solidly grounded by 'the company we keep' (1988).

A further objection is that the Bible, as a sacred text, should be treated with reverential deference, not soiled with ethical-ideological probing, and many will harbour serious misgivings about the propriety of adopting such an approach to the biblical text. The role of the reader (it is argued) is to submit to the authority of Scripture, not to question or criticize it, and the task of the biblical exegete is to affirm the values enshrined in the biblical text, not to repudiate or reject them. The fact is, however, that the Hebrew Bible often probes and questions its own values, principles and assumptions. Abraham's plea that the 'Judge of all the earth' should 'do what is just' (Gen. 18:25), Job's doubts concerning the essential justice of God, and the Psalmist's question, 'How long shall the wicked exult?' (Ps. 94:3), all belong to a tradition of questioning widely held assumptions. Such critical questioning is also characteristic of the major prophets, who constantly re-evaluated the traditions that they had inherited as they sought to make them relevant and applicable to their own age.[8] If the traditions were to remain normative and meaningful they had to be critically appraised and had to maintain their value and relevance in the face of critical questioning. There is a sense, therefore, in which a 'hermeneutic of suspicion' is encountered within the biblical tradition itself as its authors question past beliefs and query past judgments. Far from accepting passively the values that they had inherited, their strategy was to probe, challenge, modify, and even reject some of their own inherited traditions. In brief, the Hebrew Bible comes to us bearing clear traces of its own critique of tradition.[9] As Danna N. Fewell and David Gunn have remarked, 'the Bible, despite its biases of gender, race/ethnicity, and class, makes provision for its own critique' (1993: 204). By applying ethical criticism to the biblical text, we are merely allowing Scripture to challenge its own suppositions. According to this view, therefore, critique

---

8. Cf. Jonathan Magonet (1997: 4) who notes that 'the prophets were subversive activists in their time, and by recording their words and deeds, the Bible effectively repeats their provocation in every subsequent generation'.

9. For this reason, attempts to 'read against the grain' of the text is not a sign of disrespect for Scripture. As David Clines has observed, 'what is disrespectful to the text is to assume that it will say what we would like it to say' (1995a: 192).

of the Bible is not an alien principle rooted in a secular ideology; on the contrary, such a critique is sanctioned by the biblical writers themselves.[10]

Finally, it should not go unremarked that scholars who have failed to apply ethical criticism to the biblical text have sometimes ended up defending passages that are clearly indefensible. Instead of engaging in ethical criticism when faced with texts that are clearly offensive and abhorrent, they have attempted to defend the values that the text adumbrates. Perhaps nowhere has this been more apparent than in discussions of the biblical account of the conquest of Canaan. W.F. Albright, for example, not only accepted the view of the biblical text that the Canaanites were wicked, but argued that this debased and degenerate culture needed to be replaced by one that was morally superior. 'From the impartial standpoint of a philosopher of history', he observed, 'it often seems necessary that a people of markedly inferior type should vanish before a people of superior potentialities, since there is a point beyond which racial mixture cannot go without disaster' (1940: 214). Indeed, he even went on to claim that it was fortunate for the faith of Israel that the annihilation of the indigenous population took place, for the Israelite 'decimation of the Canaanites prevented the complete fusion of the two kindred folk which would almost inevitably have depressed Yahwistic standards to a point where recovery was impossible' (1940: 214). It seems astonishing that one of the leading biblical scholars of the twentieth century should imply that ethnic cleansing was a legitimate means of ensuring the religious and cultic purity of Israel. Even his pupil, John Bright, found himself desperately trying to downplay the abhorrence of the conquest narrative by emphasizing that 'the *herem* was applied only in the case of certain Canaanite cities that resisted' (1972: 138–9), as though that made everything alright!

More recently, Christopher Wright has similarly sought to defend the biblical text on the grounds that had the Israelites not annihilated the Canaanites, Israel's distinctiveness would have been severely compromised. Like Albright, he accepts without question the biblical view that the Canaanite culture was 'degraded to the point of deserving divine punishment' (2008: 106), and he proceeds to argue that this places the conquest narrative within a moral framework that distinguished it

---

10. I have argued elsewhere that the dialectical, disputatious element in Israel's faith can be regarded as providing a warrant for contemporary readers to question the morality of the biblical text (E.W. Davies 2010: 120–38). As Tod Linafelt has observed, by reading 'against the grain' of the biblical text, we merely 'engage in the quintessential Jewish activity of contending with God' (1992: 111).

from ethnocentric genocide or from violence inflicted in an arbitrary or malevolent way. Indeed, he accepts the Bible's verdict that the conquest of Canaan was 'an act of warranted judgment' (p. 107) on a people whose religion had become debased and whose life had become corrupt. Such expositions of the text seem crude and inexcusable and serve as a salutary reminder that there is such a thing as *unethical* ethical criticism. If the argument of the present chapter is accepted, the choice will be not whether or not to practice ethical criticism; rather, it will be whether we do so well or badly.

In what follows, an attempt will be made to apply ethical criticism to the character of Yahweh as depicted in two texts in 2 Samuel (12:7-25; 24:1-17)

The Character of Yahweh in 1 and 2 Samuel

Biblical scholars are by no means agreed as to the extent and prominence of Yahweh's role in 1 and 2 Samuel. Some regard these books as rather secular in outlook,[11] arguing that the characters are free to act as they please and that their fates are determined by the natural working of retribution.[12] In his detailed study of the so-called Succession Narrative (2 Sam. 9–20; 1 Kgs 1–2), Norman Whybray noted that there were comparatively few references in these chapters to Yahweh's activity, and he claimed that the events described witnessed to God's 'unseen control of human destiny through the natural course of events rather than through direct intervention' (1968: 66). K.L. Noll argued that Yahweh, far from being the focus of the story, 'was only the narrative necessity required for the thematic development of the plot' (1999: 39). David Gunn also warned against exaggerating the significance of the few passages in the books

---

11. K.L. Noll, for example, comments that 'if it is not too anachronistic, one could describe the story as essentially 'secular', or as secular as one could expect to find in an ancient Palestinian context. All elements of the tale, including the religious one, converge on the person of David, whose characterization serves a kind of 'humanistic', not theocentric, interest' (1997: 50). Elsewhere, Noll states that 1 and 2 Samuel are 'as secular as pre-Hellenistic Jewish literature could possibly be' (1999: 39). See, further, Tucker 1971: 37-8; Barton 2003: 61.

12. Klaus Koch (1983) argued in favour of the existence in the Hebrew Bible of the notion of an impersonal force in which consequences flow automatically from actions without divine intervention; deeds carried within themselves the seeds of their own consequence (*Tat-Ergehen Zusammenhang*) without the intervention of Yahweh as an outside agent.

of Samuel that imply Yahweh's intervention in human affairs (such as 2 Sam. 11:27b; 12:24; 17:14). According to Gunn, such texts merely add a providential dimension to the biblical account, and hardly warrant von Rad's claim (1966: 198–202) that Yahweh is the prime focus of interest in the story.[13]

However, such attempts to downplay Yahweh's role in the books of Samuel must be seriously questioned, for while it is true that he does not intervene directly in human affairs through dreams and visions, prophetic oracles and theophanies, there can be little doubt that his activity was regarded as having a determinative effect on the events being narrated.[14] The ominous comment in 2 Sam. 11:27b to the effect that David had 'done evil in the sight of the LORD', and Yahweh's rebuke of the king through the prophet Nathan ('you have despised me'; 12:10) clearly imply that the subsequent events that befall David and his extended family were not the result of some impersonal nemesis but the outworking of God's retributive justice. It is Yahweh who exercises ultimate control over what happens in the story: it is he who causes the death of David's illegitimate child in 12:16-23, and it is he who claims to be responsible for the calamities that were to befall David's family (12:11-12).

The tendency to downplay Yahweh's involvement in the story of David has often resulted in a failure on the part of commentators to provide a sustained critique of God as a character in the story.[15] While scholars have

---

13. Gunn 1978: 138 n. 9. For a different view, however, see James A. Wharton, who argues that von Rad was surely correct when he insisted that we pay special attention to the admittedly rare editorial asides in which the author declares Yahweh to have been at work in the story (1981: 347).

14. As Stephen Chapman has observed in his study of the role of Yahweh in 1 and 2 Samuel, just because God 'is literarily off-stage or not explicitly portrayed in a narrative episode does not mean that the narrative considers God absent or uninvolved. The narrative is all about God, all the way along' (2020: 41). A similar point is made by Barbara Green with regard to 1 Sam. 12: 'The deity participates intermittently in this narrative but implicitly and by convention is not to be understood as absent or uninvolved even when not acting tangibly and directly' (2017: 198). In his commentary on 1 and 2 Samuel, Walter Brueggemann warns against disregarding the 'hidden governance of God' and argues that exegetes must take seriously 'the inscrutable presence of Yahweh' throughout the story (1990: 3). See, also, Brueggemann 1972: 9–19.

15. As Deryn Guest has noted, while character studies have been a staple of narrative approaches to the Hebrew Bible, Yahweh seldom makes an appearance in them (2016: 184). The failure of scholars to take seriously God's function as a character in the story may be due, in no small measure, to the skill of the biblical narrators. Details which are commonly associated with other characters – such as physical

been quite prepared to comment on the immorality of David's behaviour in 2 Samuel 11, they have been noticeably more reticent to comment on the questionable nature of the divine punishment inflicted upon him by Yahweh in the following chapter. Indeed, there almost seems to have been something of a conspiracy of silence among scholars when it comes to passing judgment on Yahweh's involvement in the narrative, especially when his actions do not conform to human notions of right behaviour. Biblical scholars in theological faculties, and even some academics in secular institutions, have been so in thrall to the concept of God as a sacrosanct, transcendent being, who exists above and beyond the realm of the text, that they have failed to take Yahweh's 'literary' status seriously.[16] The fact is, however, that the God of biblical narrative is a complex literary creation who must be subject to the same kind of sustained ethical scrutiny as any other biblical character.[17]

Once critical evaluation of God's character is taken seriously and put under the spotlight, it soon emerges that there are some deeply troubling aspects to his behaviour, for even a quick perusal of the Hebrew Bible testifies to the fact that he does not always act in accord with the principles of common human morality.[18] For what kind of God is it that promises Abram many descendants only to then command him to sacrifice his

appearance, social status, personal history – are, for obvious reasons, conspicuous by their very absence when it comes to portraying the deity, and so readers are persuaded that God cannot be viewed in similar terms to other characters in the story. As Meir Sternberg has observed regarding the material aspects of God's existence, nothing is told because there is nothing to tell (1985: 323).

16. This point has been particularly emphasized by Danna Fewell and David Gunn (1993: 18–19), and by Marti J. Steussy (2000: 128). In a similar vein, David Clines has pointed out that the deity portrayed in biblical narratives is not 'the God of Christian worship and theology' (1995a: 202). Gunn (1990: 61–2) has criticized Sternberg's *The Poetics of Biblical Narrative* because of its failure to draw a distinction between 'God as character' and the 'God of faith', a failure which he regards as constituting a major source of confusion in Sternberg's work.

17. A different view is advocated by John Barton, who emphasizes the inscrutability of Yahweh and claims that 'God is not susceptible to human judgment on his actions, and they cannot be classified as moral or immoral; they are simply God's actions' (2010: 133). This, however, seems to be an abdication of the scholar's responsibility to apply ethical criticism to God's words and actions as presented in the text.

18. David Gunn has argued that biblical scholars should not shy away from challenging the moral probity of God as depicted in the Hebrew Bible, and he notes that 'Christian readings are particularly prone to a glib side-stepping of this issue in the interests of a cleaned-up, morally tidy, divinity' (1997: 553).

only son (Gen. 12:2-3; 22:2)?[19] What kind of God is it who is prepared to punish indiscriminately the innocent as well as the guilty (Gen. 18:22-33; Job 9:22; Lam. 2:20; 3:34-36)? What kind of God is it who appears more concerned about his own reputation than about the welfare of his people (Num. 14:13-19)? And what kind of God is it who commands his people to annihilate completely the native inhabitants of Canaan (Deut. 20:16-18: Josh. 10:40)? Of course, what Norman Whybray (2000: 2) and David Gunn (1980: 129) refer to as the 'dark side' of God's involvement with humans should not be overemphasized, for the positive aspects – his mercy, faithfulness and steadfast love – clearly outnumber the negative features of his character as portrayed in the Hebrew Bible.[20] Nevertheless, it cannot be denied that divine intervention in the Hebrew Bible is by no means always viewed as a comforting experience for the characters concerned, and there are certainly aspects of Yahweh's activity that are distasteful to modern sensibilities, not the least of which are the narratives that imply that God does not always act in accord with the principles of common human morality. Such narratives often serve to disorient their readers, violating their sense of justice: the deeply ingrained human instinct that requires God to act justly is destabilised, and readers are forced to recognize that he does not always grant the virtuous their reward or the villainous their comeuppance.[21]

19. Fewell and Gunn argue that in the episode concerning the sacrifice of Isaac, Yahweh is, at best, 'simply unfathomable'; at worst, he is 'depraved and sadistic' (1993: 53). As Mary Mills has observed, the fact that God utters such a command, and that Abram acquiesces without demur, suggests that neither emerge from the story with their reputations untarnished (2001: 38).

20. It was, at least in part, the negative aspects of Yahweh's character that led Marcion in the second century CE to reject the Hebrew Bible as Christian Scripture and to deny the identity of its God with the God of Christianity. In more recent times, these aspects of God's character have provided useful ammunition for the so-called new atheists, who have happily exploited such texts to point to the malign influence of the Hebrew Bible on contemporary society and in doing so have perpetuated its stereotype as a predominantly violent book. For a considered and spirited defence of the Hebrew Bible against the attacks of the new atheists, see Katharine Dell 2017.

21. For discussions of passages in the Hebrew Bible where God appears to be depicted in an immoral or amoral way, see Whybray 1996, 2000; P.J. Williams 2007; Barton 2010; and for a discussion of the problematic nature of God in the books of Samuel, see Steussy 2000; Chapman 2020. Some have sought to put a positive gloss on passages that appear to impugn God's character (cf. Kaiser 1983: 247–69), though such attempts have not generally been persuasive (cf. Rogerson 2000: 121–2).

When we turn specifically to narratives contained in 1 and 2 Samuel, the way in which Yahweh often interacts with humans to bring about his desired ends is often highly questionable from the moral point of view.[22] He desires to kill Eli's disobedient sons (1 Sam. 2:25) and he brings an 'evil' spirit upon Saul (1 Sam. 16:14-16; 18:10) and incites him to commit an evil act (1 Sam. 19:9-10); he turns the wise counsel of Ahithophel to folly so that he might bring ruin upon Absalom (2 Sam. 17:14); he instructs Samuel to deceive any inquirers by causing them to believe that he was going to Jerusalem to offer a sacrifice rather than to anoint a rival king (1 Sam. 16:1-5); he kills Nabal (1 Sam. 25:38), and he strikes Uzzah dead simply because he had tried to prevent the ark from falling to the ground and being defiled (2 Sam. 6:6-7). Questions might even be raised concerning the wisdom of Yahweh's choice of David as his anointed, for the very one singled out by him as the founder of an enduring dynasty, and described as a man 'after God's own heart' (1 Sam. 13:14), is reduced to committing adultery and is the architect of the murder of one of his loyal soldiers.[23] As David Gunn has remarked, Yahweh may well be displeased with David, but 'ultimately, he must bear some measure of responsibility; David is the one whom he has chosen and protected, and will continue to protect (17:14)' (1975: 20; 1978: 98). Indeed, it is by no

22. Marti J. Steussy estimates that about three-fifths of God's reported actions in 1 and 2 Samuel are accomplished by destructive action (2000: 135), and she concludes that 'God engages in smiting and terror far more often than healing or encouragement' (p. 136).

23. K.L. Noll notes that 'Yahweh, as a story-world character, has not proven to be the most reliable judge of character', and on the basis of various incidents in 1 and 2 Samuel, he claims that 'the reader has learned to reserve judgment concerning the reliability of Yahweh's judgment' (1997: 52). Randall Bailey similarly views God's choice of Samuel, Saul and David as somewhat questionable, and asks: 'Is Yhwh one who chooses less than competent people?' (1995: 222). He points to Yahweh's admission of regret for choosing Saul in 1 Sam. 15:10-11, and views this as a clear indication that 'Yhwh makes mistakes in choosing leaders' (p. 225). April Westbrook claims that 'the reader must recognize the uncomfortable idea that YHWH's choice of a person to be king does not necessarily guarantee that he will always follow right motives, decisions and actions – a concept already proven by the character of Saul, who was, himself, a king chosen by YHWH (1 Sam. 10:1-25)' (2015: 53). Terence Fretheim seeks to overcome the theological problem by arguing in favour of a concept which he claims permeates much of the thought of the Hebrew Bible, namely, that of limited divine foreknowledge; on this basis, he contends that it should not be assumed that God could clearly predict what the outcome of Saul's kingship would be, for he 'could see only the possibilities' (1985: 599–600).

means clear why David is deemed worthy of divine patronage and, in view of the king's egregious behaviour, 'the reader wonders why, given the offenses of David, Yahweh's patience does not end, and his patronage of the hero cease' (Noll 1997: 45). David may well have been, in Walter Brueggemann's words, Yahweh's 'trusted creature' (1969), but was his trust misplaced? Admittedly, both David and Saul had major flaws, but, all in all, might Saul not have been the better choice to be the founder of an enduring dynasty?[24]

In what follows we will focus on two narratives in which the integrity and morality of Yahweh must be called in question, for both passages appear to undermine the most basic belief in the essential justice and goodness of God. In 2 Samuel 12, Yahweh determines to punish David for his adultery with Bathsheba and for orchestrating the murder of Uriah, her husband; yet, it is David's family, rather than David himself, who are made to bear the brunt of the punishment. In 2 Samuel 24, Yahweh instructs David to take a census of the people only then to inflict a dire punishment upon the nation simply because David obeyed the divine command. In the former narrative, we witness the action of a vindictive God whose punishment appears entirely disproportionate to the offences committed; in the latter, we are introduced to an arbitrary and capricious deity whose intemperate behaviour runs completely counter to the general human understanding of what seems right and proper. Such texts imply, at the very least, that God is 'on the wrong side of a moral divide' (P.J. Williams 2007: 175).

The Character of Yahweh in 2 Samuel 12:7-25

2 Samuel 11 depicts David's affair with Bathsheba and his bungled attempt to cover up for his misdemeanour by having Uriah, her husband, killed in battle. In ch. 12, Nathan, the prophet, announces that the divine punishment for David's crimes will be far-reaching in its effect, for although it was David who had sinned, it was his descendants who would

---

24. Noll opines that 'if the reader is compelled to choose between Yahweh's first two human kings, no doubt judgment will fall with Saul, who seems more worthy for the throne than David' (1997: 45). This view is shared by others; see, e.g., Thomas R. Preston, who claims that in the rise and fall of Saul the narrator has created 'the story of a tragic hero who towers above the man who will displace him, David' (1982: 31). Cheryl Exum similarly views Saul as a 'towering figure', far superior to David (1992: 142–3).

have to pay the price. David's family would henceforth be under the sword (vv. 10-12), since it was by the sword (albeit that of the Ammonites, v. 9b) that David had struck Uriah the Hittite. The following chapters recount how David's family were caught up in the cycle of violence occasioned by his sin. The taking of Bathsheba and the murder of Uriah are replayed, with various permutations, in David's family: one of his sons rapes one of his daughters; that son is then killed by another son, who then attempts to seize his father's throne; this, in turn, leaves the door open for two more sons to compete for the throne, and for one to murder the other in order to secure his position.[25] In brief, the account of David's family turns out to be a long tale of conspiracy, internecine struggle and murder, and the story of the founding of a great dynasty now becomes, paradoxically, the story of the fall of that dynasty. But if the punishment for killing Uriah had far-reaching consequences, the punishment imposed by Yahweh for David's act of adultery with Bathsheba sounds equally ominous: 'I will take your wives before your eyes, and give them to your neighbour, and he shall lie with your wives in the sight of this very sun. For you did it secretly, but I will do this thing before all Israel, and before the sun' (12:11b-12). Since David had committed adultery in private, others will lie with his wives in public, for all to see, a prophecy that was fulfilled in the subsequent behaviour of Absalom towards David's harem in 2 Sam. 16:20-22.[26]

Now any objective assessment of this sorry episode would surely have to conclude that the punishment imposed by Yahweh was completely out of proportion to the wrongs committed.[27] Yet, remarkably, many

---

25. Cheryl Exum draws a contrast between the fate of Saul's sons and that of the sons of David. In the former case, Saul's children suffer simply because they belonged to a fated house and thus, in a sense, theirs was an 'hereditary guilt', but David's children contributed to his tragedy by re-enacting his sins as part of his punishment (1992: 70).

26. According to 2 Sam. 16:22, a tent was pitched on the palace roof, where Absalom had sex with his father's concubines. They, in turn, would suffer not only the indignity of being raped in public ('in the sight of all Israel') but would have to face the dire consequence, which was to be 'shut up until the day of their death, living as if in widowhood' (2 Sam. 20:3).

27. Randall Bailey questions whether the punishment inflicted upon David was right and appropriate, and questions the morality of Yahweh's behaviour: 'The reader is left with a vindictive deity who waited until after the death of Uriah to intervene and is then going to have other wives pay the price' (1995: 229). Cheryl Exum agrees that Yahweh's punishment for the David–Bathsheba affair seems 'savage' and even

commentators appear to blandly assume that in this case the punishment fits the crime. That the blood-stained sword will reappear time and time again throughout the later history of David's family is regarded as condign punishment for the appalling actions which David committed in respect of Bathsheba and her husband. Indeed, William McKane (1963: 234) sees here an example of the operation of the principle of the *lex talionis*, whereby the punishment fits the crime, a view echoed by Robert Gordon, although he concedes that, in this instance, the principle is rather 'taken to the limit' (1986: 258). Walter Brueggemann concurs that 'the sentence fits the affront', although he admits that 'one might not expect one single act and its cover-up to hover so ominously and for so long' (1990: 281). Even the notion that David's wives would be raped by another on account of his adultery fails to excite the ire of commentators; on the contrary, they not only raise no protest at the injustice of the punishment but appear to positively condone the type of punishment imposed. Thus, John Mauchline states that the open shame that is to befall David's wives is a 'fit penalty' for the secret act of shame which he committed with Bathsheba (1971: 254). H.W. Hertzberg similarly views Yahweh's words in 12:11-12 as a 'fitting punishment' for David's adultery, and he even claims that in this episode 'God's righteousness is clearly shown forth' (1964: 314).

The incident related in 12:15b-23 indicates that a further punishment would be inflicted upon David, and one that would involve his immediate family. In 2 Sam. 12:13a, David confesses his guilt, and Nathan assures him that God has put away his sin (v. 13b). What follows, however, entails a serious ethical conundrum, for while God determines that the sinful king will live, he pronounces that the innocent child must die.[28] According to the law, the death penalty was the prescribed punishment for adultery, but the death penalty was intended for the perpetrator of the adultery, not for the innocent child born of the union.[29] Furthermore, the law stated that children should not be put to death for their parent's crimes, only for their own (Deut. 24:16). It is David who is culpable

'perverse', and she claims that, in the series of unmitigated disasters that befall David's house, we witness the 'hostile transcendence that accompany David's guilt' (1992: 141–2).

28. The child's death appears to be a case of visiting the sins of the fathers upon the children (Exod. 20:5), an idea contradicted explicitly in Ezek. 18.

29. The penalty for adultery in ancient Israel was death (Deut. 22:22), though whether this penalty was ever carried out in practice is by no means certain; see Henry McKeating 1979.

but – far from being punished – he appears to be rewarded by Yahweh by having Bathsheba as his wife and by having another child whom God 'loves'.[30] The basic injustice is well summarized by Norman Whybray: 'The impression of David which is left with the reader is of a man who, whether by luck or providence, survived the consequences of his own blundering and folly to end his days in the enjoyment of a success and achievement which he did not deserve' (1968: 49). In a similar vein, David Gunn asks, not unreasonably, why the most notorious episode in David's life is rewarded with the gift of an heir?[31] Surprisingly, however, most commentators seem unperturbed by the injustice of the incident. The child 'has, as it were, been accepted as a sacrifice', says Hertzberg, and so David can emerge from the incident both 'judged and redeemed' (1964: 316).[32] John Mauchline concurs that, with the death of the child, the penalty for David's sin has been paid (1971: 256). That David's punishment should be transferred to the child is clearly both theologically and ethically problematic; yet it is a problem that most commentators seem reticent to address.[33] However heinous were David's

---

30. Some scholars suggest that the reward was given 'because of David's repentance' (Childs 1985: 80); however, as Walter Brueggemann (1997: 370) rightly observes, the text says nothing about David repenting or asking for forgiveness, although forgiveness is promptly granted by Yahweh through Nathan (12:13b). Ps. 51, however, which is based on 2 Sam. 12, describes a gesture of deep contrition on the part of David that the narrative lacks, as he becomes fully aware of the magnitude of his misdeeds: 'Wash me thoroughly from my iniquity, and cleanse me from my sin. For I know my transgressions, and my sin is ever before me. Against you, you alone, have I sinned, and done what is evil in your sight, so that you are justified in your sentence and blameless when you pass judgment. Indeed, I was born guilty, a sinner when my mother conceived me' (vv. 2-5). Vivian L. Johnson regards these words as 'a confession of guilt incomparable to any other in the Hebrew Bible' (2009: 39). Interestingly, the words 'against you, you alone, have I sinned' is similar to David's terse statement in 2 Sam. 12:13, 'I have sinned against the LORD'. As R.C. Heard has observed, the effect of such words was to discount the human victims of David's sins, the sin being against God alone (2010: 167–8).

31. Gunn 1978: 110. As Antony Campbell has observed, 'casuistry has to be at its mind-numbing worst to offer a justification for the death of the first child and the favor shown the second' (2005: 118).

32. Cf. Fokkelman (1981: 93), who notes that 'the child dies as a substitute, and God relieves David of his own death sentence'.

33. Cheryl Exum may well be correct when she claims that so much attention is given, both in the narrative itself and by subsequent commentators, to David's

crimes, it must surely be questioned whether the divine punishment in this case was just and appropriate.

Now it is clear that, in the context of ch. 12, ethical criticism must operate on two levels. In the first place, serious questions must be raised concerning the portrait of Yahweh that emerges here. Indeed, in contrast to Yahweh's seemingly vengeful behaviour, David – despite his appalling misdemeanours – now emerges in a positive light, and it is he who comes to occupy the moral high-ground. He seems guiltily aware that the punishment is unjust, and he does what he can to influence God to spare the child's life ('Who knows? The LORD may be gracious to me, and the child may live'; v. 22). David fasts and prays without respite for the sick child and he is consumed with concern for the innocent victim of his sin. But all attempts to placate God and to ward off the threatened loss of the child come to nothing, and his hoped-for intervention by God is in vain. Yahweh had determined that the child should die, and neither David's prayers nor his confession can reverse the divine decision. Sin must inevitably bring retribution in its train, and nothing that David can do or say can absolve him of the consequence of his actions. Realizing that his supplication had not been answered, David accepts God's verdict, and goes to the 'house of the LORD' to worship (12:20).[34] The death of the child brings about a recognition of his own mortality, and the reader's sympathies are enlisted with David as he realizes that the path to the grave is a one-way journey ('I shall go to him, but he will not return to me'; 12:23).[35]

---

unusual behaviour during the child's illness and death (12:16-23), that it has deflected attention from the fact that it was Yahweh who had caused the child to die (1992: 127–49).

34. As many commentators have observed, David's reaction to the death of his child stands in marked contrast to his cynical indifference when he hears of the deaths of other soldiers besides Uriah (11:25). Fokkelman regards his changed attitude as an indication of 'how thoroughly Nathan's intervention has worked' (1981: 91).

35. Some have suggested that the fact that David was able to pragmatically resume his normal activities and abandon his grieving as soon as the child had died casts doubt on the genuineness of his remorse. Leo Perdue asks: 'Are these the words of a grief-stricken father, or of a callous ruler realizing he had failed to negate Nathan's prophecy predicting trouble from the king's own house, a prediction whose initial sign was the death of the child?' (1984: 77). David Clines takes a similar view, arguing that David fasts and prays only because he believes he can affect God's determination of the outcome; as soon as the child dies David realizes that he has been defeated and 'abandons his weapon of a self-serving piety' (1995a: 230). This, however, seems to be an overly cynical view of David's behaviour.

On another level, ethical criticism must raise questions concerning the way in which interpreters have dealt with this episode in David's life. They have demonstrated a surprising propensity to suppress any misgivings they may have felt about the injustice of the punishment imposed by Yahweh and have even sought to defend the indefensible.[36] How can commentators possible affirm that the raping of David's wives by his neighbour is a 'fitting punishment' for his sin?[37] There seems to be an assumption that God's punishment is just and deserved but, in truth, is this the kind of justice that is worth preserving (cf. Linafelt 1992: 108)?

The Character of Yahweh in 2 Samuel 24:1-17

The narrative contained in 2 Sam. 24:1-17 raises further questions concerning Yahweh's seemingly irrational actions and provides a further example of the 'demonic or vicious side to his behaviour' (Whybray 2000: 1). The chapter begins ominously by stating that 'the anger of the LORD was kindled against Israel' (v. 1), though the cause of Yahweh's displeasure is not made clear. As a form of punishment, God incites David to take a census of the people of Israel and Judah, and David obeys, instructing a reluctant Joab and the commanders of his army to number them (v. 2).[38] David recognizes, belatedly, that taking a census was a sin against God, and he is filled with remorse, praying that Yahweh might 'take away the

---

36. David R. Blumenthal is particularly critical of attempts to censor passages that seem to our advanced ethical consciousness to be unpalatable: 'to censor them out because they are not "ethical" is to limit our understanding of the complexity of human and divine existence' (1993: 245).

37. Tod Linafelt suggests that, due to the androcentric nature of biblical interpretation, commentators have usually ignored the injustice perpetrated against women in 2 Sam. 12:11, and they seem 'reticent to deal with the implications of this for the character of Yhwh' (1992: 108).

38. A census was usually taken either for taxation purposes, or in connection with the allocation of land or, as here, to determine the strength of the national militia. The result of the census is recorded in v. 9: the number of soldiers 'able to draw the sword' in Israel was 800,000, and the number in Judah amounted to 500,000. As many commentators have observed, the numbers are clearly exaggerated, for they would imply a total population in excess of five million (cf. A.A. Anderson 1989: 285; Gordon 1986: 319). The number of those registered for Israel appears larger still in 1 Chron. 21:5, which records 1,100,000, whereas the number for Judah, 470,000, is slightly less. On the large numbers in the census returns recorded in the Hebrew Bible, see E.W. Davies 1995: 449–69; 2017: 49–53.

guilt of your servant, for I have done very foolishly' (v. 10).³⁹ But David's remorse is disregarded, and his plea goes unheeded; consequently, he must accept the punishment ordained by Yahweh. The nature of that punishment is communicated through the prophet Gad, who, rather bizarrely, lets David choose the type of punishment to be inflicted: either three years of famine in the land,⁴⁰ or three months during which David must flee from his enemies, or three days of pestilence. The reading of MT does not contain a record of the punishment chosen by David, though he appears to decide against the second option, anxious to avoid punishment by a human agency ('let me not fall into human hands'; v. 14). He thus leaves it to Yahweh to decide between the first and third options, and Yahweh opts for the third, sending a pestilence on Israel 'from that morning until the appointed time', whereupon 70,000 of the people died (v. 15).⁴¹ When the angel of the Lord stretches out his hand to destroy Jerusalem, however, Yahweh relents, and no further destruction takes place (v. 16).

There are clearly profound ethical (as well as theological) issues at stake in this episode, not the least of which is the portrait of a seemingly irrational deity who is intent upon punishing David for conducting the very census which he had commanded him to take.⁴² Biblical commentators have usually been at pains to put a positive gloss on the account, playing down the element of divine unpredictability. William McKane, for example, merely makes a passing reference to the 'quaint theology'(!) of v. 1 (1963: 302), while A.A. Anderson argues that the significance of the

---

39. The census was probably regarded as sinful because it implied a lack of trust in Yahweh's ability to conquer the enemy, relying instead on the human resources at one's disposal. That census-taking could therefore have unpleasant consequences is reflected in Exod. 30:11-12, where payment of a ransom is made to avert a plague.

40. The NRSV follows LXX and 1 Chron. 21:12 by reading 'three years' of famine instead of the MT's 'seven years'. Given that the number 'three' appears in connection with the other two alternatives, the emendation seems entirely plausible, and it may gain further support if, as some suggest, there is a covert allusion to the three years of famine in 2 Sam. 21:1.

41. While the MT refrains from stating what David's choice was, the LXX states that he chose the pestilence option, and adds that the incident occurred during the time of the wheat harvest. The phrase rendered by NRSV 'until the appointed time' is difficult; it cannot mean the end of the three-day period, since the pestilence had ended before that. The LXX reads 'until the time of the evening meal' (hence NEB's 'the hour of dinner'), a reading favoured by Kyle McCarter (1984: 506).

42. The irrational nature of God's command and his punishment of the people is well expressed by David Penchansky: 'It was the will of YHWH that YHWH's people violate the will of YHWH! And then when they obeyed the will of YHWH by sinning, YHWH punished them for violating the divine will!' (1999: 44).

account for all later generations is that it offers 'a model whereby deliverance may become a possibility, even a reality through the mercy of God' (1989: 287). But the accolade for providing the most sanitized version of the episode must surely go to Walter Brueggemann, for he unashamedly seeks to brush the unsavoury aspects of the episode under the carpet. According to him, the unexplained anger of God in v. 1, the options of divine punishment in vv. 11-13, and the description of the destroying angel sent and then recalled in v. 16, are merely distractions from the main point of the account; the focus should rather be on David's confession of sin and acknowledgment of his own foolishness in vv. 10, 17, and on God's mercy and readiness to repent in vv. 14, 16.[43]

Such attempts to salvage God's reputation are, of course, by no means new. Even the Chronicler was evidently offended by the idea of attributing to Yahweh the command to conduct a census for which Israel would subsequently be punished, for 1 Chron. 21:1 attributes the command to Satan. There can be little doubt, however, that in the passage as it stands in 2 Sam. 24:1-17, it is God who both commands David and punishes the people, actions that appear to be both 'arbitrary and incomprehensible' (Hertzberg 1964: 411). As David Penchansky has observed, 'if a census was a wicked/foolish act, it was wicked and foolish for God to ask for one' (1999: 43). Indeed, Penchansky has argued that this is the most Kafkaesque episode in the entire Hebrew Bible since, as in Kafka's *The Trial*, we find ourselves sympathizing and identifying 'with the bewilderment of the protagonist, who has lost confidence in a fair universe' (p. 35). David emerges in the narrative as the hapless, helpless victim, the instrument of Yahweh's anger, who obeys, suffers and repents for no apparent reason. As in 12:15b-23, it is David, rather than Yahweh, who occupies the moral high-ground in the narrative by protesting that innocent people had been punished for a sin which he had committed: 'I alone have sinned, and I alone have done wickedly; but these sheep, what have they done? Let your hand, I pray, be against me and against my father's house' (v. 17). Attempts to exonerate God by emphasizing his mercy and readiness to halt the angel from bringing destruction upon

---

43. Brueggemann 1990: 354. Other scholars attempt to exonerate the deity by emphasizing the supposed negative traits in David's character as exemplified in this chapter. Thus, he is variously described as boastful, proud and guilty of the sins of self-aggrandizement, self-reliance and self-sufficiency. However, as Stuart Lasine has pointed out, the text of 2 Sam. 24 offers little or no direct evidence to support this negative view of David, and he wonders whether such attempts simply reflect the desire of readers to justify God 'by condemning the humans with whom God interacts' (2012: 221).

Jerusalem rather overlook the fact that this is said to have happened not so that the inhabitants of the city could be spared[44] but simply to ensure that the threshing floor of Araunah the Jebusite would not be polluted.[45]

At this point it seems propitious to consider why such a story should have been told and preserved? Why would the biblical narrators, in their imaginative reconstruction of God's character, want to present him as such an arbitrary, unpredictable, and morally questionable deity? Ancient readers of the story would no doubt have been familiar with other accounts in which God lashes out in understandable outrage at the sinfulness of his people, but in this case there is no indication that Israel had done anything wrong, and no explanation is provided to account for the divine anger. If God was angry with his people, why was it not made clear to them the reason they were being punished? And why did God not punish them immediately instead of inciting David to sin, thus giving the impression that it was all his fault? Why would he incite David to take a census only then to punish him for having done so? The narrator appears to exhibit no discomfort at presenting Yahweh in such a way; yet, the thought that the

---

44. As Norman Whybray has observed, attempts to justify Yahweh because he mitigated the disaster by making the destroying angel stay his hand are unsatisfactory, since 'it is surely a tardy mitigation that occurs after 70,000 innocent Israelites have already been slaughtered!' (2000: 11). In a similar vein, Marti J. Steussy notes that, however positive a spin is given to the divine action in this narrative, 'we may fairly question whether this particular withdrawal of divine affliction should be credited to God as blessing' (2000: 135).

45. 2 Sam. 24:18-25 states that David bought the threshing floor in order to build an altar to Yahweh, while 1 Chron. 22:6-16 mentions that it was on this threshing floor that Solomon's temple was later to be built. 1 Chron. 21 represents the Chronicler's only negative portrayal of David, and scholars have naturally wondered why this episode should have been included, especially given that the other unflattering traditions concerning David in Samuel–Kings have been deliberately omitted. Most scholars assume that the Chronicler was anxious not to omit an event that was crucial in the founding of the Jerusalem cult, for it was on the basis of this event that the location for the altar and the temple was established. See the bibliography cited by J.W. Wright 1993: 88–9 n. 4. Wright himself offers a different explanation, based on the premise that throughout Chronicles the census is viewed positively as a legitimate means of royal military control. He argues that in 1 Chron. 21:7-15 God smites Israel not because David numbered the people but because Joab refused to complete the census as commanded by David by failing to include Levi and Benjamin in the numbering (v. 6); it was on account of Joab's disobedience to the divinely chosen king rather than because of the census itself that Israel was made to suffer Yahweh's punishment. Even if Wright's argument is accepted, however, the ethical issue remains, for the people are made to suffer through no fault of their own.

world was governed by a seemingly unprincipled deity who was prepared to coerce and manipulate others in order to have his own way must have been apparent both to the narrator and to readers of the narrative. Few could have read the story without contemplating the basic unfairness of the punishment and concluding that God does not always act morally, reasonably or consistently.[46] The story was probably intended to invite a sustained reflection on the character of Yahweh and his involvement in human affairs, and to suggest that the intemperate behaviour of an angry and capricious God should not go unchallenged. It was not without significance that the divine action earned a rebuke from David, who argued that it was wrong that innocent Israelites should be punished because of what he had done: 'I alone have sinned, and I alone have done wickedly; but these sheep, what have they done?' (v. 17). As such, the story may be regarded as part of a theology of protest deeply ingrained in the Hebrew Bible, a theology that acknowledges that the divine behaviour could – and should – occasionally be questioned and challenged, and that God himself could be called to account and reprimanded when he fails to act according to the criteria of basic human justice.[47]

Conclusion

In this chapter we have argued that ethical criticism must become a necessary part of the practice of critical biblical scholarship, even if that means transforming our perception of what that practice entails. The idea that the biblical scholar must adopt a 'neutral' stance towards the text, in an effort to emulate the objective methods of the physical sciences, has been widely questioned (especially by feminist biblical critics), and

---

46. Graeme Auld (2011: 614–15) argues that the punishment recorded in this chapter was entirely appropriate to the offence: David had gloried in the number of his people and is punished by losing many of them. The fact is, however, that the punishment was anything but appropriate, a fact recognized by David himself in his entreaty in v. 17.

47. Stuart Lasine has suggested that the tautology implicit in Yahweh's words to Moses in Exod. 33:19 ('I will be gracious to whom I will be gracious, and will show mercy on whom I will show mercy') may have been intended to portray God as rather cleverly asserting his unaccountability (2016: 469). However, there is no shortage of narratives in the Hebrew Bible in which the divine intervention in human affairs is deemed worthy of critical questioning by the biblical writers. Eli's words to the effect that God 'must do what seems good to him' (1 Sam. 3:18) was probably not regarded as a satisfactory response; indeed, on the contrary, God himself must on occasion be held to account.

the idea that academic respectability demands that our scholarly output should remain descriptive rather than evaluative will hold little sway in this postmodern age. In recent years there has been so much emphasis on appraising the text's historical or literary worth that its ideological and ethical aspects have, to a large extent, been regarded as secondary. While various other forms of biblical criticism have been discussed almost to the point of tedium, ethical criticism has remained the Cinderella of biblical studies. However, once scholars feel able to free themselves from the shackles of the historical-critical approach, which has held sway for most of the twentieth century, there is no reason why they cannot challenge, question and criticize the moral norms enshrined in the text. There is certainly no shortage of passages in the Hebrew Bible that call for moral critique, and if biblical scholarship is not to remain self-centred and self-serving, it must articulate clearly the ethical ramifications of such texts, and the concrete implications of the ideology that they promote.

In order to demonstrate how such a critique might be applied to the Hebrew Bible, the present chapter has focussed on the nature and character of Yahweh as portrayed in 2 Sam. 12:7-25 and 24:1-17. The character of God has not generally been the subject of critical scrutiny, partly no doubt because scholars have too often regarded the figure of God as sacrosanct, and raising awkward questions about the supposedly benign deity of the Jewish and Christian traditions is regarded by many as out of bounds. But once it is recognized that the God of biblical narratives is not to be identified with the transcendent God of religious faith, and that he is no more and no less than a construct of the biblical narrator, there is no reason why interpreters should not confront the problematic character of God as portrayed in the Hebrew Bible, and apply to the deity the same kind of ethical scrutiny that would be applied to all the other characters in the story. Indeed, given that the ethics of the Hebrew Bible is almost entirely religious in character, it is inevitable that the character of God himself should enter into the discussion.

The two narratives discussed in this chapter clearly demonstrate that God's intervention in human affairs was not always marked by justice, equity and reliability; on the contrary, the punishment that he meted out to David's family on account of David's sins, and his annihilation of the people because David had conducted a census which Yahweh himself had commanded, suggest that the deity was more than capable of acting in a capricious manner. That the punishment inflicted by God in these narratives could be imposed indiscriminately without regard to the guilt or innocence of the individuals must have raised disturbing questions in the minds of readers, for it could hardly be denied that there was an unpredictable and irrational aspect to Yahweh's behaviour. Why did David's innocent child have to pay the price for his father's adultery? Why were thousands of Israelites slain because David took a census in response to a divine command? Of course, the presence of such narratives in the Hebrew Bible inevitably raises the question: why was God portrayed is such unflattering terms? Why was such a negative view of the deity not omitted or suppressed by the final editors or by the compilers of the narratives? It is almost as if they *wanted* readers to ponder the unsavoury aspects of God's character, and to consider the obvious disconnect between divine justice and divine retribution. That David himself is depicted as reproaching the deity for inflicting a punishment on the people that was completely undeserved (24:17) would have suggested to the readers that the divine activity could, indeed, be open to human scrutiny, and that doubts could legitimately be raised concerning the nature of God's retribution for human wrongdoing. Belief in God did not entail the abrogation of moral concern, and by inviting its readers to ponder on the divine punishment inflicted on the various characters in such passages as 2 Sam. 12:7-25 and 24:1-17, they may well have been led to discover that Yahweh would prove to be 'the most challenging character of all' (Green 2017: 198).

Chapter 7

CONCLUSION

In this volume we have attempted to provide a 'close reading' of some of the narratives concerning David in 1 and 2 Samuel. These stories have been chosen because they provide a good illustration of how biblical narratives can function in ethical deliberation, for they demonstrate that there are moral problems with no easy solutions and moral complications that cannot easily be resolved. Of course, detailed attention to these stories can be found in the standard commentaries, but the discussion has often been largely concerned with text-critical and historical questions, or with the compositional techniques and literary structure of the text, and this has – perhaps inevitably – led to a failure to appreciate the rich ethical content enshrined in the narratives. Thus, our aim has been to bring a focussed attentiveness to bear on the moral aspects of the stories in an attempt to make readers more receptive to the ethical issues embodied in the text. We have argued that, as narratives concerning issues of moral significance, they demand a particularly vigilant type of reading that is alert to the tone and ambiguity of the text. Consequently, in analysing these narratives, we have given attention to the ambivalence of characterization, the subtleties and ambiguities of plot, the significance of narrative point of view, and how the behaviour of the characters has been evaluated both within the text itself and by subsequent commentators.

The characters encountered in these stories usually reveal themselves through dialogue and especially through their actions, without the imposition of an intrusive authorial 'voice-over'. By deliberately refraining from comment and withholding judgment, the narrator invites readers to do their own reflection on the story and to draw their own conclusions. We are encouraged to explore the ethical dilemmas faced by the characters and to consider whom we should pity and why, which misfortunes are deserved, and which are not. Such decisions are not always easy due to the narrator's technique of leaving ambiguous the motives of the various characters, motives which we, as readers, often wish had been made crystal clear. The tantalisingly brief account of the illicit liaison between David and Bathsheba (2 Sam. 11:2-5), discussed in Chapter 3, provides an excellent example of deliberately cultivated ambiguity on the part of the narrator, for the reader is left to ponder whether Bathsheba should be viewed as the archetypal scheming temptress or as the innocent victim of male lust. The ambiguity present in the narratives not only engages its readers to make moral judgments, but it also encourages them to become actively involved in the events recounted. As readers, we are immediately drawn into the moral tangle of the story, not only by our natural readerly tendency to take sides, identifying with one character against another, but also by our decision as to how we construe the characters, their actions and motivations.

Part of the fascination of the stories we have studied is that they reflect the ambiguities and complexities of human existence. Often the competing values and moral conflicts depicted in the stories are those we might encounter in our daily lives; hence we are able to position ourselves as characters in the story, exploring the ethical dilemmas that they face, and assess various possibilities for ourselves as we consider how we might respond in similar situations. By cultivating our ability to experience vicariously another person's situation, and by picturing ourselves in another person's place, we bring to the text our own hopes, fears and confusions, and begin to reflect on our own lives in light of the stories we read. These stories invite and require identification with the characters, and we can recognize our affinities with them precisely because they are fallible human individuals who share the same needs, emotions and frailties as ourselves. David is certainly not portrayed as a paragon of resplendent virtue (if he were he would be insufferable!); rather, we have an intensely human portrait of a character endeavouring to make the best of life's opportunities and then floundering in a welter of bad decisions, just as we might do. The result is that such narratives elicit in us as readers an acknowledgment of our own flaws and imperfections, for we recognize that the characters encountered exemplify the strengths and weaknesses of the human condition.

Although this volume has focussed on a few isolated incidents in the life of David, our overall evaluation of his character will clearly depend on whether we view the larger expanse of narrative in 1 and 2 Samuel, and allow ourselves to see associations between texts and make retrospective connections. Scholars who have attended to the broader outline of David's life as reflected throughout 1 and 2 Samuel have suggested that it may even be possible to trace a development in his character, though two contrasting views of David have usually emerged (cf. Perdue 1984). According to some, he begins his reign with kindness and magnanimity (showing compassion, for example, to surviving members of the house of Saul; 2 Sam. 9), but with Absalom's death he changes, and the merciful king becomes the ruthless manipulator, the portrait of David thus being one of 'degenerating moral integrity' (Mills 2001: 59). Others contend that he had a ruthless and deceitful streak from the beginning but that he later morphed into the weak, indulgent father, manipulated by his own sons and unable or unwilling to punish or reprimand them for their wrongdoing (cf. 2 Sam. 13:21).

Viewed in this broader context, David emerges as the most complex and elaborately presented of all the characters in the Hebrew Bible, a man full of surprises and contradictions (cf. Bowman 2002). At times he seems sympathetic and compassionate, at times cruel and motivated by a voracious self-interest; at times he is depicted as a formidable warrior and tactical military strategist, at times a foolhardy and deluded king; at times he is politically savvy, shrewd and calculating, at times (especially with regard to his own children) he is weak, indecisive and naïve. In fact, it is difficult to avoid the irony in the portrait of David: the man who refused to harm Yahweh's anointed (1 Sam. 24:6-7; 26:1-25) turns out to be a vicious murderer (1 Sam. 27: 9-12); the man favoured by Yahweh (1 Sam. 13:13-14) turns out to be capable of the most heinous crimes (2 Sam. 8:3-5, 18; 10:18); the man who enjoyed the adulation of his people (1 Sam. 18:6-8; 21:11) turns out to be one who violates the trust and loyalty of his subjects (2 Sam. 11:6-25). The ultimate irony, of course, is that the adulterer and murderer later came to be viewed as the paradigmatic monarch against whom later kings would be measured and found wanting (1 Kgs 15:11; 2 Kgs 18:1-3).

Throughout the volume, Martha Nussbaum has proved to be an insightful and helpful conversation partner, for her study of ancient Greek tragedy and modern fiction has enabled us to explore the moral issues in the narratives in the light of contemporary philosophical concerns. We have attempted to demonstrate how adopting her approach can serve to challenge traditional readings, offer alternative interpretations, and suggest different perspectives on the biblical narrative. For example, we have seen how the morality of lies and deception, loyalty and treachery, exemplified in the stories concerning David, Michal, Jonathan, and Saul in 1 Samuel 19 and 20 (discussed in Chapter 2) can be informed and elucidated by philosophical debates concerning the ethics of loyalty and truth-telling. Such stories leave the reader to ponder whether certain circumstances – such as when an innocent life is threatened – can mitigate or extenuate a lie and remove moral blame, and whether respect for the truth should trump family loyalty and family solidarity. Nussbaum's discussion of the incommensurability of certain values, and the dilemma of establishing priorities between conflicting obligations when there is no loss-free and perhaps even no guilt-free course available, has helped to sharpen and clarify the issues at stake in these two narratives, enabling the interpreter to explore the complexity of moral choices and the repercussions of moral dilemmas from various angles.

Furthermore, Nussbaum's Aristotelian understanding of the role of emotion in reading works of fiction has enriched our interpretation of the narrative contained in 2 Samuel 12 (discussed in Chapter 4). The parable uttered by Nathan clearly plays on the emotion and sentiment of the reader (the lamb was 'like a daughter' to the poor man and 'lay in his bosom'; v. 3), and the emotional impact of the chapter reaches a climax in the account of David's distress during his child's illness and his mourning for his dead son, as he becomes bleakly aware of his own inevitable mortality ('I shall go to him but he will not return to me'; v. 23). Such a story has the capacity to stimulate empathetic understanding on our part as we become emotionally invested in the actions and fate of the character, and by involving ourselves in David's suffering, we learn something of our own emotional repertoire.

Moreover, following the lead of Martha Nussbaum, attention to the details and the particularity of the stories concerning David has served to open up the text to a multiplicity of readings and prevented any temptation to reduce these narratives to moral platitudes or to draw the moral 'message' too simplistically or too narrowly. All too often there has been a tendency to provide a neat, oversimplified account of the ethical conundrums faced by the characters, and to force the text into a narrow moral straitjacket, neglecting its complexities and the various ways it speaks to the reader. Our discussion of David's adultery with Bathsheba and his murder-by-proxy of her husband has served as a salutary reminder that, as we read, we must become alert to various and conflicting possibilities, and eschew the glib analysis and simplistic moralizing that ignores the subtleties of the narrative. Readers who conclude that the moral of the story is merely that adultery and murder are wrong would have to be blunt and unimaginative readers indeed! Such stories defy simple analysis in terms of their message. Indeed, they have been selected for analysis precisely because they resist reduction to a simple moral 'lesson'; rather, they repay re-reading and revisiting time and again in order to tease out the moral import of the text.

There are undoubtedly aspects of the stories concerning David in 1 and 2 Samuel that merit further consideration, not the least of which is the extent to which the characters portrayed are free agents and responsible for their own actions. Do they act as they wish, unconstrained by divine intervention, or is God working providentially behind the scenes? Are the events recorded merely the outworking of an impersonal nemesis or an indication of God's control over human destiny? The account of the rape of Tamar and the death of Amnon (discussed in Chapter 5) raises the question whether the events described in 2 Samuel 13 were the fulfilment of God's punishment announced through the prophet Nathan ('I will raise up trouble against you from within your own house'; 2 Sam. 12:11), in which case Tamar must be regarded as the victim not only of Amnon's lust, but of David's sin and Yahweh's judgment. This inevitably raises uncomfortable questions regarding the conduct of Yahweh as depicted in the narratives of 1 and 2 Samuel. The 'dark side' of his character is evident in the story of the death of David's son (2 Sam. 12:7-25) and in the punishment that was inflicted upon the people because David had conducted a census which Yahweh himself had expressly commanded (discussed in Chapter 6). The fact that God's punishment of innocent Israelites earned a rebuke from David (2 Sam. 24:17) suggests that the divine behaviour could – and should – occasionally be questioned and challenged, and that God himself could be called to account and reprimanded when he failed to act in accordance with the basic principles of human justice. It was argued that the actions of the deity, just like the actions of any other character, must be subjected to sustained analysis, and that ethical criticism must remain firmly on the agenda of the biblical scholar.

The present study has demonstrated that biblical narratives can be an effective vehicle for ethical reflection, and our aim has been to provide some fresh insights and to inspire a more fruitful reading of the text, together with a greater appreciation and deeper understanding of its moral implications. Such stories as those considered in this volume can play a guiding role in moral deliberation as we consider the lessons they wish to impart and the insights they struggle to articulate. Though some of the characters portrayed in 1 and 2 Samuel may be fictional, the way the narrator invests their lives with meaning, and their actions with consequences, invites us to question our own ethical stance and to re-evaluate our own moral conduct. Reading, and thinking reflectively about what we have read, inevitably invites a certain type of self-scrutiny. The stories may induce in us a heightened moral sensibility and alter our moral vision; or they may simply deepen our understanding of what we already know and enrich the knowledge we already possess. As such, they can shape our values and influence our decision-making often in indirect and complex ways, so that, in the words of Martha Nussbaum, reading becomes 'a preparation for life that is lived at one remove from life' (1990: 188).

Bibliography

Abasili, Alexander I. (2011), 'Was it Rape? The David and Bathsheba Pericope Re-examined', *VT* 61: 1–15.
Ackerman, James S. (1990), 'Knowing Good and Evil: A Literary Analysis of the Court History in 2 Samuel 9–20 and 1 Kings 1–2', *JBL* 109: 41–60.
Ackerman, Susan (2005), *When Heroes Love: The Ambiguity of Eros in the Stories of Gilgamesh and David*, New York: Columbia University Press.
Ackroyd, Peter R. (1971), *The First Book of Samuel*, CBC, Cambridge: Cambridge University Press.
Ackroyd, Peter R. (1977), *The Second Book of Samuel*, CBC, Cambridge: Cambridge University Press.
Ackroyd, Peter R. (1981), 'The Succession Narrative (so-called)', *Int* 35: 383–96.
Adler, Jonathan E. (1997), 'Lying, Deceiving or Falsely Implicating', *JPhil* 94: 435–52.
Albright, William Foxwell (1940), *From the Stone Age to Christianity: Monotheism and the Historical Process*, Baltimore: The Johns Hopkins University Press.
Albright, William Foxwell (1946), *Archaeology and the Religion of Israel*, 2nd edn, Baltimore: The Johns Hopkins University Press.
Alter, Robert (1980), 'Sacred History and the Beginnings of Prose Fiction', *Poetics Today* 1: 143–62.
Alter, Robert (1981), *The Art of Biblical Narrative*, London: George Allen & Unwin.
Alter, Robert (1992), *The World of Biblical Literature*, London: SPCK.
Alter, Robert (1999), *The David Story: A Translation with Commentary of 1 and 2 Samuel*, London: W.W. Norton.
Anderson, A.A. (1989), *2 Samuel*, WBC 11, Dallas: Word Books.
Anderson, Lyle V. (1985), 'Moral Dilemmas, Deliberation, and Choice', *JPhil* 82: 139–62.
Andersson, Greger (2009), *Untameable Texts: Literary Studies and Narrative Theory in the Books of Samuel*, LHBOTS 514, London: T&T Clark.
Andrew, Maurice E. (1963), 'Falsehood and Truth: An Amplified Sermon on Exodus 20:16', *Int* 17: 425–38.
Andruska, Jennifer L. (2017), '"Rape" in the Syntax of 2 Sam. 11: 4', *ZAW* 129: 103–9.
Arendt, Hannah (1968), *Between Past and Present: Eight Exercises in Political Thought*, New York: Viking.
Auld, A. Graeme (2011), *I & II Samuel*, OTL, Louisville, KY: Westminster John Knox Press.
Avioz, Michael (2009), 'The Motif of Beauty in the Books of Samuel and Kings', *VT* 59: 341–59.
Bach, Alice (1993), 'Signs of the Flesh: Observations on Characterization in the Bible', *Semeia* 63: 61–79.

Bach, Alice (1997), *Women, Seduction, and Betrayal in Biblical Narrative*, Cambridge: Cambridge University Press.
Bailey, Randall C. (1990), *David in Love and War: The Pursuit of Power in 2 Samuel 10–12*, JSOTSup 75, Sheffield: Sheffield Academic Press.
Bailey, Randall C. (1995), 'The Redemption of YHWH: A Literary Critical Function of the Songs of Hannah and David', *BibInt* 3: 213–31.
Bal, Mieke (1985), *Narratology: Introduction to the Theory of Narrative*, trans. Christine Van Boheemen, Toronto: University of Toronto Press.
Bal, Mieke (1987), *Lethal Love: Feminist Literary Readings of Biblical Love Stories*, Bloomington, IN: Indiana University Press.
Bar-Efrat, Shimon (1980), 'Some Observations on the Analysis of Structure in Biblical Narrative', *VT* 30: 154–73.
Bar-Efrat, Shimon (1989), *Narrative Art in the Bible*, trans. Dorothea Shefer-Vanson, JSOTSup 70, BLS 17, Sheffield: Almond Press.
Barnes, J.A. (1994), *A Pack of Lies: Towards a Sociology of Lying*, Cambridge: Cambridge University Press.
Barr, James (1969), 'The Symbolism of Names in the Old Testament', *BJRL* 52: 11–29.
Barr, James (2006), 'Is God a Liar? (Genesis 2–3) – and Related Matters', *JTS*, NS, 57: 1–22.
Barton, John (1995), 'Reading for Life: The Use of the Bible in Ethics and the Work of Martha C. Nussbaum', in J.W. Rogerson, M. Davies, and M. Daniel Carroll R. (eds), *The Bible in Ethics: The Second Sheffield Colloquium*, 66–76, JSOTSup 207, Sheffield: Sheffield Academic Press.
Barton, John (1998), *Ethics and the Old Testament*, London: SCM Press.
Barton, John (2000), 'Disclosing Human Possibilities: Revelation and Biblical Stories', in G. Sauter and J. Barton (eds), *Revelation and Story: Narrative Theology and the Centrality of Story*, 53–60, Aldershot: Ashgate.
Barton, John (2003), *Understanding Old Testament Ethics: Approaches and Explorations*, Louisville, KY: Westminster John Knox Press.
Barton, John (2004), 'Dating the "Succession Narrative"', in John Day (ed.), *In Search of Pre-Exilic Israel*, 95–106, JSOTSup 406, London: T&T Clark International.
Barton, John (2010), 'The Dark Side of God in the Old Testament', in K.J. Dell (ed.), *Ethical and Unethical in the Old Testament: God and Humans in Dialogue*, 122–34, LHBOTS 528, London: T&T Clark International.
Barton, John (2014), *Ethics in Ancient Israel*, Oxford: Oxford University Press.
Bar-Yosef, Eitan (2006), '"It's the Old Story": David and Uriah in II Samuel and *David Copperfield*', *MLR* 101: 957–65.
Bechtel, Lyn M. (1994), 'What if Dinah is not Raped (Genesis 34)?', *JSOT* 62: 19–36.
Benton, Robert J. (1982), 'Political Expediency and Lying: Kant vs Benjamin Constant', *JHI* 43: 135–44.
Berlin, Adele (1982), 'Characterization in Biblical Narrative: David's Wives', *JSOT* 23: 69–85.
Berlin, Adele (1994), *Poetics and Interpretation of Biblical Narrative*, Winona Lake, IN: Eisenbrauns.
Bewer, Julius A. (1962), *The Literature of the Old Testament*, 3rd rev. edn, New York: Columbia University Press.
Biddle, Mark E. (2002), 'Ancestral Motifs in 1 Samuel 25: Intertextuality and Characterization', *JBL* 121: 617–38.

Birch, Bruce C. (1988), 'Old Testament Narrative and Moral Address', in G.M. Tucker, D.L. Petersen, and R.R. Wilson (eds), *Canon, Theology, and Old Testament Interpretation: Essays in Honor of Brevard S. Childs*, 75–91, Philadelphia: Fortress Press.

Birch, Bruce C. (1991), *Let Justice Roll Down: The Old Testament, Ethics and Christian Life*, Louisville, KY: Westminster John Knox Press.

Birch, Bruce C. (1998), 'The First and Second Books of Samuel', *The New Interpreter's Bible* 2:949–1383, Nashville: Abingdon Press.

Blenkinsopp, Joseph (1966), 'Theme and Motif in the Succession History (2 Sam. xi. 2ff.) and the Yahwist Corpus', *Volume du Congrès: Genève*, 44–57, VTSup 15, Leiden: Brill.

Blumenthal, David R. (1993), *Facing the Abusing God: A Theology of Protest*, Louisville, KY: Westminster John Knox Press.

Bodi, Daniel (2005), *The Michal Affair: From Zimri-Lim to the Rabbis*, HBM 3, Sheffield: Sheffield Phoenix Press.

Bodi, Daniel (2010), *The Demise of the Warlord: A New Look at the David Story*, HBM 26, Sheffield: Sheffield Phoenix Press.

Bodner, Keith (2005), *David Observed: A King in the Eyes of His Court*, HBM 5, Sheffield: Sheffield Phoenix Press.

Bodner, Keith (2008), *1 Samuel: A Narrative Commentary*, Sheffield: Sheffield Phoenix Press.

Bok, Sissela (1989), *Lying: Moral Choice in Public and Private Life*, 2nd edn, New York: Vintage Books.

Booth, Wayne C. (1983), *The Rhetoric of Fiction*, 2nd edn, Chicago: University of Chicago Press.

Booth, Wayne C. (1988), *The Company We Keep: An Ethics of Fiction*, Berkeley: University of California Press.

Booth, Wayne C. (2006), *The Essential Wayne Booth*, ed. and with an Introduction by W. Jost, Chicago: University of Chicago Press.

Bosworth, David A. (2011), 'Faith and Resilience: King David's Reaction to the Death of Bathsheba's Firstborn', *CBQ* 73: 691–707.

Bovati, Pietro (1994), *Re-establishing Justice: Legal Terms, Concepts and Procedures in the Hebrew Bible*, trans. Michael J. Smith, JSOTSup 105, Sheffield: JSOT Press.

Bowman, Richard G. (2002), 'The Complexity of Character and the Ethics of Complexity: The Case of King David', in W.P. Brown (ed.), *Character and Scripture; Moral Formation, Community, and Biblical Interpretation*, 73–97, Grand Rapids, MI: Eerdmans.

Boyle, Marjorie O'Rourke (2001), 'The Law of the Heart: The Death of a Fool (1 Samuel 25)', *JBL* 120: 401–27.

Brenner, Athalya (2000), 'Introduction', in A. Brenner (ed.), *Samuel and Kings: A Feminist Companion to the Bible*, 13–20, 2nd Series, Sheffield: Sheffield Academic Press.

Bright, John (1967), *The Authority of the Old Testament*, London: SCM Press.

Bright, John (1972), *A History of Israel*, 2nd rev. edn, London: SCM Press.

Brueggemann, Walter (1969), 'The Trusted Creature', *CBQ* 31: 484–98.

Brueggemann, Walter (1972), 'On Trust and Freedom: A Study of Faith in the Succession Narrative', *Int* 26: 3–19.

Brueggemann, Walter (1985), *David's Truth in Israel's Imagination and Memory*, Minneapolis, MN: Fortress Press.

Brueggemann, Walter (1990), *First and Second Samuel*, IBC, Louisville, KY: John Knox Press.

Brueggemann, Walter (1997), *Theology of the Old Testament: Testimony, Dispute, Advocacy*, Minneapolis, MN: Fortress Press.
Brueggemann, Walter (2004), 'Truth-telling as Subversive Obedience', in W.P. Brown (ed.), *The Ten Commandments: The Reciprocity of Faithfulness*, 291–300, Louisville, KY: Westminster John Knox Press.
Camp, Claudia V. (1981), 'The Wise Women of 2 Samuel: A Role Model for Women in Early Israel?', *CBQ* 43: 14–29.
Campbell, Antony F. (2005), *2 Samuel*, FOTL 8, Grand Rapids, MI: Eerdmans.
Carlson, R.A. (1964), *David, the Chosen King: A Traditio-Historical Approach to the Second Book of Samuel*, trans. Eric J. Sharpe and Stanley Rudman, Stockholm: Almqvist & Wiksell.
Carson, Thomas L. (2006), 'The Definition of Lying', *Nous* 40: 284–306.
Carson, Thomas L. (2010), *Lying and Deception: Theory and Practice*, Oxford: Oxford University Press.
Chankin-Gould, J. D'ror et al. (2008), 'The Sanctified "Adulteress" and her Circumstantial Clause: Bathsheba's Bath and Self-Consecration in 2 Samuel 11', *JSOT* 32: 339–52.
Chapman, Stephen B. (2016), *1 Samuel as Christian Scripture: A Theological Commentary*, Grand Rapids, MI: Eerdmans.
Chapman, Stephen B. (2020), 'Worthy to be Praised: God as a Character in Samuel', in K. Bodner and B.J.M. Johnson (eds), *Characters and Characterization in the Book of Samuel*, 25–41, LHBOTS 669, London: Bloomsbury: T&T Clark.
Childs, Brevard S. (1970), *Biblical Theology in Crisis*, Philadelphia: Westminster Press.
Childs, Brevard S. (1985), *Old Testament Theology in a Canonical Context*, London: SCM Press.
Chun, S. Min (2014), *Ethics and Biblical Narrative: A Literary and Discourse-Analytical Approach to the Story of Josiah*, Oxford: Oxford University Press.
Clements, Ronald E. (1999), 'Worship and Ethics: A Re-examination of Psalm 15', in M. Patrick Graham, Rick R. Marrs, and Steven L. McKenzie (eds), *Worship and the Hebrew Bible. Essays in Honour of John T. Willis*, 78–94, Sheffield: Sheffield Academic Press.
Clines, David J.A. (1991), 'Michal Observed: An Introduction to Reading her Story', in David J.A. Clines and Tamara C. Eskenazi (eds), *Telling Queen Michal's Story: An Experiment in Comparative Interpretation*, 24–63, JSOTSup 119, Sheffield: Sheffield Academic Press.
Clines, David J.A. (1995a), *Interested Parties: The Ideology of Writers and Readers of the Hebrew Bible*, JSOTSup 205, Sheffield: Sheffield Academic Press.
Clines, David J.A. (1995b), 'Ethics as Deconstruction, and, the Ethics of Deconstruction', in J.W. Rogerson, M.E. Davies, and M. Daniel Carroll R. (eds), *The Bible in Ethics: The Second Sheffield Colloquium*, 77–106, JSOTSup 207, Sheffield: Sheffield Academic Press.
Coats, George W. (1981), 'Parable, Fable, and Anecdote: Storytelling in the Succession Narrative', *Int* 35: 368–82.
Coats, George W. (1986), 'II Samuel 12:1–7a', *Int* 40: 170–4.
Cobley, Paul (2001), *Narrative*, London: Routledge.
Cohen, H. Hirsch (1965), 'David and Bathsheba', *JBR* 33: 142–8.
Collins, John J. (2005), *The Bible after Babel: Historical Criticism in a Postmodern Age*, Grand Rapids, MI: Eerdmans.
Conee, Earl (1982), 'Against Moral Dilemmas', *PhilRev* 91: 87–97.

Conroy, Charles (1978), *Absalom! Absalom! Narrative and Language in 2 Sam. 13–20*, AnBib 81, Rome: Biblical Institute.

Coxon, Peter W. (1981), 'A Note on "Bathsheba" in 2 Samuel 12, 1-6', *Bib* 62: 247–50.

Crouch, Carly L. (2016), 'Ethics', in J. Barton (ed.), *The Hebrew Bible: A Critical Companion*, 338–55, Princeton: Princeton University Press.

Daube, David (1947), *Studies in Biblical Law*, Cambridge: Cambridge University Press.

Daube, David (1982), 'Nathan's Parable', *NovT* 24: 275–88.

Davies, Eryl W. (1981), *Prophecy and Ethics: Isaiah and the Ethical Traditions of Israel*, JSOTSup 16, Sheffield: JSOT Press.

Davies, Eryl W. (1995), 'A Mathematical Conundrum: The Problem of the Large Numbers in Numbers I and XXVI', *VT* 45: 449–69.

Davies, Eryl W. (2003a), *The Dissenting Reader: Feminist Approaches to the Hebrew Bible*, Aldershot: Ashgate.

Davies, Eryl W. (2003b), 'Reader-Response Criticism and Old Testament Studies', in R. Pope (ed.), *Honouring the Past and Shaping the Future: Religious and Biblical Studies in Wales*, 20–37, Leominster: Gracewing.

Davies, Eryl W. (2005), 'The Morally Dubious Passages of the Hebrew Bible: An Examination of Some Proposed Solutions', *CBR* 3: 197–228.

Davies, Eryl W. (2006), 'The Bible in Ethics', in J.W. Rogerson and J.M. Lieu (eds), *The Oxford Handbook of Biblical Studies*, 732–53, Oxford: Oxford University Press.

Davies, Eryl W. (2010), *The Immoral Bible: Approaches to Biblical Ethics*, London: T&T Clark International.

Davies, Eryl W. (2011), 'The Ethics of the Old Testament: Historical and Literary Approaches', in Alan P.F. Sell (ed.), *The Bible in Church, Academy and Culture; Essays in Honour of the Revd John Tudno Williams*, 44–57, Eugene, OR: Pickwick Publications.

Davies, Eryl W. (2013), *Biblical Criticism: A Guide for the Perplexed*, London: Bloomsbury T&T Clark.

Davies, Eryl W. (2016), 'Political and Advocacy Approaches', in J. Barton (ed.), *The Hebrew Bible: A Critical Companion*, 507–31, Princeton: Princeton University Press.

Davies, Eryl W. (2017), *Numbers: The Road to Freedom*, London: Bloomsbury T&T Clark.

Davies, Eryl W. (2019), 'Litigation: Trial Procedure, Jurisdiction, Evidence, Testimony', in P. Barmash (ed.), *The Oxford Handbook of Biblical Law*, 45–58, Oxford: Oxford University Press.

Davies, Eryl W. (2021a), 'The Ethics of Worship', in Samuel Balentine (ed.), *The Oxford Handbook of Ritual and Worship*, 445–58, Oxford: Oxford University Press.

Davies, Eryl W. (2021b), 'The Moral Vision of the Hebrew Bible: An Examination of some Methodological Issues', in Volker Rabens, Jacqueline N. Grey, and Mariam K. Kovalishyn (eds), *Key Approaches to Biblical Ethics, An Interdisciplinary Dialogue*, 154–70, BIS 189, Leiden: Brill.

Davies, Philip R. (1995), 'Ethics and the Old Testament', in J.W. Rogerson, M.E. Davies, and M. Daniel Carroll R. (eds), *The Bible in Ethics: The Second Sheffield Colloquium*, 164–73, JSOTSup 207, Sheffield: Sheffield Academic Press.

Day, Peggy L. (1989), 'From the Child is Born the Woman: The Story of Jephthah's Daughter', in Peggy L. Day (ed.), *Gender and Difference in Ancient Israel*, Minneapolis, MN: Fortress Press.

Deferrari, Roy J., ed. (1952), Augustine's 'Lying', *Treatises on Various Subjects*, in *Fathers of the Church*, vol. xvi, New York: Fathers of the Church.

Delekat, L. (1967), 'Tendenz und Theologie der David-Salomo-Erzählung', in F. Maas (ed.), *Das ferne und nahe Wort*, 26–36, BZAW 105, Berlin: Alfred Töpelmann.
Dell, Katharine J., ed. (2010), *Ethical and Unethical in the Old Testament: God and Humans in Dialogue*, LHBOTS 528, London: T&T Clark International.
Dell, Katharine J. (2017), *Who Needs the Old Testament? Its Enduring Appeal and Why the New Atheists Don't Get It*, London: SPCK.
Dickens, Charles (1966), *David Copperfield*, ed. Trevor Blount, Harmondsworth: Penguin.
Dijk-Hemmes, Fokkelien van (1989), 'Tamar and the Limits of Patriarchy: Between Rape and Seduction (2 Samuel 13 and Genesis 38)', in M. Bal (ed.), *Anti-Covenant: Counter-Reading Women's Lives in the Hebrew Bible*, 135–56, JSOTSup 81, BLS 22, Sheffield: Almond Press.
Dodd, C. H. (1943), *The Parables of the Kingdom*, rev. edn, London: Nisbet & Co.
Dray, Carol A. (2010), 'Ethical Stance as an Authorial Issue in the Targums', in K.J. Dell (ed.), *Ethical and Unethical in the Old Testament: God and Humans in Dialogue*, 231–54, LHBOTS 528, London: T&T Clark International.
Driver, Samuel R. (1890), *Notes on the Hebrew Text of the Books of Samuel*, Oxford: Clarendon Press.
Eagleton, Terry (1978), *Criticism and Ideology: A Study in Marxist Literary Theory*, London: Verso.
Edelman, Diana V. (1991), *King Saul in the Historiography of Judah*, JSOTSup 121, Sheffield: JSOT Press.
Eissfeldt, Otto (1966), *The Old Testament: An Introduction*, trans. P.R. Ackroyd, Oxford: Basil Blackwell.
Esau, Ken (2006), 'Divine Deception in the Exodus Event?', *Direction* 35: 4–17.
Esler, Philip F. (2011), *Sex, Wives, and Warriors: Reading Old Testament Narrative with its Ancient Audience*, Cambridge: James Clarke.
Esler, Philip F. (2020), 'Abigail: A Woman of Wisdom and Decisive Action', in K. Bodner and B.J.M. Johnson (eds), *Characters and Characterization in the Book of Samuel*, 167–82, LHBOTS 669, London: Bloomsbury T&T Clark.
Exum, J. Cheryl (1992), *Tragedy and Biblical Narrative: Arrows of the Almighty*, Cambridge: Cambridge University Press.
Exum, J. Cheryl (1996), *Plotted, Shot, and Painted: Cultural Representations of Biblical Women*, JSOTSup 215, Sheffield: Sheffield Academic Press.
Exum J. Cheryl (2016), *Fragmented Women: Feminist (Sub)versions of Biblical Narratives*, 2nd edn, London: Bloomsbury T&T Clark.
Fewell, Danna Nolan, ed. (2016), *The Oxford Handbook of Biblical Narrative*, Oxford: Oxford University Press.
Fewell, Danna Nolan, and David M. Gunn (1993), *Gender, Power, and Promise: The Subject of the Bible's First Story*, Nashville: Abingdon Press.
Fish, Stanley E. (1972), *Self-Consuming Artifacts: The Experience of Seventeenth-Century Literature*, Berkeley: University of California Press.
Flanagan, James W. (1972), 'Court History or Succession Document? A Study of 2 Samuel 9–20 and 1 Kings 1–2', *JBL* 91: 172–81.
Fohrer, Georg (1970), *Introduction to the Old Testament*, trans. David Green, London: SPCK.
Fokkelman, Jan P. (1981), *Narrative Art and Poetry in the Books of Samuel: A Full Interpretation based on Stylistic and Structural Analyses, Volume 1: King David (II Sam 9–20 & 1 Kings 1–2)*, SSN 20, Assen, Netherlands: Van Gorcum.

Fokkelman, Jan P. (1986), *Narrative Art and Poetry in the Books of Samuel: A Full Interpretation based on Stylistic and Structural Analyses, Volume 2: The Crossing Fates (1 Sam 13–31 and 2 Sam 1)*, SSN 23, Assen, Netherlands: Van Gorcum.

Fontaine, Carole R. (1986), 'The Bearing of Wisdom on the Shape of 2 Samuel 11–12 and 1 Kings 3', *JSOT* 34: 61–77.

Frankfurt, Harry (2009), 'On Truth, Lies, and Bullshit', in Clancy Martin (ed.), *The Philosophy of Deception*, 37–48, Oxford: Oxford University Press.

Frei, Hans (1974), *The Eclipse of Biblical Narrative: A Study in Eighteenth and Nineteenth Century Hermeneutics*, New Haven: Yale University Press.

Fretheim, Terence E. (1985), 'Divine Foreknowledge, Divine Constancy, and the Rejection of Saul's Kingship', *CBQ* 47: 595–602.

Frymer-Kensky, Tikva (1998), 'Virginity in the Bible', in Victor H. Matthews, Bernard M. Levinson, and Tikva Frymer-Kensky (eds), *Gender and Law in the Hebrew Bible and the Ancient Near East*, 79–96, JSOTSup 262, Sheffield: Sheffield Academic Press.

Fuchs, Esther (2000), *Sexual Politics in the Biblical Narrative: Reading the Hebrew Bible as a Woman*, JSOTSup 310, Sheffield: Sheffield Academic Press.

Garbini, Giovanni (1988), *History and Ideology in Ancient Israel*, London: SCM Press.

Garsiel, Moshe (1993), 'The Story of David and Bathsheba: A Different Approach', *CBQ* 55: 244–62.

Gilmour, Rachelle (2011), *Representing the Past: A Literary Analysis of Narrative Historiography in the Book of Samuel*, Leiden: Brill.

Gilmour, Rachelle (2016), '(Hi)story Telling in the Books of Samuel', in Danna Nolan Fewell (ed.), *The Oxford Handbook of Biblical Narrative*, 192–203, Oxford: Oxford University Press.

Goldingay, John (1995), *Models for Interpretation of Scripture*, Grand Rapids, MI: Eerdmans.

Goldingay, John (2009), *Old Testament Theology, Volume 3: Israel's Life*, Downers Grove, IL: InterVarsity Press.

Good, Edwin M. (1965), *Irony in the Old Testament*, London: SPCK.

Goody, Jack (1969), *Comparative Studies in Kinship*, London and New York: Routledge.

Gordon, Robert P. (1980), 'David's Rise and Saul's Demise: Narrative Analogy in 1 Samuel 24–26', *TynB* 31: 37–64.

Gordon, Robert P. (1986), *I & II Samuel: A Commentary*, Exeter: Paternoster Press.

Gorospe, Athena E. (2007), *Narrative and Identity: An Ethical Reading of Exodus 4*, Leiden: Brill.

Gravett, Sandie (2004), 'Reading "Rape" in the Hebrew Bible: A Consideration of Language', *JSOT* 28: 279–99.

Gray, Mark (1998), 'Amnon: A Chip off the old Block? Rhetorical Strategy in 2 Samuel 13.7-15: The Rape of Tamar and the Humiliation of the Poor', *JSOT* 23: 39–54.

Green, Barbara (2017), *David's Capacity for Compassion: A Literary-Hermeneutical Study of 1–2 Samuel*, LHBOTS 641, London: Bloomsbury T&T Clark.

Gros Louis, Kenneth R.R. (1977), 'The Difficulty of Ruling Well: King David of Israel', *Semeia* 8: 15–33.

Guest, Deryn (2016), 'Judging YHWH in the Book of Judges', in D.N. Fewell (ed.), *The Oxford Handbook of Biblical Narrative*, 180–91, Oxford: Oxford University Press.

Gunkel, Hermann (1987), *The Folktale in the Old Testament*, trans. M.D. Rutter, Sheffield: Almond Press.

Gunn, David M. (1975), 'David and the Gift of the Kingdom (2 Sam 2–4, 9–20, 1 Kgs 1–2)', *Semeia* 3: 14–45.

Gunn, David M. (1976), 'Traditional Composition in the "Succession Narrative"', *VT* 26: 214–29.
Gunn, David M. (1978), *The Story of King David: Genre and Interpretation*, JSOTSup 6, Sheffield: JSOT Press.
Gunn, David M. (1980), *The Fate of King Saul: An Interpretation of a Biblical Story*, JSOTSup 14 Sheffield: JSOT Press.
Gunn, David M. (1987), 'New Directions in the Study of Biblical Hebrew Narrative', *JSOT* 39: 65–75.
Gunn, David M. (1990), 'Reading Right: Reliable and Omniscient Narrator, Omniscient God, and Foolproof Composition in the Hebrew Bible', in D.J.A. Clines, S.E. Fowl, and S.E. Porter (eds), *The Bible in Three Dimensions: Essays in Celebration of Forty Years of Biblical Studies in the University of Sheffield*, 53–64, JSOTSup 87, Sheffield: Sheffield Academic Press.
Gunn, David M. (1997), 'Reflections on David', in A. Brenner and C. Fontaine (eds), *A Feminist Companion to Reading the Bible: Approaches, Methods and Strategies*, 548–66, Sheffield: Sheffield Academic Press.
Gunn, David M., and Danna N. Fewell (1993), *Narrative in the Hebrew Bible*, Oxford: Oxford University Press.
Hagan, Harry (1979), 'Deception as Motif and Theme in 2 Sm 9–20; 1 Kgs 1–2', *Bib* 60: 301–26.
Halberstam, Chaya (2007), 'The Art of Biblical Law', *Prooftexts* 27: 345–64.
Hallo, W.W. (1977), 'New Moons and Sabbaths: A Case-Study in the Contrastive Approach', *HUCA* 48: 1–18.
Halpern, Baruch (2001), *David's Secret Demons: Messiah, Murderer, Traitor, King*, Grand Rapids, MI: Eerdmans.
Hays, Richard B. (1997), *The Moral Vision of the New Testament: A Contemporary Introduction to New Testament Ethics*, London: T&T Clark.
Hazony, Yoram (2012), *The Philosophy of Hebrew Scripture*, Cambridge: Cambridge University Press.
Heard, R.C. (2010), 'Penitent to a Fault: The Characterization of David in Psalm 51', in T. Linafelt, C.V. Camp, and T. Beal (eds), *The Fate of King David: The Past and Present of a Biblical Icon*, 163–74, LHBOTS 500, London: T&T Clark.
Hertzberg, Hans Wilhelm (1964), *I and II Samuel: A Commentary*, trans. J.S. Bowden, OTL, London: SCM Press.
Ho, Craig Y.S. (1999), 'The Stories of the Family Troubles of Judah and David: A Study of their Literary Links', *VT* 49: 514–31.
Homan, Michael M. (1999), 'Booths or Succoth? A Response to Yigael Yadin', *JBL* 118: 691–7.
Honeyman, Alexander M. (1948), 'The Evidence for Regnal Names among the Hebrews', *JBL* 67: 13–25.
Irwin, W.A. (1929), 'Truth in Ancient Israel', *JR* 9: 357–88.
Iser, Wolfgang W. (1971), 'Indeterminacy and the Reader's Response in Prose Fiction', in J. Hillis Miller (ed.), *Aspects of Narrative*, 1–45, New York: Columbia University Press.
Janzen, David (2012), 'The Condemnation of David's "Taking" in 2 Samuel 12:1–14', *JBL* 131: 209–20.
Janzen, Waldemar (1994), *Old Testament Ethics: A Paradigmatic Approach*, Louisville, KY: Westminster John Knox Press.

Jensen, Hans J.L. (1992), 'Desire, Rivalry and Collective Violence in the "Succession Narrative"', *JSOT* 55: 39–59.
Jobling, David (1978), *The Sense of Biblical Narrative*, JSOTSup 7, Sheffield: JSOT Press.
Johnson, Vivian L. (2009), *David in Distress: His Portrait through the Historical Psalms*, LHBOTS 505, London: T&T Clark.
Jones, Gwilym H. (1990), *The Nathan Narratives*, JSOTSup 80, Sheffield: JSOT Press.
Kaiser Jr., Walter C. (1983), *Toward Old Testament Ethics*, Grand Rapids, MI: Zondervan.
Kalmanofsky, Amy (2014), *Dangerous Sisters of the Hebrew Bible*, Minneapolis, MN: Fortress Press.
Kant, Immanuel (1930), *Lectures on Ethics*, London: Methuen.
Kant, Immanuel (1950), 'On a Supposed Right to Lie from Altruistic Motives', in his *Critique of Practical Reason and Other Writings in Moral Philosophy*, ed. and trans. L.W. Beck, Chicago: University of Chicago Press.
Kant, Immanuel (1964), *The Metaphysic of Morals*. Part 2, *The Doctrine of Virtue*, trans. M. Gregor, New York: Harper & Row.
Keefe, Alice A. (1993), 'Rapes of Women/Wars of Men', *Semeia* 61: 79–97.
Kessler, John (2000), 'Sexuality and Politics: The Motif of the Displaced Husband in the Books of Samuel', *CBQ* 62: 409–23.
Kim, Uriah Y. (2008), *Identity and Loyalty in the David Story: A Postcolonial Reading*, HBM 22, Sheffield: Sheffield Phoenix Press.
Kim, Hyun Chul P., and M. Fulgence Nyengele (2003), 'Murder S/he Wrote? A Cultural and Psychological Reading of 2 Samuel 11–12', in Cheryl A. Kirk-Duggan (ed.), *Pregnant Passion: Gender, Sex, and Violence in the Bible*, 95–116, Atlanta, GA: Society of Biblical Literature.
Kirk-Duggan, Cheryl A. (2003), 'Slingshots, Ships, and Personal Psychosis: Murder, Sexual Intrigue, and Power in the Lives of David and Othello', in Cheryl A. Kirk-Duggan (ed.), *Pregnant Passion: Gender, Sex, and Violence in the Bible*, 37–70, Atlanta, GA: Society of Biblical Literature.
Klein, Lillian R. (2003), *From Deborah to Esther: Sexual Politics in the Hebrew Bible*, Minneapolis, MN: Fortress Press.
Koch, Klaus (1983), 'Is there a Doctrine of Retribution in the Old Testament?', in James L. Crenshaw (ed.), *Theodicy in the Old Testament*, 57–87, London: SPCK.
Krause, Martin (1983), '2 Sam. 11: 4 und das Konzeptionsoptimum', *ZAW* 95: 434–7.
Lalleman, Hetty (2004), *Celebrating the Law? Rethinking Old Testament Ethics*, Milton Keynes: Paternoster Press.
Landay, Jerry M. (1998), *David: Power, Lust and Betrayal in Biblical Times*, Berkeley, CA: Seastone.
Lasine, Stuart (2012), *Weighing Hearts: Character, Judgment, and the Ethics of Reading the Bible*, LHBOTS 568, London: T&T Clark International.
Lasine, Stuart (2016), 'Characterizing God in His/Our Image', in D.N. Fewell (ed.), *The Oxford Handbook of Biblical Narrative*, 465–77, Oxford: Oxford University Press.
Lategan, Bernard C. (1985), 'Reference: Reception, Redescription, and Reality', in B.C. Lategan and W.S. Vorster, *Text and Reality: Aspects of Reference in Biblical Texts*, 67–93, Atlanta, GA: Scholars Press.
Leithart, Peter J. (2001), 'Nabal and his Wine', *JBL* 120: 525–7.
Lemche, Niels Peter (1979), 'David's Rise', *JSOT* 10: 2–25.
Lemche, Niels Peter (1998), *The Israelites in History and Tradition*, London: SPCK.
Lemmon, E.J. (1962), 'Moral Dilemmas', *PhilRev* 71: 139–58.

Létourneau, Anne (2018), 'Beauty, Bath and Beyond: Framing Bathsheba as a Royal Fantasy in 2 Sam. 11, 1-5', *SJOT* 32: 72–91.
Levenson, Jon D. (1978), '1 Samuel 25 as Literature and as History', *CBQ* 40: 11–28.
Levenson, Jon D., and Baruch Halpern (1980), 'The Political Import of David's Marriages', *JBL* 99: 507–18.
Linafelt, Tod (1992), 'Taking Women in Samuel: Readers/Responses/Responsibility', in D.N. Fewell (ed.), *Reading Between Texts: Intertextuality and the Hebrew Bible*, 99–113, Literary Currents in Biblical Interpretation, Louisville, KY: Westminster John Knox Press.
Linafelt, Tod (2016), 'Poetry and Biblical Narrative', in D.N. Fewell (ed.), *The Oxford Handbook of Biblical Narrative*, 84–92, Oxford: Oxford University Press.
Lodge, David (1992), *The Art of Fiction Illustrated from Classic and Modern Texts*, London: Penguin.
Long, Burke O. (1985), 'Historical Narrative and the Fictionalizing Imagination', *VT* 35: 405–16.
Macwilliam, Stuart (2009), 'Ideologies of Male Beauty and the Hebrew Bible', *BibInt* 17: 265–87.
Magonet, Jonathan (1997), *The Subversive Bible*, London: SCM Press.
Mahon, James E. (2011), 'The Truth about Kant on Lies', in Clancy Martin (ed.), *The Philosophy of Deception*, 201–24, Oxford: Oxford University Press.
Marcus, David (1986), 'David the Deceiver and David the Dupe', *Prooftexts* 6: 163–71.
Marcus, Ruth B. (1980), 'Moral Dilemmas and Consistency', *JPhil* 77: 121–36.
Martin, Clancy (2009) (ed.), *The Philosophy of Deception*, Oxford: Oxford University Press.
Mauchline, John (1971), *1 and 2 Samuel*, NCB, London: Oliphants.
McCarter Jr., P. Kyle (1980), *I Samuel: A New Translation with Introduction, Notes and Commentary*, AB 8, Garden City, NY: Doubleday.
McCarter Jr., P. Kyle (1981), '"Plots True of False": The Succession Narrative as Court Apologetic', *Int* 35: 355–67.
McCarter Jr., P. Kyle (1984), *II Samuel: A New Translation with Introduction, Notes and Commentary*, AB 9, Garden City, NY: Doubleday.
McConnell, Terrance (1978), 'Moral Dilemmas and Consistency in Ethics', *CJPhil* 7: 269–88.
McKane, William (1963), *I and II Samuel: Introduction and Commentary*, TBC, London: SCM Press.
McKeating, Henry (1979), 'Sanctions against Adultery in Ancient Israelite Society, with some Reflections on Methodology in the Study of Old Testament Ethics', *JSOT* 11: 57–72.
McKenzie, Steven L. (2000), *King David: A Biography*, Oxford: Oxford University Press.
Mein, Andrew (2001), *Ezekiel and the Ethics of Exile*, Oxford: Oxford University Press.
Miller, Gerald R., and James B. Stiff (1993), *Deceptive Communication*, London: Sage Publications.
Miller, J. Hillis (1987), *The Ethics of Reading: Kant, de Man, Eliot, Trollope, James, and Benjamin*, New York: Columbia University Press.
Mills, Mary E. (2001), *Biblical Morality: Moral Perspectives in Old Testament Narratives*, Aldershot: Ashgate.
Moore, Stephen D. (2016), 'Biblical Narrative Analysis from the New Criticism to the New Narratology', in D.N. Fewell (ed.), *The Oxford Handbook of Biblical Narrative*, 27–50, Oxford: Oxford University Press.

Newkirk, Matthew (2015), *Just Deceivers: An Exploration of the Motif of Deception in the Books of Samuel*, Eugene, OR: Pickwick Publications.

Nicol, George G. (1988), 'Bathsheba: A Clever Woman?', *ExpTim* 99: 360–3.

Nicol, George G. (1997), 'The Alleged Rape of Bathsheba: Some Observations on Ambiguity in Biblical Narrative', *JSOT* 73: 43–54.

Nicol, George G. (1998), 'David, Abigail and Bathsheba, Nabal and Uriah: Transformations within a Triangle', *SJOT* 12: 130–45.

Nietzsche, Friedrich (1967), *The Will to Power*, ed. Walter Kaufmann, New York: Random House.

Noll, K.L. (1997), *The Faces of David*, JSOTSup 242, Sheffield: Sheffield Academic Press.

Noll, K.L. (1999), 'Is there a Text in this Tradition? Readers' Response and the Taming of Samuel's God', *JSOT* 83: 31–51.

North, Christopher R. (1946), *The Old Testament Interpretation of History*, London: Epworth Press.

Nussbaum, Martha C. (1986), *The Fragility of Goodness: Luck and Ethics in Greek Tragedy and Philosophy*, Cambridge: Cambridge University Press.

Nussbaum, Martha C. (1990), *Love's Knowledge: Essays on Philosophy and Literature*, Oxford: Oxford University Press.

Otto, Eckart (1994), *Theologische Ethik des Alten Testaments*, Stuttgart: Kohlhammer.

Parry, Robin A. (2004), *Old Testament Story and Christian Ethics: The Rape of Dinah as a Case Study*, Milton Keynes: Paternoster Press.

Patrick, Dale (1986), *Old Testament Law*, London: SCM Press.

Penchansky, David (1999), *What Rough Beast? Images of God in the Hebrew Bible*, Louisville, KY: Westminster John Knox Press.

Perdue, Leo G. (1984), '"Is there anyone left of the House of Saul?" Ambiguity and the Characterization of David in the Succession Narrative', *JSOT* 30: 67–84.

Pfeiffer, Robert H. (1948), *Introduction to the Old Testament*, London: Adam and Charles Black.

Phillips, Anthony (1966), 'The Interpretation of 2 Samuel xii 5-6', *VT* 16: 242–4.

Phillips, Anthony (1970), *Ancient Israel's Criminal Law: A New Approach to the Decalogue*, Oxford: Basil Blackwell.

Phillips, Anthony (1975), 'NEBALA – a Term for Serious Disorderly and Unruly Conduct', *VT* 25: 237–42.

Polzin, Robert A. (1993), *David and the Deuteronomist: A Literary Study of the Deuteronomic History: Part 3: 2 Samuel*, Bloomington, IN: Indiana University Press.

Powell, Mark A. (1993), *What is Narrative Criticism?*, London: SPCK.

Powis Smith, J.M. (1933), 'The Character of King David', *JBL* 52: 1–11.

Preston, Thomas R. (1982), 'The Heroism of Saul: Patterns of Meaning in the Narrative of the Early Kingship', *JSOT* 24: 27–46.

Propp, William H. (1993), 'Kinship in 2 Samuel 13', *CBQ* 55: 39–53.

Prouser, Ora Horn (1994),'The Truth about Women and Lying', *JSOT* 61: 15–28.

Proust, Marcel (2003), *Time Regained*, trans. A. Mayor, T. Kilmartin, and D.J. Enright, New York: Modern Library.

Pyper, Hugh S. (1996), *David as Reader: 2 Samuel 12:1-15 and the Poetics of Fatherhood*, BIS 23, Leiden: Brill.

Rad, Gerhard von (1966), 'The Beginnings of Historical Writing in Ancient Israel', in G. von Rad, *The Problem of the Hexateuch and Other Essays*, 166–204, trans. E.W. Trueman Dicken, Edinburgh: Oliver and Boyd.

Rad, Gerhard von (1972), *Wisdom in Israel*, trans. J.D. Martin, London: SCM Press.
Reis, Pamela Tamarkin (2002), *Reading the Lines: A Fresh Look at the Hebrew Bible*, Peabody, MA: Hendrickson.
Resseguie, James L. (2005), *Narrative Criticism of the New Testament: An Introduction*, Grand Rapids, MI: Baker Academic.
Rich, Adrienne (1979), 'Women and Honor: Some Notes on Lying', in *On Lies, Secrets, and Silence: Selected Prose 1966–1978*, 185–94, London: W.W. Norton.
Roberts, J.J.M. (1988), 'Does God Lie? Divine Deceit as a Theological Problem in Israelite Prophetic Literature', in J.A. Emerton (ed.), *Congress Volume*, 211–20, VTSup 40, Leiden: Brill.
Rodd, Cyril S. (2001), *Glimpses of a Strange Land: Studies in Old Testament Ethics*, Edinburgh: T&T Clark.
Rogerson, John W. (2000), 'Old Testament Ethics', in A.D.H. Mayes (ed.), *Text in Context: Essays by Members of the Society for Old Testament Study*, 116–37, Oxford: Oxford University Press.
Rosenberg, Joel (1986), *King and Kin: Political Allegory in the Hebrew Bible*, Indianapolis: Indiana University Press.
Rosenberg, Joel (1989), 'The Institutional Matrix of Treachery in 2 Samuel 11', *Semeia* 46: 103–16.
Rost, Leonhard (1982), *The Succession to the Throne of David*, trans. M.D. Rutter and D.M. Gunn, with Introduction by E. Ball, Sheffield: Almond Press (originally published as *Die Überlieferung von Thronnachfolge Davids*, BWANT 3/6, Stuttgart: Kohlhammer, 1926).
Roth, Wolfgang (1960), 'NBL', *VT* 10: 394–409.
Rowe, Jonathan Y. (2011), *Michal's Moral Dilemma: A Literary, Anthropological and Ethical Interpretation*, London: T&T Clark International.
Sarna, Nahum (1991), *Exodus*, Philadelphia, PA: Jewish Publication Society.
Schipper, Jeremy (2007), 'Did David Overinterpret Nathan's Parable in 2 Samuel 12:1-6?', *JBL* 126: 383–91.
Scholes, Robert, and Robert Kellogg (1966), *The Nature of Narrative*, Oxford: Oxford University Press.
Schüssler Fiorenza, Elisabeth (1988), 'The Ethics of Biblical Interpretation: Decentering Biblical Scholarship', *JBL* 107: 3–17.
Schüssler Fiorenza, Elisabeth (1999), *Rhetoric and Ethic: The Politics of Biblical Studies*, Minneapolis, MN: Fortress Press.
Schüssler Fiorenza, Elisabeth (2001), *Wisdom Ways: Introducing Feminist Biblical Interpretation*, Maryknoll, NY: Orbis Books.
Schwartz, Regina M. (1991), 'Adultery in the House of David: The Metanarrative of Biblical Scholarship and the Narratives of the Bible', *Semeia* 54: 35–55.
Schwartz, Regina M. (1997), *The Curse of Cain: The Violent Legacy of Monotheism*, Chicago: University of Chicago Press.
Seebass, Horst (1974), 'Nathan und David in II Sam 12', *ZAW* 86: 203–11.
Shemesh, Yael (2003), 'Measure for Measure in the David Stories', *SJOT* 17: 89–109.
Simon, Uriel (1967), 'The Poor Man's Ewe-Lamb: An Example of a Juridical Parable', *Bib* 48: 207–42.
Smith, Duane E. (2010), '"Pisser against a Wall": An Echo of Divination in Biblical Hebrew', *CBQ* 72: 699–717.
Smith, Henry Preserved (1899), *A Critical and Exegetical Commentary on the Books of Samuel*, ICC, Edinburgh: T&T Clark.

Smith, Richard G. (2009), *The Fate of Justice and Righteousness during David's Reign: Narrative Ethics and Rereading the Court History according to 2 Samuel 8:15–20:26*, LHBOTS 508, London: T&T Clark.
Smith, Sidney (1931), 'What were the Teraphim?', *JTS* 33: 33–6.
Spohn, William C. (1995), *What are they Saying about Scripture and Ethics?*, 2nd rev. edn, New York: Paulist Press.
Sternberg, Meir (1985), *The Poetics of Biblical Narrative: Ideological Literature and the Drama of Reading*, Bloomington, IN: Indiana University Press.
Steussy, Marti J. (2000), 'The Problematic God of Samuel', in D. Penchansky and P.L. Redditt (eds), *Shall not the Judge of all the Earth do What is Right? Studies on the Nature of God in Tribute to James L. Crenshaw*, 127–61, Winona Lake, IN: Eisenbrauns.
Stiebert, Johanna (2013), *Fathers and Daughters in the Hebrew Bible*, Oxford: Oxford University Press.
Stiebert, Johanna (2016), *First-Degree Incest and the Hebrew Bible: Sex in the Family*, LHBOTS 596, London: Bloomsbury T&T Clark.
Stone, Ken (1996), *Sex, Honor, and Power in the Deuteronomistic History*, JSOTSup 234, Sheffield: Sheffield Academic Press.
Strudler, Alan (2011), 'Deception and Trust', in Clancy Martin (ed.), *The Philosophy of Deception*, 139–52, Oxford: Oxford University Press.
Sussman, David (2011), 'On the Supposed Duty of Truthfulness: Kant on Lying in Self-Defence', in Clancy Martin (ed.), *The Philosophy of Deception*, 225–43, Oxford: Oxford University Press.
Thatcher, Adrian (2008), *The Savage Text: The Use and Abuse of the Bible*, Chichester: Wiley-Blackwell.
Thompson, Thomas L. (1992), *Early History of the Israelite People: From the Written and Archaeological Sources*, Leiden: Brill.
Toorn, Karel van der (1990), 'The Nature of the Biblical Teraphim in the Light of the Cuneiform Evidence', *CBQ* 52: 203–22.
Trible, Phyllis (1984), *Texts of Terror: Literary-Feminist Readings of Biblical Narratives*, OBT, Philadelphia: Fortress Press.
Tsevat, Matitiahu (1958), 'Marriage and Monarchical Legitimacy in Ugarit and Israel', *JSS* 3: 237–43.
Tucker, Gene M. (1971), *Form Criticism of the Old Testament*, Philadelphia: Fortress Press.
Van Seters, John (1983), *In Search of History: Historiography in the Ancient World and the Origins of Biblical History*, New Haven: Yale University Press.
Vaux, Roland de (1961), *Ancient Israel: Its Life and Institutions*, trans. J. McHugh, London: Darton, Longman & Todd.
Veijola, T. (1979), 'Salomo – der Erstgeborene Bathshebas', *VTSup* 30: 230–50.
Vogel, Jane (1977), *Allegory in Dickens*, Alabama: University of Alabama Press.
Vorster, Willem S. (1985), 'Reader-response, Redescription, and Reference: "You are the Man" (2 Sam 12: 7)', in B.C. Lategan and W.S. Vorster, *Text and Reality: Aspects of Reference in Biblical Texts*, Atlanta, GA: Scholars Press.
Weiss, Shira (2018), *Ethical Ambiguity in the Hebrew Bible: Philosophical Analysis of Scriptural Narrative*, Cambridge: Cambridge University Press.
Wellhausen, Julius (1885), *Prolegomena to the History of Israel*, trans. J.S. Black and A. Menzies, Edinburgh: Adam & Charles Black.
Wenham, Gordon J. (1972), '*Betûlāh* "A Girl of Marriageable Age"', *VT* 22: 326–48.

Wenham, Gordon J. (2000), *Story as Torah: Reading the Old Testament Ethically*, Edinburgh: T&T Clark.
Wenham, Gordon J. (2005), 'The Ethics of the Psalms', in P.S. Johnston and D.G. Firth (eds), *Interpreting the Psalms: Issues and Approaches*, 175–94, Leicester: Apollos.
Wenham, Gordon J. (2012), *Psalms as Torah: Reading Biblical Song Ethically*, Grand Rapids, MI: Baker Academic.
Westbrook, April D. (2015), *'And He will Take your Daughters...' Woman Story and the Ethical Evaluation of Monarchy in the David Narrative*, LHBOTS 610, London: Bloomsbury T&T Clark.
Wharton, James A. (1981), 'A Plausible Tale: Story and Theology in II Samuel 9–20, I Kings 1–2', *Int* 35: 341–54.
White, Ellen (2007), 'Michal the Misinterpreted', *JSOT* 31: 451–64.
Whitelam, Keith W. (1979), *The Just King: Monarchical Judicial Authority in Ancient Israel*, JSOTSup 12, Sheffield: JSOT Press.
Whitelam, Keith W. (1984), 'The Defence of David', *JSOT* 29: 61–87.
Whybray, R. Norman (1968), *The Succession Narrative: A Study of II Samuel 9–20; 1 Kings 1 and 2*, SBT 2nd Series 9. London: SCM Press.
Whybray, R. Norman (1974), *The Intellectual Tradition in the Old Testament*, BZAW 135, Berlin: de Gruyter.
Whybray, R. Norman (1996), 'The Immorality of God: Reflections on Some Passages in Genesis, Job, Exodus and Numbers', *JSOT* 72: 89–120.
Whybray, R. Norman (2000), '"Shall not the Judge of all the Earth do what is Just?": God's Oppression of the Innocent in the Old Testament', in D. Penchansky and P.L. Redditt (eds), *Shall not the Judge of all the Earth do What is Right? Studies on the Nature of God in Tribute to James L. Crenshaw*, 1–19, Winona Lake, IN: Eisenbrauns.
Williams, Bernard (2002), *Truth and Truthfulness: An Essay in Genealogy*, Princeton: Princeton University Press.
Williams, Michael J. (2001), *Deception in Genesis: An Investigation into the Morality of a Unique Biblical Phenomenon*, StBL 32, New York: Peter Lang.
Williams, Peter J. (2007), 'Is God Moral? On the Saul Narratives as Tragedy', in R.P. Gordon (ed.), *The God of Israel*, 175–89, Cambridge: Cambridge University Press.
Wright, Christopher J.H. (1983), *Living as the People of God: The Relevance of Old Testament Ethics*, Leicester: Inter-Varsity Press.
Wright, Christopher J.H. (2004), *Old Testament Ethics for the People of God*, Leicester: Inter-Varsity Press.
Wright, Christopher J.H. (2008), *The God I Don't Understand: Reflections on Tough Questions of Faith*, Grand Rapids, MI: Zondervan.
Wright, John Wesley (1993), 'The Innocence of David in 1 Chronicles 21', *JSOT* 60: 87–105.
Würthwein, Ernst (1974), *Die Erzählung von der Thronfolge Davids – theologische oder politische Geschichtsschreibung?*, Zurich: Theologische-Verlag.
Yadin, Yigael (1955), 'Some Aspects of the Strategy of Ahab and David (1 Kings 20, 2 Sam. 11)', *Bib* 36: 332–51.
Yee, Gale A. (1981), 'A Form-Critical Study of Isaiah 5: 1-7 as a Song and a Juridical Parable', *CBQ* 43: 30–40.
Yee, Gale A. (1988), '"Fraught with Background": Literary Ambiguity in 2 Samuel 11', *Int* 42: 240–53.
Zimmerli, Walther (1978), *Old Testament Theology in Outline*, trans. D.E. Green, Edinburgh: T&T Clark.

Index of References

Hebrew Bible/ Old Testament

Genesis
3:12	82
4:25	104
6:9	16
12	40
12:2-3	152
12:4-5	12
12:10-20	12
13:13	16
16:11	104
17:17	12
18:4	63
18:22-33	12, 29, 152
18:25	13, 147
19	17
19:1-8	93
19:37-38	104
20	40
20:1-18	12
20:2	42
20:12	119
21:8-14	13
22:1-19	12
22:2	152
24:16	112
24:28-33	93
25	40
25:29-34	13
25:34	13
26	40
29:21-30	13
31	40, 50
34	121, 124, 128, 139
34:2	81, 121
34:5	133
34:7	114, 123
38	40, 77, 80, 121
38:26	16
42	40
43:24	63
44	40

Exodus
1:15-21	40
2:22	104
3:18	40
10:28	116
20:5	156
20:12	50
20:16	39
22:1-6	28
22:1	93, 94
22:17	123
30:11-12	160
33:19	163

Leviticus
11–15	36
15:18	121
15:24	121
18:9	119, 121, 125
18:11	119, 121, 125
18:15	121
19:35-36	39
20:17	119, 121, 125
21:13	112

Numbers
5:13	121
5:19	121
14:13-19	152
22:21-35	99
23:19	41
28:11-15	36
30	49

Deuteronomy
19:14	39
20:16-18	152
22:14	112
22:19	127
22:21	114
22:22	156
22:23-27	81
22:23-24	123
22:24	126
22:25	81
22:28-29	122, 125, 128
23:10-15	63
24:16	156
25:13-15	39
27:17	39
27:22	119, 125

Joshua
7:15	114
10:40	152

Judges
1:20	18
9:7-15	99
9:50-55	65
19	17, 111

19:16-21	93	19:15	34	25:36	21
19:24	123	19:17	34, 49	25:37	18
19:39	112	20	35, 46, 53,	25:38	153
20:6	114, 123		55, 56,	25:39	21, 115
20:10	114		168	25:44	120
21:12	112	20:1-34	22, 32, 35,	26:1-25	168
			47, 48, 53	26:16	93
Ruth		20:1	35, 53	27:8-11	18
3	80	20:3	36	27:9-12	168
3:4	63	20:4	53		
3:7	63	20:8	53	*2 Samuel*	
3:11	16	20:13	53	2:1-4	18
		20:14-15	53	2:12-32	67
1 Samuel		20:17	53, 54	3:2	112
2:25	153	20:23	53	3:3	112, 136
3:18	163	20:26	36	3:13-14	120
8:1-4	110	20:27	54	3:20-23	67
8:20	66	20:28-29	54	3:22-30	64
10:1-25	153	20:28	54	4	53
12	150	20:29	36	6:6-7	153
13:13-14	168	20:30-33	47, 55	6:16-23	37
13:14	88, 153	20:30-31	54	7	94
15:10-11	153	20:31	54, 93	8:3-5	168
16	75	20:33	54, 55	8:15	102
16:1-5	41, 153	20:35	54	8:18	168
16:14-16	153	20:41	54	9–20	5, 149
18:1	48	20:42	53	9	53, 168
18:3	53	21:1-6	6	10:17	67
18:10	153	21:5-6	63	10:18	168
18:11	35	24:6-7	168	11–20	108
18:17-25	46	24:19	34	11–12	59, 60,
18:17	45	24:20	53		104, 132,
18:19	45	25	17, 19		133, 142
18:20	48	25:3	16, 19	11	22, 26,
18:21	46	25:7	17		59–61,
18:22	46	25:8	17		73–7, 79,
18:25	35, 46	25:10	18		81, 85, 87,
19	46, 48,	25:11	18		92, 96–8,
	168	25:13	18		101, 105-
19:4	35	25:16	21		107, 109,
19:9-10	153	25:17	20		110, 151,
19:11-17	22, 32, 33,	25:21-22	18		154
	35, 37, 43,	25:22	19	11:1-27	30, 92, 97,
	46–8, 50,	25:25	20		101
	52, 55, 56,	25:28-31	18	11:1-5	71
	58	25:28	20	11:1	61, 67, 70,
19:14	33, 34	25:30	20		92, 97

2 Samuel (cont.)

11:2–12:24	97	12:1	92, 98	12:23	106, 158, 169
11:2-5	85, 87, 167	12:2-5	157	12:24-25	89, 140
		12:2	93	12:24	104, 109, 150
11:2	76	12:3	93, 97, 169		
11:3	62, 67, 71	12:4	93	12:25	92
11:4	62, 70, 79, 81, 82, 92, 97	12:5-6	93, 98	13–20	9, 109
		12:5	8, 27, 92, 93	13–14	109
				13	59, 81, 108, 109, 142, 170
11:5	77, 78	12:6	94		
11:6-27	71	12:7-25	31, 143, 149, 154, 164, 165, 170	13:1-39	30
11:6-25	168			13:1-14	122
11:6	71, 92, 97			13:1-2	85
11:8	63			13:1	81, 115, 132
11:9	63, 68	12:7-14	72		
11:10	64	12:7-12	8, 92		
11:11	63, 64, 70, 97, 103	12:7-8	72	13:2	112, 121, 139
		12:7	8, 94, 96, 98		
11:13	63, 64, 68			13:3	112, 130
11:14	92, 97	12:8	94, 95	13:4	113
11:15	64	12:9	72, 95, 155	13:5-7	135
				13:5-6	113, 139
11:17	64, 71				
11:20-21	65	12:10-12	89, 155	13:5	113
11:21	78	12:10-11	142	13:6	113, 139
11:22-25	65	12:10	150	13:7-8	127, 129
11:22	65	12:11-12	72, 150, 155, 156	13:8-9	113
				13:8	85, 127
11:23	65	12:11	95, 170	13:9-10	139
11:24	71, 95	12:12-23	26	13:9	116, 123
11:25	65, 71, 95, 106, 158	12:13-15	92	13:10-16	8
11:26-27	76, 79, 105	12:13	72, 73, 89, 92, 95, 156, 157	13:10	114, 129
				13:11	108, 139
11:26	66	12:14	95, 105	13:12-13	22, 111, 129
11:27	15, 66, 71, 74, 75, 85, 90, 91, 97, 150	12:15-25	92, 103, 105	13:12	78, 111, 114, 123, 124, 126, 127, 129
		12:15-23	156, 161		
		12:15	97		
12–20	60	12:16-23	6, 106, 150, 158	13:13	119, 124, 125, 141
12	22, 92, 97, 106, 111, 154, 157, 158, 169	12:16-17	103	13:14	115, 121, 128, 140
		12:18	103		
12:1-25	30, 92	12:19-20	103	13:15	115, 140
12:1-15	92, 97	12:20	158	13:16	111, 116, 123, 129
12:1-7	92, 93	12:21	103		
12:1-6	8, 26	12:22	158	13:17	111, 116, 140
12:1-4	93, 97-100				

13:18	112	24:1-17	31, 143, 149, 159, 161, 164, 165	21:5	159
13:19	116			21:6	162
13:20	117, 122, 136			21:7-15	162
				21:12	160
13:21	108, 117, 133, 168	24:1	159-61	22:6-16	162
		24:2	159	22:9	104
13:22	117, 136, 137	24:9	159		
		24:10	160, 161	2 Chronicles	
13:24-25	117	24:11-13	161	12:14	16
13:26-27	133, 135	24:14	160, 161	20:35	16
13:26	118	24:15	160	36:10	61
13:28-29	95	24:16	160, 161		
13:28	118, 137	24:17	161, 163, 165, 170	Job	
13:30	108			1:1	16
13:31	118	24:18-25	162	1:8	16
13:32-33	133	33:11-17	131	2:9-10	82
13:32	118, 130, 137			9:22	152
		1 Kings		31:5-6	39
13:33	118	1–2	5, 9, 77, 79, 80, 87, 149	31:9-11	95
13:34-36	130				
13:35	118			Psalms	
13:37	134	1	79, 80	5:6	39
13:39	134	2	59, 75	5:9	39
14	98	2:13-25	95	39:8	115
14:1-20	98, 99	6–7	4	51	74, 157
14:17	106	15:5	88	58:3	39
14:20	106	15:11	168	73:22	115
14:26	137	20:22	61	74:22	115
14:27	118	20:26	61	94:3	147
15:1-15	97	20:35-43	98, 99	109:2	39
15:2-4	135, 141	21:18-24	101		
15:12	62	22:5-23	40	Proverbs	
16:20-22	155			6:16-19	39
16:21-22	81, 94, 95	2 Kings		6:31	94
16:22	155	9–10	53	12:22	39
17:14	150, 153	12–20	59	30:20	79
17:25	20	14:9	99		
18:9-15	95	18:1-3	168	Song of Songs	
18:33	106	18:3	16	4:1	33
19:1-4	106	21:16	16		
20:3	155	22:1–23:30	17	Isaiah	
20:8-10	64			1:13	36
21:1	160	1 Chronicles		5:1-7	98, 99
23:13-17	6	2:17	20	5:3-4	98
23:34	62	20:1	61	5:18	39
24	161	21	162		
		21:1	161		

Jeremiah		NEW TESTAMENT		BABYLONIAN TALMUD	
3:1-5	98, 99	*Matthew*		*Sanhedrin*	
4:10	41	1	66	107a	73
15:18	41	1:3	66		
29:23	114	1:5	66	*Yoma*	
		1:6	66	22b	94
Lamentations					
2:20	152	*Luke*		ANCIENT CHRISTIAN	
3:34-36	152	19:8	93	LITERATURE	
				Augustine	
Ezekiel		*1 Timothy*		*Summa Theologiae*	
18	156	1:9-10	39	IIa IIae, Q. 69, 1	42
23:8	121			IIa IIae, Q. 69, 2	42
		Revelation			
Hosea		22:15	39		
1–2	82				
2:13	36	MISHNAH			
		Shabbat			
Joel		56a	73		
1:8	112				
		Niddah			
		31b	62		

Index of Authors

Abasili, A.I. 81, 85
Ackerman, J.S. 6, 11, 81, 134
Ackerman, S. 35, 52
Ackroyd, P.R. 18, 33, 71, 76, 99, 109, 112, 114–16, 120, 137
Adler, J.E. 42
Albright, W.F. 33, 148
Alter, R. 2, 8, 9, 34, 36, 37, 50, 52, 60, 62, 71, 78, 80, 83, 92, 94, 100, 103, 112–17, 119, 120, 131, 134, 160
Anderson, A.A. 27, 61, 62, 89, 93, 97–9, 103, 109, 111, 112, 114, 121, 122, 136, 159, 161
Anderson, L.V. 55
Andersson, G. 86, 88
Andrew, M.E. 39
Andruska, J.L. 81
Arendt, H. 39
Auld, A.G. 35, 50, 61, 62, 76, 78, 82, 93, 97, 112, 127, 137, 163
Avioz, M. 62

Bach, A. 62, 73, 83, 84
Bailey, R.C. 62, 78, 79, 85, 92, 96, 153, 155
Bal, M. 1, 69, 70, 78, 81
Bar-Efrat, S. 71, 110, 112–16, 122, 131, 132, 137, 139, 140
Bar-Yosef, E. 26
Barnes, J.A. 47
Barr, J. 20, 38, 39
Barton, J. 2, 3, 7, 23, 27–9, 61, 101, 102, 105, 149, 151, 152
Bechtel, L.M. 121
Benton, R.J. 44
Berlin, A. 13, 16, 19, 20, 69, 70, 72, 77, 79, 105
Bewer, J.A. 6
Biddle, M.E. 18

Birch, B.C. 1, 18, 27, 28, 80, 83, 89, 99, 121, 122, 130, 134, 136
Blenkinsopp, J. 77
Blumenthal, D.R. 159
Bodi, D. 33, 34, 37, 52, 63, 64, 66, 73, 75, 76, 93–5, 99
Bodner, K. 50, 60–2, 65, 97
Bok, S. 44, 46, 47, 57
Booth, W.C. 31, 143, 147
Bosworth, D.A. 105, 106
Bovati, P. 93
Bowman, R.G. 168
Boyle, M. O'R. 18, 19
Brenner, A. 83
Bright, J. 6, 145, 148
Brueggemann, W. 6, 11, 18, 19, 21, 27, 37, 39, 41, 54, 62, 71, 73, 74, 85, 88, 98, 105, 107, 115, 117, 123, 131, 134, 136, 150, 154, 156, 157, 161

Camp, C.V. 98
Campbell, A.F. 60, 78, 82, 93, 97, 126, 131, 133, 157
Capote, T. 7
Carlson, R.A. 59, 94, 97, 109
Carson, T.L. 43, 45
Chankin-Gould, J. D'ror 62
Chapman, S.B. 41, 150, 152
Childs, B.S. 1, 157
Chun, S.M. 2, 16, 17
Clements, R.E. 2
Clines, D.J.A. 34, 35, 47, 74–6, 81, 144, 147, 151, 158
Coats, G.W. 99
Cobley, P. 7
Cohen, H.H. 75
Collins, J.J. 5
Conee, E. 55
Conroy, C. 109, 111, 113, 117, 125, 137

Coxon, P.W. 94, 97
Crouch, C.L. 5

Daube, D. 78, 96, 120
Davies, E.W. 2, 99, 145, 146, 148, 159
Davies, P.R. 144
Day, P.L. 112
Deferrari, R.J. 42
Delekat, L. 96
Dell, K.J. 152
Dickens, C. 26
Dijk-Hemmes, F. van 121, 127, 132, 133, 139
Dodd, C. H. 101
Dray, C.A. 41
Driver, S.R. 94, 116, 121

Eagleton, T. 143
Edelman, D.V. 34
Eissfeldt, O. 9
Esau, K. 40
Esler, P.F. 19, 61, 66, 67, 110, 113, 126, 130, 131, 136
Exum, J.C. 52, 62, 78, 81, 83–7, 101, 154–6, 157, 158

Fewell, D.N. 2, 114, 136, 144, 147, 151, 152
Fish, S.E. 145, 146
Flanagan, J.E. 122
Fohrer, G. 6
Fokkelman, J.P. 26, 37, 48–50, 52, 54, 55, 59, 70, 76, 78, 82, 93, 96, 97, 99, 102, 109, 110, 115, 121, 127, 129, 131, 132, 134, 157, 158
Fontaine, C.R. 66, 76
Frei, H. 5
Fretheim, T.E. 153
Frymer-Kensky, T. 112, 121, 122
Fuchs, E. 122, 128, 129, 137, 138, 142

Garbini, G. 7
Garsiel, M. 67, 68
Gilmour, R. 9, 22, 136
Goldingay, J. 1, 13
Good, E.M. 77
Goody, J. 119
Gordon, R.P. 20, 59, 61–3, 71, 78, 79, 97, 98, 112, 115, 123, 134, 137, 156, 159
Gorospe, A.E. 2

Gravett, S. 81, 121
Gray, M. 109, 110, 119, 135
Green, B. 72, 99, 118, 123, 134, 150, 165
Gros Louis, K.R.R. 109
Guest, D. 150
Gunkel, H. 64, 97
Gunn, D.M. 3, 6, 9, 10, 18, 19, 21, 64, 67, 83, 97, 98, 100, 105, 106, 109, 114, 116, 136, 144, 147, 149–53, 157

Hagan, H. 37, 98, 132
Halberstam, C. 100
Hallo, W.W. 36
Halpern, B. 18, 134
Harman, G. 30
Hays, R.B. 1
Hazony, Y. 29, 30
Heard, R.C. 157
Heller, J. 83
Hertzberg, H.W. 6, 20, 59, 62, 63, 68, 77, 80, 82, 87, 92, 94, 96, 101, 109, 119, 136, 156, 161
Ho, C.Y.S. 77
Homan, M.M. 70
Honeyman, A.M. 104

Irwin, W.A. 40
Iser, W.W. 61

James, H. 23–5, 31
Janzen, D. 72
Janzen, W. 2
Jensen, H.J.L. 5
Jobling, D. 55
Johnson, V.L. 74, 157
Jones, G.H. 104

Kafka, F. 161
Kaiser, W.C., Jr. 2, 28, 152
Kalmanofsky, A. 119, 121, 131, 133
Kant, I. 23, 43, 44, 55, 56
Keefe, A.A. 121, 129
Kellogg, R. 60
Keneally, T. 7
Kennedy, A.R.S. 76
Kenny, A. 30
Kessler, J. 20, 21, 76, 80
Kim, H.C.P. 78, 79, 82
Kim, U.Y. 71
Kirk-Duggan, C.A. 62, 75, 76

Klein, L.R. 79, 80
Koch, K. 149
Krause, M. 62

Lalleman, H. 2
Landay, J.M. 78, 80, 85
Lasine, S. 26, 27, 161, 163
Lategan, B.C. 99
Leithart, P.J. 19
Lemche, N.P. 7, 18
Lemmon, E.J. 55
Létourneau, A. 84, 85
Levenson, J.D. 18–20, 94
Linafelt, T. 2, 148, 159
Lodge, D. 7
Long, B.O. 9

Macwilliam, S. 62
Magonet, J. 12, 147
Mahon, J.E. 44
Mantel, H. 7
Marcus, D. 46
Marcus, R.B. 55
Mauchline, J. 34, 61, 62, 64, 68, 76, 82, 95, 109, 119, 134, 156, 157
McCarter, P.K., Jr. 33, 62–4, 70, 73, 76, 92, 94, 97, 98, 109, 113, 114, 121, 160
McConnell, T. 55
McKane, W. 33, 37, 54, 63, 74, 76, 136, 156, 160
McKeating, H. 95, 156
McKenzie, S.L. 18–20, 46, 47, 55, 62, 107
Mein, A. 2
Miller, G.R. 44
Miller, J.H. 143
Mills, M.E. 2, 12, 13, 101, 107, 152, 168
Moore, S.D. 1
Murdoch, I. 23

Newkirk, M. 34, 37, 39–41, 46, 54, 132
Nicol, G.G. 19–21, 77–9, 84, 85–7
Nietzsche, F. 45
Noll, K.L. 81, 149, 153, 154
North, C.R. 6
Nussbaum, M.C. 4, 23–6, 28–31, 56, 61, 104, 143, 168, 169, 171
Nyengele, M.F. 78, 79, 82

Orwell, G. 42
Otto, E. 2

Parry, R.A. 2, 16
Patrick, D. 39
Penchansky, D. 160, 161
Perdue, L.G. 70, 158, 168
Pfeiffer, R.H. 6
Phillips, A. 39, 93, 102, 114, 124
Polzin, R.A. 36, 67, 97
Powell, M.A. 1
Powis Smith, J.M. 76
Preston, T.R. 76, 81, 154
Propp, W. H. 109, 111, 119, 120, 123, 124, 135
Prouser, O.H. 40
Proust, M. 23, 26
Pyper, H.S. 26, 94, 96, 101–3

Rad, G. von 6, 99, 130, 131, 136, 150
Reis, P.T. 120, 121, 126, 127
Resseguie, J.L. 1
Rich, A. 47
Roberts, J.J.M. 40
Rodd, C.S. 1
Rogerson, J.W. 152
Rosenberg, J. 86, 119, 120
Rost, L. 5
Roth, W. 114, 124
Rowe, J.Y. 33, 35, 48–52, 57

Sarna, N. 40
Schipper, J. 96
Scholes, R. 60
Schüssler Fiorenza, E. 144
Schwartz, R.M. 95, 101, 109, 119, 133
Seebass, H. 27, 93, 101, 102
Shemesh, Y. 46
Simon, U. 73, 98–100
Smith, D.E. 19
Smith, H.P. 62, 63, 67, 119, 123, 136, 140
Smith, R.G. 66, 70, 87, 109, 110, 122, 124, 125, 137, 140
Smith, S. 33
Spohn, W.C. 146
Sternberg, M. 8, 14, 61–4, 66, 68, 69, 77, 78, 80, 85, 86, 99, 151
Steussy, M.J. 41, 151–3, 162
Stiebert, J. 120–3, 126, 127, 131, 132
Stiff, J.B. 44

Stone, K. 67, 71, 79, 112, 119, 121, 123, 125, 132, 135
Strudler, A. 44
Sussman, D. 44

Thatcher, A. 145
Thompson, T.L. 7
Toorn, K. van der 34
Trible, P. 109, 114, 116, 118, 132-4
Tsevat, M. 94
Tucker, G.M. 6, 149

Van Seters, J. 7
Vaux, R. de 36, 120
Veijola, T. 103, 104
Vogel, J. 26
Vorster, W.S. 97

Weiss, S. 32, 40
Wellhausen, J. 5

Wenham, G.J. 2, 14, 112
Westbrook, A.D. 10, 18, 20, 52, 80, 110, 111, 129, 135, 153
Wharton, J.A. 75, 150
White, E. 34
Whitelam, K.W. 89, 100, 102
Whybray, R.N. 6, 9, 10, 76, 79, 109, 113, 119, 120, 130, 149, 152, 157, 159, 162
Williams, B. 31, 42
Williams, M.J. 37, 40
Williams, P.J. 152, 154
Wright, C.J.H. 1, 148, 149
Wright, J.W. 162
Würthwein, E. 78

Yadin, Y. 70
Yee, G.A. 15, 60, 61, 69-71, 81, 99

Zimmerli, W. 123

www.ingramcontent.com/pod-product-compliance
Lightning Source LLC
Chambersburg PA
CBHW061830300426
44115CB00013B/2324